Our Best

Recipes from Nebraska 4-H

Published by
Nebraska 4-H Development Foundation
114 Agricultural Hall, University of Nebraska
Lincoln, Nebraska 68583-0700

Designed, Edited, and Manufactured by
Favorite Recipes® Press
P.O. Box 305142
Nashville, Tennessee 37230
1-800-358-0560

ISBN: 0-9652002-0-5
Library of Congress Number: 96-84226
Manufactured in the United States of America
First Printing: 1996 10,000 copies

Cover Photograph:
A young man picks flowers on the way in from the field to share with someone special.

—Becky Weekly, Lincoln County

TABLE OF CONTENTS

To 4-H Families and Friends	4
A Proud Past . . . A Future of Opportunity	5
Nebraska 4-H	6
The Pictures of Nebraska 4-H'ers	7
Nutritional Profile Guidelines	8
Friends of Nebraska 4-H *Formal Dinner Menu*	9
Appetizers and Beverages *Patio Party Menu*	27
Soups, Salads and Vegetables *Salad Luncheon Menu*	37
Meat Main Dishes *Tailgate Party Menu*	55
More Main Dishes *Sunday Brunch Menu*	89
Breads and Rolls *Coffee with Friends Menu*	107
Desserts *Dessert Buffet Menu*	125
Fast, Easy and Fun *After the Game Party Menu*	151
Appendix	163
Index	171
Order Information	175

☘ Recipes from *The 4-H Friends' Cookbook.*

TO 4-H FAMILIES AND FRIENDS

Sharing our Best from Nebraska 4-H represents the participation of hundreds of individuals across Nebraska with a special interest in the 4-H program. Publication of this unique cookbook would not have been possible without the support, advice, and assistance of numerous individuals.

It is with sincere appreciation that we thank the many 4-H friends who submitted recipes to be considered for publication. We regret that all the recipes could not be used. Generally, all published recipes were selected by the staff of Favorite Recipes® Press under their established guidelines.

The actual production challenge would not have been met without the special efforts of the Nebraska 4-H Development Foundation staff, as well as the participation of the cookbook planning and marketing committees and the efforts of many others.

Many Extension professionals throughout the state played a part in bringing this project to completion. We acknowledge their participation and support with this special publication.

A special thank you for the encouragement and enthusiasm of the Executive Council of the Nebraska 4-H Development Foundation and Del Dearborn, Nebraska State 4-H Program Leader in including *Sharing our Best Recipes from Nebraska 4-H* as part of the fund-raising efforts to benefit Nebraska's young people.

Cookbook Planning Committee

Jane Tonjes, Chairperson
Sue Friesen
Duane Grugel
Jane Krause
Kay McKinzie
Jan Mehl
Terri Uden

Marketing Committee

Danita Diamond, Co-Chair
Carin Gerdes, Co-Chair
Jane Krause
Linda Lovgren
Amy Malchow
Sandy Rockwood
Marilyn Schepers
Terri Uden
Marlene Wagoner

The University of Nebraska, the Nebraska 4-H Development Foundation and Favorite Recipes® Press are not responsible for the nutritional profile provided at the end of each recipe if ingredients are substituted. Nor can they be held responsible for any product listed in this book. The recipes are home-tested and are not endorsed by the University of Nebraska or the Nebraska 4-H Development Foundation. This cookbook is a collection of our favorite recipes and are not necessarily original recipes.

A PROUD PAST . . . A FUTURE OF OPPORTUNITY

It was 1893, and E. C. Bishop sat at his teacher's desk in Seward County, Nebraska, pondering how best to make education more relevant for his pupils. Visiting the farm of one of his students, he decided that school would be more challenging if the students' lessons were based on farm life and work. Over the next several years he experimented with a variety of activities focusing on agriculture and home economics.

In 1903, Bishop collected ears of corn from Central Nebraska farmers, distributed a quart of seed corn to many boys in York, Fillmore, and Seward counties, and provided them a lesson on how to grow it. They were instructed to plant their corn and bring back ten ears of their 1904 crop to a State Corn Show.

From that simple beginning of a quart of corn and a lesson on how to grow it, Boys' and Girls' Clubs spread across Nebraska. In 1908, the four-leaf clover was accepted as the organization's emblem, and 4-H became its name.

Today, one out of every three youth in Nebraska is a 4-H member, experiencing youth development activities through community clubs, special interest groups, and school enrichment programs.

They're involved in projects beyond corn, cooking, and cows. The youth in today's 4-H program are addressing the issues that will continue to challenge them in the future, such as water quality, conservation of natural resources, child development, home environment, garbology, and food safety.

Over the years, 4-H members have focused not only on learning specific subject matter skills, but have worked at learning life skills as well. When 4-H alumni reflect upon their years in the program, they often credit the 4-H program for the development of communication skills, organizational and record-keeping abilities, and knowledge of how to conduct an effective meeting. Because of the skills they learned during 4-H leadership and citizenship activities, 4-H alumni take an active role in their communities.

Today's 4-H program continues that tradition as it reaches out to youth at risk in both urban and rural settings, offers opportunities to mentally and physically challenged youth, crosses cultural and ethnic lines, and develops linkages with business and industry.

Past, present, and future, Nebraska 4-H works in many ways to enrich the lives of its members and their families. It will continue to grow and develop the heads, hearts, hands, and health of Nebraska youth as they strive to "Make the Best Better" for their club, their community, their country, and their world.

NEBRASKA 4-H

The Nebraska 4-H Youth Development program combines traditional programming with innovation, rural with urban audiences, domestic with international activities, art with science and technology, and inquisitive youth with caring responsible adults. Today, 4-H is truly more than you ever imagined.

The Nebraska 4-H Youth Development program is proud to be a part of the *Sharing our Best* cookbook. Some recipes represent the oldest of family traditions, while others provide quick and healthy ways to meet the needs of today's busy Nebraska families. All contain a nutritional summary, an important resource for maintaining "Nebraska the Good Life." Striving to "Make the Best Better," 4-H youth have been involved in providing the photos, supplying the recipes, promoting the cookbook, and prioritizing the programs that will benefit from its returns.

Thanks for purchasing this cookbook. Together we can show our encouragement for and support of Nebraska youth as they "Learn by Doing."

Delwyn Dearborn
Nebraska State 4-H Program Leader

NEBRASKA 4-H DEVELOPMENT FOUNDATION

The Nebraska 4-H Development Foundation provides an opportunity for 4-H friends and alumni from across the state and nation to support the enhancement of the Nebraska 4-H Youth Development program. A nonprofit organization, the Foundation's private funds are used to assist in program marketing, member recruitment and retention, management and development of 4-H camps, volunteer leader enhancement and recognition, and incentives to support youth development.

The *Sharing our Best* cookbook is a special Foundation project; its main purpose is to assist Nebraska 4-H program development at the county and club level. Three-fourths of the net revenues will support county and/or club youth development activities at the local level. The majority of profits from individual county cookbook sales will remain with that county for programming efforts. The remaining portion will be used to create a Program Development Grant Fund, which will be used to provide "seed" money for counties to use in innovative program development.

Thank you for joining us in our efforts to support the Nebraska 4-H program. Together we can assist in providing positive development activities and experiences as we prepare Nebraska youth for the twenty-first century.

Sherman Berg, president
Nebraska 4-H Development Foundation

Jane Tonjes, cookbook chairperson
Nebraska 4-H Development Foundation

THE PICTURES OF NEBRASKA 4-H'ERS

The photography throughout this publication shares the beauty and essence of Nebraska as seen through the eyes of 4-H'ers.

We appreciate the opportunity to use these outstanding photographs that were submitted by Nebraska 4-H members. These were chosen from the 24 photographs selected at the 1995 Nebraska State Fair in the 4-H Photography Division. We hope you enjoy these contributions as much as we have.

BECKY WEEKLY
Lincoln County

MEGHAN BURGESS
Gage County

REBECCA WATKINS
Perkins County

KRIS EGGERS
Nemaha County

MANDY GALE
Cherry County

JIM RAHRS
Hamilton County

JENNY HEFTI
Jefferson County

KYLE ELLISON
Sarpy County

JASON HIRSCHFELD
York County

NUTRITIONAL PROFILE GUIDELINES

The editors have attempted to present these family recipes in a form that allows approximate nutritional values to be computed. Persons with dietary or health problems or whose diets require close monitoring should not rely solely on the nutritional information provided. They should consult their physicians or a registered dietitian for specific information.

Abbreviations for Nutritional Profile

Cal - Calories	Fiber - Dietary Fiber	Sod - Sodium
Prot - Protein	T Fat - Total Fat	g - grams
Carbo - Carbohydrates	Chol - Cholesterol	mg - milligrams

Nutritional information for these recipes is computed from information derived from many sources, including materials supplied by the United States Department of Agriculture, computer databanks, and journals in which the information is assumed to be in the public domain. However, many specialty items, new products, and processed foods may not be available from these sources or may vary from the average values used in these profiles. More information on new and/or specific products may be obtained by reading the nutrient labels. Unless otherwise specified, the nutritional profile of these recipes is based on all measurements being level.

- **Artificial sweeteners** vary in use and strength so should be used "to taste," using the recipe ingredients as a guideline. Sweeteners using aspartame (NutraSweet and Equal) should not be used as a sweetener in recipes involving prolonged heating, which reduces the sweet taste. For further information on the use of these sweeteners, refer to package.
- **Buttermilk**, **sour cream**, and **yogurt** are the types available commercially.
- **Cake mixes** which are prepared using package directions include 3 eggs and 1/2 cup oil.
- **Chicken**, cooked for boning and chopping, has been roasted; this method yields the lowest caloric values.
- **Cottage cheese** is cream-style with 4.2% creaming mixture. Dry curd cottage cheese has no creaming mixture.
- **Eggs** are all large. To avoid raw eggs that may carry salmonella, as in eggnog or 6-week muffin batter, use an equivalent amount of commercial egg substitute.
- **Flour** is unsifted all-purpose flour.
- **Garnishes**, serving suggestions, and other optional additions and variations are not included in the profile.
- **Margarine** and **butter** are regular, not whipped or presoftened.
- **Milk** is whole milk, 3.5% butterfat. Lowfat milk is 1% butterfat. Evaporated milk is whole milk with 60% of the water removed.
- **Oil** is any type of vegetable cooking oil. **Shortening** is hydrogenated vegetable shortening.
- **Salt** and other ingredients to taste as noted in the ingredients have not been included in the nutritional profile.
- If a choice of ingredients has been given, the nutritional profile reflects the first option. If a choice of amounts has been given, the nutritional profile reflects the greater amount.

Friends of Nebraska 4-H

A Stately Occasion

Formal Dinner Menu

Strawberry Spinach Salad
page 49

Italian Roast Beef
page 57
or
Festive Holiday Lamb
page 15

Three-Cheese Scalloped Potatoes
page 18

Butterhorn Rolls
page 119

Blintzes with Raspberry Sauce
page 147
or
Bavarian Apple Cheesecake
page 144

PHOTOGRAPH BY REBECCA WATKINS
Perkins County

BROCCOLI RAISIN SALAD

Florets of 19 heads fresh broccoli
3 (1-pound) packages carrots, peeled, shredded
2 pounds bacon, crisp-fried, crumbled
3 (15-ounce) packages raisins
3 cups sunflower kernels
1 gallon French dressing or Dorothy Lynch dressing

Combine the broccoli florets, shredded carrots, crumbled bacon, raisins and sunflower kernels in a large bowl; toss to mix. Add the dressing; toss to mix. Refrigerate, covered, until serving time.

Yield: 150 servings.

Approx Per Serving: Cal 177; T Fat 13 g; 65% Calories from Fat; Prot 2 g; Carbo 14 g; Fiber 2 g; Chol 17 mg; Sod 405 mg

Jim Bell, camp manager
Eastern Nebraska 4-H Center

"BOHEMIAN" TERIYAKI BEEF

2 pounds (1-inch thick) top sirloin
1/2 cup soy sauce
1/4 cup packed brown sugar
2 tablespoons plum jelly
2 tablespoons olive oil
1 teaspoon ginger
1/4 teaspoon lemon pepper
1/4 teaspoon garlic salt

Cut the sirloin into 1/4-inch strips; place in a shallow dish. Combine the soy sauce, brown sugar, plum jelly, olive oil, ginger, lemon pepper and garlic salt in a bowl; mix well. Pour over the sirloin, stirring to coat. Marinate, covered, in the refrigerator for 2 hours; drain, reserving the marinade. Arrange the sirloin on skewers. Cook on a hot grill for 8 to 10 minutes or until done to taste, turning and brushing with the reserved marinade frequently. Serve with additional plum jelly.

My wife, Pat, won first place with this recipe at the 1990 Nebraska State Fair Celebrity Beef Cook-Off.

Yield: 4 servings.

Approx Per Serving: Cal 416; T Fat 18 g; 43% Calories from Fat; Prot 43 g; Carbo 21 g; Fiber <1 g; Chol 119 mg; Sod 2329 mg

Jim Exon, United States senator

CHILI

2 pounds beef chuck
2 teaspoons chili powder
2 cloves of garlic, minced
3 tablespoons flour
1 medium onion, chopped
1/4 cup shortening
2 teaspoons salt
1 1/2 quarts hot water
1 (8-ounce) can tomato purée

Cut the beef into bite-size pieces. Combine the chili powder, garlic and flour in a shallow bowl; mix well. Coat the beef with the flour mixture. Sauté the onion in the shortening in a deep large saucepan until clear. Add the beef. Cook for 15 minutes, stirring frequently. Stir in the salt. Add the hot water gradually, stirring to mix. Simmer for 45 minutes or until the beef is tender and cooking thermometer registers 165 degrees, stirring occasionally. Stir in the tomato purée.

The ingredients of this recipe are easy to assemble and the chili needs very little attention while cooking. It is also delicious.

Yield: 6 servings.

Approx Per Serving: Cal 445; T Fat 30 g; 60% Calories from Fat; Prot 35 g; Carbo 9 g; Fiber 1 g; Chol 112 mg; Sod 943 mg

Carl T. Curtis

Carl T. Curtis, former United States senator

COMPANY MEATBALLS

3 pounds ground beef
2 cups rolled oats
1 cup evaporated milk
1 cup finely chopped onion
2 teaspoons chili powder
3/4 teaspoon pepper
2 teaspoons salt
1/2 teaspoon garlic powder
2 cups catsup
1 cup packed brown sugar
2 tablespoons liquid smoke
1/2 teaspoon garlic powder
1/2 cup chopped onion

Combine the ground beef, oats, evaporated milk, 1 cup chopped onion, chili powder, pepper, salt and garlic powder in a large bowl; mix well. Shape into 1-inch balls; place in a single layer in two 9x13-inch baking pans. Bake, covered, at 350 degrees for 30 minutes; drain. Combine the catsup, brown sugar, liquid smoke, garlic powder and 1/2 cup chopped onion in a bowl; mix well. Pour over the meatballs. Bake, uncovered, for 30 minutes longer or until no pink remains in the center of the meatballs.

These meatballs freeze well, so a meal for unexpected guests can be prepared quickly and easily. They are tasty.

Yield: 10 servings.

Approx Per Serving: Cal 522; T Fat 22 g; 38% Calories from Fat; Prot 36 g; Carbo 47 g; Fiber 3 g; Chol 109 mg; Sod 1115 mg

Arlene Viersen

Arlene Viersen
National 4-H Alumni winner

MEATBALLS IN GINGERSNAP SAUCE

- 1 pound lean ground beef
- 1 egg
- 3/4 cup soft bread crumbs
- 1/4 cup finely chopped onion
- 2 teaspoons beef bouillon granules
- 1 1/2 cups boiling water
- 1/3 cup packed brown sugar
- 1/4 cup raisins
- 2 tablespoons lemon juice
- 1/2 cup coarse gingersnap crumbs

Mix the first 3 ingredients in a bowl. Shape into 1-inch balls; place in a hot heavy skillet. Cook over medium heat, browning on all sides; drain. Dissolve the bouillon in the boiling water and brown sugar. Stir in the raisins and lemon juice. Pour over the meatballs. Simmer, covered, for 15 to 20 minutes or until no pink remains in the center of the meatballs. Add the gingersnap crumbs. Cook until the sauce is thick and smooth, stirring constantly. Serve hot with noodles, mashed potatoes or brown rice.

Yield: 6 servings.

Approx Per Serving: Cal 291; T Fat 12 g; 38% Calories from Fat; Prot 19 g;Carbo 26 g; Fiber 1 g; Chol 92 mg; Sod 426 mg

Warren Nielson

Warren Nielson, radio and TV communicator

BARRETT'S HEARTY HAM AND VEGETABLE CASSEROLE

- 1 (20-ounce) package frozen cauliflowerets
- 1 (20-ounce) package frozen broccoli florets
- Salt to taste
- 1/4 cup butter
- 3 tablespoons flour
- 3 cups milk
- 1 1/2 cups shredded Cheddar cheese
- 1 cup grated Parmesan cheese
- 1/2 teaspoon salt
- 3 cups chopped cooked ham
- 3 cups fresh bread crumbs
- 1/4 cup melted butter

Cook the cauliflower and broccoli in salted water just until tender-crisp using package directions; drain. Melt 1/4 cup butter in a 1-quart saucepan. Stir in the flour, blending well. Add the milk gradually. Cook until thickened, stirring constantly. Add the Cheddar cheese, Parmesan cheese and 1/2 teaspoon salt. Cook over low heat until the cheese melts, stirring constantly. Place the vegetables in an ungreased 4-quart baking dish; sprinkle with the ham. Pour the cheese sauce over the top. Combine the bread crumbs and melted butter in a bowl, tossing to coat. Sprinkle in a border around the edge of the baking dish. Bake, uncovered, at 350 degrees for 20 to 30 minutes or until the bread crumbs are light brown and a cooking thermometer registers 165 degrees.

Yield: 10 servings.

Approx Per Serving: Cal 383; T Fat 24 g; 55% Calories from Fat; Prot 26 g; Carbo 18 g; Fiber 3 g; Chol 85 mg; Sod 1201 mg

Bill Barrett

Bill Barrett, United States congressman

FRUITED PORK ROAST

- 1 (3-pound) boneless pork loin roast
- 1 (10-ounce) can apricot filling
- 4 cups coarsely chopped potatoes
- 4 cups coarsely chopped carrots

Place the roast in a roasting pan. Cover with apricot filling. Bake, covered, at 325 degrees for 1 hour. Add the potatoes and carrots. Bake for 45 minutes longer or until the vegetables are tender and a meat thermometer registers 160 degrees for medium or 170 degrees for well-done. May substitute prune filling or sauerkraut for the apricot filling.

Yield: 8 servings.

Approx Per Serving: Cal 311; T Fat 8 g; 23% Calories from Fat; Prot 34 g; Carbo 25 g; Fiber 3 g; Chol 82 mg; Sod 71 mg

Doug Bereuter

Doug Bereuter, United States congressman

HOMEMADE PORK AND BEANS

- $1^1/_2$ cups dried red beans
- 2 to $2^1/_4$ pounds boneless pork shoulder
- 8 ounces slab bacon
- 2 tablespoons olive oil
- 2 cups chopped yellow onions
- 2 cups defatted chicken broth
- 1 (28-ounce) can plum tomatoes, drained, crushed
- 4 cloves of garlic, chopped
- 2 tablespoons Worcestershire sauce
- 1 bay leaf
- $^1/_8$ teaspoon Tabasco sauce
- Salt and pepper to taste
- $^1/_8$ teaspoon red wine vinegar
- 2 tablespoons chopped parsley

Rinse and sort the beans. Soak the beans in water to cover in the refrigerator overnight. Drain. Cut the pork into $1^1/_2$-inch cubes and the bacon into $^1/_4$-inch cubes. Brown the pork a small amount at a time in olive oil in a skillet over medium heat. Remove to a 2-quart baking dish. Add the bacon to the skillet. Cook over medium heat for 2 minutes. Remove to the baking dish. Cook the onions in the pan drippings for 5 minutes or until clear; drain. Add to the baking dish. Combine the chicken broth, tomatoes, garlic, Worcestershire sauce, bay leaf, Tabasco sauce, salt and pepper in a saucepan. Bring to a boil over medium heat. Pour into the baking dish. Mix in the vinegar and beans. Bake, covered, at 350 degrees for $1^1/_4$ hours. Stir the beans. Bake, uncovered, for 15 minutes longer or until a cooking thermometer registers 165 degrees. Discard the bay leaf. Garnish with parsley.

Yield: 6 servings.

Approx Per Serving: Cal 584; T Fat 24 g; 37% Calories from Fat; Prot 52 g; Carbo 40 g; Fiber 13 g; Chol 131 mg; Sod 681 mg

David Bracht

David Bracht
Nebraska 4-H Development Foundation, honorary member

FESTIVE HOLIDAY LAMB

- 3/4 teaspoon dried rosemary, crushed
- 1/2 teaspoon garlic powder
- 1 (4- to 5-pound) leg of lamb
- 1/3 cup sugar
- 1/3 cup vinegar
- 3 tablespoons light corn syrup
- 3 tablespoons water
- 1 (2-inch) cinnamon stick
- 1/2 teaspoon whole cloves
- 1/4 teaspoon ginger
- 3 medium apples, cored, sliced
- 1/2 cup packed brown sugar
- 1/3 cup frozen orange juice concentrate
- 2 teaspoons prepared mustard
- 3/4 teaspoon cinnamon

Combine the rosemary and garlic powder in a small bowl; mix well. Rub the mixture over the surface of the lamb. Place the lamb on a rack in a shallow roasting pan. Roast, uncovered, at 325 degrees for 2 1/4 to 2 1/2 hours or until a meat thermometer registers 160 degrees. Combine the 1/3 cup sugar, vinegar, corn syrup, water, cinnamon stick, cloves and ginger in a medium skillet. Bring to a boil over medium heat. Simmer, covered, over low heat for 4 minutes, stirring occasionally. Add the apple slices. Simmer for 4 minutes. Remove the apple slices, reserving 2 tablespoons of the poaching liquid. Cut 4 of the apple slices into halves. Combine the brown sugar, orange juice concentrate, mustard, cinnamon and reserved poaching liquid in a bowl; mix well. Cut 3-inch slits in the top of the lamb. Insert apple slice halves into the slits. Spoon a small amount of the brown sugar glaze over roast. Roast at 325 degrees for 10 minutes longer, basting with the remaining glaze twice. Arrange the lamb on a serving platter, drizzling with any remaining glaze. Arrange the apple slices around the edge of the platter. May double the amount of glaze if desired.

Adorned with poached apple slices, this leg of lamb makes an impressive holiday feast.

Yield: 10 servings.

Approx Per Serving: Cal 375; T Fat 11 g; 26% Calories from Fat; Prot 39 g; Carbo 30 g; Fiber 1 g; Chol 121 mg; Sod 117 mg

Sherman Berg

Sherman Berg
Nebraska 4-H Development Foundation, president

TACO TURKEY CORN BREAD

- **$2^1/_2$ cups yellow cornmeal**
- **2 tablespoons sugar**
- **1 tablespoon baking powder**
- **$^3/_4$ teaspoon baking soda**
- **$^1/_2$ teaspoon salt**
- **$2^1/_2$ cups buttermilk**
- **2 egg whites, slightly beaten**
- **1 pound ground turkey breast or chicken breast**
- **$^1/_3$ cup water**
- **1 envelope taco seasoning**
- **1 large onion, chopped**
- **1 cup shredded low-fat Cheddar cheese**

Mix the cornmeal, sugar, baking powder, baking soda and salt in a bowl. Add a mixture of the buttermilk and egg whites, stirring just until moistened. Brown the turkey in a skillet sprayed with nonstick cooking spray. Stir in the water and taco seasoning. Simmer until the liquid is absorbed, stirring frequently. Layer $^1/_2$ of the corn bread batter, the turkey mixture, onion, cheese and remaining batter in a baking pan sprayed with nonstick cooking spray. Bake at 400 degrees for 20 minutes; spray the top with nonstick cooking spray. Bake for 10 to 15 minutes longer or until brown and a cooking thermometer registers 165 degrees.

Eating healthy helps my performance on tour. This is a low-fat recipe that I enjoy.

Yield: 10 servings.

Approx Per Serving: Cal 281; T Fat 6 g; 19% Calories from Fat; Prot 19 g; Carbo 38 g; Fiber 2 g; Chol 33 mg; Sod 800 mg

Val Skinner
Professional golfer

HONEY BARBECUE-STYLE BAKED BEANS

- **2 (16-ounce) cans baked beans**
- **$^3/_4$ cup barbecue sauce**
- **2 tablespoons chopped onion**
- **3 slices crisp-fried bacon, crumbled**
- **2 tablespoons honey**
- **$^3/_4$ teaspoon paprika**
- **$^3/_4$ teaspoon dry mustard**

Combine the baked beans, barbecue sauce, onion, bacon, honey, paprika and dry mustard in a bowl and mix well. Spoon into a 9x9-inch heat-resistant pan. Place the pan on a grill rack over indirect heat; close the lid. Grill for 1 hour or until heated through and a cooking thermometer registers 165 degrees. May bake in a 2-quart baking dish at 350 degrees for 1 hour or until of the desired consistency.

All American, traditional, seasoned . . . and the beans are pretty good too!

Yield: 6 servings.

Approx Per Serving: Cal 227; T Fat 5 g; 17% Calories from Fat; Prot 10 g; Carbo 41 g; Fiber 10 g; Chol 13 mg; Sod 932 mg

Jon Christensen
United States congressman

CELERY AND WATER CHESTNUT CASSEROLE

- 4 cups chopped celery
- 1 (8-ounce) can sliced water chestnuts, drained
- 1 (10-ounce) can cream of chicken soup
- 1 (4-ounce) can mushroom bits and pieces, drained
- 1 (2-ounce) jar pimento strips, drained
- 1/2 cup seasoned bread crumbs
- 1/4 cup slivered almonds

Combine the celery with enough water to cover in a saucepan. Cook until tender-crisp; drain. Combine the celery, water chestnuts, soup, mushrooms and pimento in a bowl and mix well. Spoon into a greased 2-quart baking dish; sprinkle with the bread crumbs and almonds. Bake at 350 degrees for 35 minutes.

Yield: 4 servings.

Approx Per Serving: Cal 224; T Fat 10 g; 36% Calories from Fat; Prot 8 g; Carbo 30 g; Fiber 5 g; Chol 6 mg; Sod 1163 mg

Virginia D. Smith

Virginia D. Smith
former United States congresswoman

SCALLOPED CORN

- 1/4 cup chopped onion
- 1/4 cup chopped green bell pepper
- 2 tablespoons margarine
- 2 tablespoons flour
- 1 teaspoon salt
- 1/2 teaspoon paprika
- 1/4 teaspoon dry mustard
- 1/8 teaspoon pepper
- 3/4 cup milk
- 2 cups whole kernel corn
- 1 egg, beaten
- 1/3 cup cracker crumbs
- 1 tablespoon margarine

Sauté the onion and green pepper in 2 tablespoons margarine in a skillet. Remove from heat. Stir in the flour, salt, paprika, dry mustard and pepper. Cook over low heat until bubbly, stirring constantly. Remove from heat. Stir in the milk. Bring to a boil, stirring constantly. Boil for 1 minute, stirring constantly. Stir in the corn and egg. Spoon into an ungreased 1-quart baking dish. Sprinkle with the cracker crumbs; dot with 1 tablespoon margarine. Bake at 350 degrees for 30 to 50 minutes or until a cooking thermometer registers 165 degrees. May substitute crumbled potato chips for the crackers.

Yield: 4 servings.

Approx Per Serving: Cal 240; T Fat 13 g; 47% Calories from Fat; Prot 7 g; Carbo 26 g; Fiber 3 g; Chol 59 mg; Sod 774 mg

Ben Nelson

Ben Nelson, Nebraska governor

ROGER'S MASHED POTATOES

6 medium new potatoes, peeled, cut into quarters
1/8 teaspoon salt
1/2 cup low-fat or skim milk
2 tablespoons margarine, softened
2 teaspoons minced onion

Combine the potatoes with enough cold water to cover in a 4-quart saucepan. Add salt. Simmer, covered, for 20 minutes or until tender. Drain, reserving liquid for gravy if desired. Combine the potatoes, milk, margarine and onion in a mixer bowl. Beat until of the desired consistency, scraping the bowl occasionally. May substitute 1/2 teaspoon minced garlic for onion.

Yield: 4 servings.

Approx Per Serving: Cal 236; T Fat 6 g; 24% Calories from Fat; Prot 5 g; Carbo 41 g; Fiber 3 g; Chol 2 mg; Sod 158 mg

Roger Welsch

Roger Welsch, author

THREE-CHEESE SCALLOPED POTATOES

6 baking potatoes, peeled, sliced
Salt to taste
1 tablespoon chopped garlic
1 tablespoon chopped shallot
1 tablespoon butter
2 cups cream
2 cups milk
1 tablespoon chopped fresh basil
Pepper to taste
2 tablespoons (about) cornstarch
1 cup shredded Cheddar cheese
1 cup shredded Monterey Jack cheese
1 cup grated Parmesan cheese

Combine the potatoes and salt with enough water to cover in a saucepan. Cook until tender but firm; drain. Sauté the garlic and shallot in the butter in a saucepan until tender. Stir in the cream, milk, basil, salt and pepper. Bring to a boil. Stir in the cornstarch and mix well. Cook until of the consistency of a cream soup, stirring constantly. Layer the potatoes, sauce, Cheddar cheese, Monterey Jack cheese and Parmesan cheese alternately in a baking pan until all of the ingredients are used. Bake at 350 degrees for 45 to 60 minutes or until brown and bubbly. Let stand for 20 to 30 minutes before serving. May substitute your favorite herb or combination of herbs for the basil. May substitute 1 1/2 teaspoons dried herbs for 1 tablespoon chopped fresh.

Yield: 10 servings.

Approx Per Serving: Cal 413; T Fat 31 g; 66% Calories from Fat; Prot 14 g; Carbo 22 g; Fiber 1 g; Chol 105 mg; Sod 374 mg

Gerald R. Ford

Gerald R. Ford
former United States president

TEXAS POTATOES

3 or 4 (3-pound) packages frozen hash brown potatoes, thawed
1 (50-ounce) can cream of chicken soup
3 to 4 cups shredded Cheddar cheese
2 cups sour cream
1½ cups melted margarine
1 cup chopped onion
3 to 4 tablespoons salt
Pepper to taste

Combine the hash brown potatoes, soup, cheese, sour cream, margarine, onion, salt and pepper in a bowl and mix well. Spoon into baking pans sprayed with nonstick cooking spray. Bake at 350 degrees for 2 hours or until brown and bubbly.

Yield: 30 servings

Approx Per Serving: Cal 369; T Fat 21 g; 51% Calories from Fat; Prot 9 g; Carbo 37 g; Fiber <1 g; Chol 26 mg; Sod 1473 mg

Bernie Lorkovic, camp manager
Nebraska State 4-H Camp

ARLENE'S MACARONI AND CHEESE

2 quarts water
2¾ cups macaroni
½ teaspoon salt
1 tablespoon chopped onion
2 tablespoons melted butter
1¼ pounds American cheese, chopped
3 cups milk
Salt and pepper to taste
4 ounces American cheese, shredded

Bring the water to a boil in a saucepan. Add the macaroni and ½ teaspoon salt. Cook for 8 to 10 minutes or until tender but firm; drain. Sauté the onion in the butter in a saucepan. Add 1¼ pounds cheese and milk. Cook until the cheese melts, stirring constantly. Season with salt to taste and pepper. Add to the macaroni in a bowl and mix well. Spoon into a baking pan; sprinkle with 4 ounces cheese. Bake at 350 degrees for 35 minutes.

The kids love this family favorite. It's quick and easy to make for a family on the go.

Yield: 8 servings.

Approx Per Serving: Cal 533; T Fat 33 g; 56% Calories from Fat; Prot 27 g; Carbo 33 g; Fiber 1 g; Chol 100 mg; Sod 1425 mg

Danny Nee
University of Nebraska men's head basketball coach

CORNISH SAFFRON CHRISTMAS BREAD

2 envelopes dry yeast
1 teaspoon sugar
1 cup lukewarm (110 to 115 degrees) water
1 cup boiling water
1 to 2 teaspoons saffron tea leaves
1 1/2 cups lukewarm water
1 tablespoon lemon extract
2 1/2 cups sugar
1 teaspoon salt
3/4 cup shortening
3 eggs, beaten
8 to 10 cups flour
1 1/2 cups raisins
1/2 cup currants

Dissolve the yeast and 1 teaspoon sugar in 1 cup lukewarm water and mix well. Pour 1 cup boiling water over the saffron tea leaves in a bowl. Let stand until cool; strain into a large bowl. Stir in 1 1/2 cups lukewarm water and the lemon extract. Add 2 1/2 cups sugar and salt and mix well. Stir in the yeast mixture. Stir in the shortening and eggs until blended. Add 1/2 of the flour, beating until blended. Stir in the remaining flour. Add the raisins and currants and mix well; knead. Let rise, covered, in a warm place until doubled in bulk. Punch the dough down; the dough should be slightly sticky. Let rise until doubled in bulk if desired, or shape and place on a baking sheet, letting rise until doubled in bulk. Bake at 350 degrees for 35 to 40 minutes or until golden brown.

The traditional shape is a large bun (half a loaf) with a miniature bun perched on the top. This recipe was brought by my great-great-grandmother from Cornwall, England, to the United States. Giving buns as gifts and enjoying them in our homes with our family is a Christmas tradition.

Yield: 50 servings.

Approx Per Serving: Cal 182; T Fat 4 g; 18% Calories from Fat; Prot 3 g; Carbo 34 g; Fiber 1 g; Chol 13 mg; Sod 48 mg

Delwyn Dearborn

Delwyn D. Dearborn
Nebraska State 4-H Program Leader & Director of
The Nebraska 4-H Development Foundation

HOUSKA-CZECH BRAIDED BREAD

2 envelopes dry yeast
1 teaspoon sugar
½ cup lukewarm (110 to 115 degrees) water
2½ cups milk, scalded, cooled
½ cup sugar
½ cup melted shortening
3 egg yolks, beaten
1 tablespoon salt
8 cups (about) flour

Combine the yeast, 1 teaspoon sugar and lukewarm water in a bowl. Let stand for 10 minutes or until bubbly. Combine the yeast mixture, milk, ½ cup sugar, shortening, egg yolks and salt in a bowl and mix well. Add just enough flour to make a medium-stiff dough; knead. Let rise, covered, in a warm place until doubled in bulk. Punch the dough down. Divide the dough into 4 equal portions. Divide each portion into 2 portions. Set aside all but 2 portions. Divide 1 of these 2 portions into thirds. Roll each third into a 12-inch strip; braid on a baking sheet. Divide the second portion of dough into ⅓ and ⅔ portions. Divide the ⅔ portion into 3 equal portions. Roll each portion into a 10-inch strip; braid. Place on the prepared braided layer, making an indention in the prepared layer for it to rest on. Divide the remaining ⅓ portion into 2 portions. Roll each portion into a thin strip; twist together loosely. Arrange on top of the prepared layers; tuck the ends under the loaf. Repeat the procedure with the remaining dough portions. Bake at 350 degrees for 30 to 40 minutes or until brown; may cover with foil during the last 15 minutes of the baking time to prevent overbrowning.

I won the country demonstration contest and received a special award at the State Fair Demonstration Contest with this recipe.

Yield: 48 servings.

Approx Per Serving: Cal 115; T Fat 3 g; 24% Calories from Fat; Prot 3 g; Carbo 19 g; Fiber 1 g; Chol 15 mg; Sod 140 mg

Melissa Loftis

Melissa Loftis
Nebraska 4-H Development Foundation, fall 1995 intern

CARAMEL CINNAMON ROLLS

1 envelope yeast
2 teaspoons sugar
1/2 cup lukewarm (110 to 115 degrees) water
1 1/2 cups milk
1/2 cup sugar
1/4 cup shortening
1 teaspoon salt
6 cups sifted flour
2 eggs, beaten
1 teaspoon grated lemon peel
1/4 cup margarine, softened
1/4 to 1/3 cup packed brown sugar
Cinnamon to taste
1/2 cup cream
1 cup packed brown sugar

Dissolve the yeast and 2 teaspoons sugar in the lukewarm water and mix well. Scald the milk in a saucepan. Stir in 1/2 cup sugar, shortening and salt. Let stand until cool. Combine the sugar mixture with just enough of the flour in a bowl to make a thick batter. Add the yeast mixture and mix well. Stir in the eggs and lemon peel. Add enough of the remaining flour to make a soft dough and mix well. Place the dough on a lightly floured surface; cover with a bowl. Let rest for 10 minutes; knead. Place the dough in a greased bowl, turning to coat the surface. Let rise, covered, for 20 minutes. Roll into a 1/4-inch thick rectangle on a lightly floured surface. Spread with the margarine; sprinkle with 1/4 to 1/3 cup brown sugar and cinnamon. Roll to enclose the filling. Cut into 1 1/2-inch slices. Grease a 9x13-inch baking pan. Pour the cream into the pan. Crumble 1 cup brown sugar into the cream. Place the slices cut side down in the prepared pan. Bake at 350 degrees for 25 to 30 minutes or until brown. May omit the lemon peel and may sprinkle the dough with white granulated sugar instead of brown sugar. May substitute evaporated milk for the cream.

I used to help my mother make these cinnamon rolls for 4-H Club treats and to put in school lunches at the one-room school I attended.

Yield: 48 servings.

Approx Per Serving: Cal 115; T Fat 4 g; 28% Calories from Fat; Prot 2 g; Carbo 19 g; Fiber <1 g; Chol 13 mg; Sod 65 mg

Rich Hawkins

Rich Hawkins, KRVN Radio

CRESCENT ROLLS

$4^1/_2$ cups flour
1 envelope dry yeast
1 cup milk
$^1/_3$ cup sugar
$^1/_3$ cup margarine
$^1/_2$ teaspoon salt
2 eggs
$^1/_4$ cup melted margarine

Combine 2 cups of the flour and the yeast in a mixer bowl and mix well. Combine the milk, sugar, $^1/_3$ cup margarine and salt in a microwave-safe dish. Microwave until the mixture is warm and the margarine is almost melted or to 120 degrees on a cooking thermometer. Stir into the flour mixture. Add the eggs. Beat at low speed for 30 seconds, scraping the bowl constantly. Beat at high speed for 3 minutes, scraping the bowl frequently. Stir in enough of the remaining flour to make an easily handled dough. Knead the dough on a lightly floured surface for 6 to 8 minutes or until smooth and elastic. Shape into a ball. Place in a greased bowl, turning to coat the surface. Let rise, covered, in a warm place for 1 to $1^1/_2$ hours or until doubled in bulk. Punch the dough down. Divide the dough into 2 equal portions. Roll each portion into a 12-inch circle on a lightly floured surface. Brush with $^1/_4$ cup margarine. Cut each circle into 12 wedges. Roll the wedges up from the wide end. Shape into crescents on a baking sheet. Let rise until almost doubled in bulk. Bake at 375 degrees for 10 to 12 minutes or until golden brown. May double or quadruple this recipe and freeze for future use.

This recipe has been a favorite of my family for years. Our daughters used this recipe for Harlan County and Nebraska State Fair entries, often winning purple ribbons for the rolls.

Yield: 24 servings.

Approx Per Serving: Cal 149; T Fat 5 g; 33% Calories from Fat; Prot 3 g; Carbo 21 g; Fiber 1 g; Chol 19 mg; Sod 107 mg

Larene Bantam, camp manager
South Central 4-H Center

COCONUT PECAN CAKE

1 (2-layer) package yellow cake mix
1 (3-ounce) package vanilla instant pudding mix
$1\frac{1}{3}$ cups water
4 eggs
$\frac{1}{4}$ cup vegetable oil
2 cups flaked coconut
1 cup chopped pecans
Coconut Frosting

Combine the cake mix, instant pudding mix and water in a mixer bowl; beat well. Add the eggs and oil; mix well. Stir in the coconut and pecans. Spoon into 3 greased and floured 9-inch cake pans. Bake at 350 degrees for 35 minutes or until the cake tests done. Cool in the pans for several minutes; remove to a wire rack to cool completely. Spread the Coconut Frosting between the layers and over the top and side of the cake. Sprinkle with the reserved browned coconut.

COCONUT FROSTING

2 cups flaked coconut
2 tablespoons margarine
8 ounces cream cheese, softened
2 tablespoons margarine
2 teaspoons milk
$3\frac{1}{2}$ cups confectioners' sugar
$\frac{1}{2}$ teaspoon vanilla extract

Sauté the coconut in 2 tablespoons margarine in a skillet until brown. Cream the cream cheese and remaining 2 tablespoons margarine in a mixer bowl. Add the milk; mix well. Add the confectioners' sugar gradually. Add the vanilla; mix well. Reserve $\frac{1}{4}$ cup of the browned coconut. Stir in the remaining browned coconut.

This is not fat-free, but it can be made as a lower-fat version by using egg substitute or egg whites, safflower oil, skim milk, low-fat cream cheese and light margarine.

Yield: 12 servings.

Approx Per Serving: Cal 696; T Fat 37 g; 46% Calories from Fat; Prot 7 g; Carbo 89 g; Fiber 4 g; Chol 92 mg; Sod 526 mg

Tom Osborne

Tom Osborne
University of Nebraska head football coach

MELBA'S OATMEAL CAKE

$1^1/_2$ cups boiling water
1 cup quick-cooking oats
1 cup packed brown sugar
1 cup sugar
$^1/_2$ cup margarine, softened
2 eggs
$1^1/_4$ cups sifted flour
1 teaspoon baking soda
1 teaspoon nutmeg
$^1/_2$ teaspoon salt
$^1/_2$ teaspoon cinnamon
1 cup chopped walnuts
1 cup flaked coconut
$^1/_2$ cup sugar
6 tablespoons margarine
$^1/_4$ cup packed brown sugar
$^1/_4$ cup light cream
$^1/_4$ teaspoon vanilla extract

Pour the boiling water over the oats in a bowl and mix well. Beat 1 cup brown sugar, 1 cup sugar and $^1/_2$ cup margarine in a mixer bowl until creamy. Beat in the eggs until blended. Add the oats mixture and mix well. Stir in a sifted mixture of the flour, baking soda, nutmeg, salt and cinnamon. Spoon into a greased 9x13-inch cake pan. Bake at 350 degrees for 30 to 35 minutes or until the cake tests done. Let stand until cool. Combine the walnuts, coconut, $^1/_2$ cup sugar, 6 tablespoons margarine, $^1/_4$ cup brown sugar and light cream in a saucepan. Cook until bubbly, stirring constantly. Stir in the vanilla. Spread over the baked layer. Broil for 5 minutes or until golden brown.

Melba Glock, a Nebraska farm wife, is a dear friend of Senator Kerry. He is always happy to enjoy her legendary oatmeal cake.

Yield: 15 servings.

Approx Per Serving: Cal 381; T Fat 20 g; 45% Calories from Fat; Prot 4 g; Carbo 49 g; Fiber 2 g; Chol 33 mg; Sod 269 mg

Bob Kerrey, United States senator

LOW-FAT BROWNIES

1 (22-ounce) package brownie mix
$^1/_3$ cup low-fat plain yogurt
2 egg whites
1 teaspoon vanilla extract

Combine the brownie mix, yogurt, egg whites and vanilla in a bowl and mix well. Spoon into a 9x13-inch baking pan. Bake at 350 degrees for 22 to 24 minutes or until the brownies test done. Cool in pan. Cut into bars. May substitute $^1/_4$ cup egg substitute for the egg whites.

These brownies are the answer to a low-fat, cholesterol-free dessert.

Yield: 36 servings.

Approx Per Serving: Cal 57; T Fat 1 g; 17% Calories from Fat; Prot 1 g; Carbo 10 g; Fiber <1 g; Chol <1 mg; Sod 64 mg

Angela Beck
University of Nebraska women's head basketball coach

DATE NUT BALLS

- 1 cup sugar
- 8 ounces chopped pitted dates
- 1/2 cup plus 2 tablespoons margarine
- 2 cups crisp rice cereal
- 1 cup chopped walnuts
- 1 teaspoon vanilla extract
- 1/4 cup (or more) confectioners' sugar

Combine the sugar, dates and margarine in a saucepan. Cook over low heat until the margarine melts and the sugar dissolves, stirring frequently. Remove from heat. Stir in the cereal, walnuts and vanilla. Cool to room temperature. Shape into 1-inch balls. Coat with the confectioners' sugar. Place on a serving platter.

These are easy to make for friends and parties.

Yield: 36 servings.

Approx Per Serving: Cal 98; T Fat 5 g; 46% Calories from Fat; Prot 1 g; Carbo 13 g; Fiber 1 g; Chol 0 mg; Sod 57 mg

Terry Pettit

Terry Pettit
University of Nebraska women's head volleyball coach

FAVORITE OATMEAL COOKIES

- 1 cup raisins
- 1 teaspoon baking soda
- 1 cup shortening
- 1 cup sugar
- 2 eggs
- 1 teaspoon vanilla extract
- 2 cups flour
- 1/2 teaspoon salt
- 1/2 teaspoon nutmeg
- 1/2 teaspoon cinnamon
- 1/2 teaspoon allspice
- 2 cups rolled oats
- 1 cup chopped walnuts or pecans

Combine the raisins with enough water to cover in a saucepan. Bring to a boil. Boil for several minutes. Drain, reserving 5 tablespoons of the liquid. Combine the reserved liquid and baking soda in a bowl and mix well. Beat the shortening and sugar in a mixer bowl until creamy. Add the eggs and vanilla, beating until blended. Add a sifted mixture of the flour, salt, nutmeg, cinnamon and allspice and the liquid mixture and mix well. Stir in the raisins, oats and walnuts. Drop by teaspoonfuls onto a cookie sheet. Bake at 350 degrees for 10 to 12 minutes or until brown. Remove to a wire rack to cool. Store in a covered food-graded container or freeze for future use.

These cookies have always been a favorite family treat with milk or coffee on winter evenings.

Yield: 48 servings.

Approx Per Serving: Cal 115; T Fat 6 g; 48% Calories from Fat; Prot 2 g; Carbo 14 g; Fiber 1 g; Chol 9 mg; Sod 43 mg

Dave Howe

Dave R. Howe, Nebraska Farmer

Appetizers and Beverages

A Taste of Summer

Patio Party Menu

Tex-Mex Dip
page 30

Buffalo Wings Original New York-Style
page 32

Mozzarella Sticks
page 32

Pasta Chicken Salad
page 46

Amazing Corn Cake
page 127

Harvest Popcorn
page 155

Slush Punch
page 35

Photograph by Meghan Burgess
Gage County

BERRY GOOD DIP

8 ounces fresh or frozen strawberries, thawed
4 ounces nonfat cream cheese, softened
1/4 cup reduced-fat sour cream
1 tablespoon sugar

Process the strawberries in a securely covered blender container until puréed. Beat the cream cheese in a small bowl until smooth. Stir in the strawberries, sour cream and sugar. Chill, covered, in the refrigerator until serving time. Serve with fresh fruit or angel food cake cubes.

Kids love this dip.

Yield: 12 servings.

Approx Per Serving: Cal 25; T Fat 1 g; 25% Calories from Fat; Prot 2 g; Carbo 3 g; Fiber <1 g; Chol 4 mg; Sod 59 mg

Makayla Hirschman, St. Paul

FRUIT DIP

8 ounces cream cheese, softened
3/4 cup packed brown sugar
1/2 cup confectioners' sugar
1 tablespoon vanilla extract
1 tablespoon milk

Combine the cream cheese, brown sugar, confectioners' sugar, vanilla and milk in a bowl; mix well. Refrigerate until serving time. Serve with sliced apples or other fruit.

Yield: 16 servings.

Approx Per Serving: Cal 99; T Fat 5 g; 45% Calories from Fat; Prot 1 g; Carbo 13 g; Fiber 0 g; Chol 16 mg; Sod 46 mg

Julie Kresl, Hemingford

SALSA SAUCE

1 (28-ounce) can stewed tomatoes, chopped
1/2 medium onion, chopped
1 (4-ounce) can mild chile peppers
2 tablespoons vinegar
1/4 cup sugar
Tabasco sauce to taste
Pepper to taste

Combine the tomatoes, onion, chile peppers, vinegar, sugar, Tabasco sauce and pepper in a 2-quart saucepan. Simmer over medium-low heat for 1 1/4 hours, stirring occasionally. Serve warm or cold with tortilla chips.

Yield: 12 servings.

Approx Per Serving: Cal 38; T Fat <1 g; 2% Calories from Fat; Prot 1 g; Carbo 10 g; Fiber 1 g; Chol 0 mg; Sod 279 mg

Kara Ayers, York

MELISSA'S TACOS GRINGO-STYLE

- **4 ounces cream cheese, softened**
- **1/2 cup sour cream**
- **1 tablespoon hot sauce**
- **2 tablespoons taco seasoning mix**
- **1/2 pound ground beef**
- **1 1/2 teaspoons taco seasoning mix**
- **1 onion, chopped**
- **1 tomato, chopped**
- **1/4 head lettuce, shredded**
- **1/2 cup shredded Cheddar cheese**
- **1/4 cup sliced olives**
- **1/2 cup chopped green bell pepper**

Combine the cream cheese, sour cream, hot sauce and 2 tablespoons taco seasoning mix in a bowl; mix well. Brown the ground beef in a skillet until no pink remains, stirring until crumbly; drain. Stir in remaining 1 1/2 teaspoons taco seasoning mix. Layer the cream cheese mixture, ground beef, onion, tomato, lettuce, cheese, olives and green pepper in an 8x8-inch serving dish. Serve immediately with tortilla chips.

This recipe came from a 4-H presentation.

Yield: 16 servings.

Approx Per Serving: Cal 102; T Fat 8 g; 66% Calories from Fat; Prot 5 g; Carbo 3 g; Fiber <1 g; Chol 25 mg; Sod 227 mg

Pam Goshorn, Ainsworth

TEX-MEX DIP

- **2 (9-ounce) cans bean dip**
- **3 avocados, peeled**
- **2 tablespoons lemon juice**
- **1/2 teaspoon salt**
- **1/4 teaspoon pepper**
- **1 cup sour cream**
- **1/2 cup mayonnaise**
- **1 (1 1/4-ounce) package taco seasoning mix**
- **2 cups shredded Cheddar cheese**
- **1 cup sliced black olives**
- **3 green onions and tops, sliced**
- **1 large tomato, seeded, chopped**

Spread bean dip on a 12-inch serving plate. Mash the avocados with lemon juice, salt and pepper in a bowl. Spread over the bean dip, leaving a small margin around edge. Combine the sour cream, mayonnaise and taco seasoning mix in a bowl. Layer over the avocados; sprinkle with cheese, olives, green onions and tomato. Refrigerate until serving time. Serve with tortilla chips.

If you have lovers of Tex-Mex foods, this will disappear so fast you won't believe it. It is as festive looking as it is tasty.

Yield: 10 servings.

Approx Per Serving: Cal 429; T Fat 35 g; 71% Calories from Fat; Prot 11 g; Carbo 21 g; Fiber 6 g; Chol 41 mg; Sod 1384 mg

Fran Obermire, Atkinson

DRIED BEEF LOG

- 8 ounces cream cheese, softened
- 1/4 cup grated Parmesan cheese
- 1 tablespoon horseradish
- 1/3 cup chopped pimento-stuffed olives
- 2 1/2 ounces dried beef, finely chopped

Combine the cream cheese, Parmesan cheese and horseradish in a bowl; mix well. Stir in the olives. Shape into two 6-inch rolls with a diameter of 1 1/2 inches. Refrigerate, wrapped in plastic wrap, for 8 to 10 hours. Roll each log in the dried beef. Place on a serving plate. Serve with crackers.

Yield: 24 servings.

Approx Per Serving: Cal 45; T Fat 4 g; 78% Calories from Fat; Prot 2 g; Carbo <1 g; Fiber <1 g; Chol 13 mg; Sod 199 mg

Wade Miller, Aurora

CHEESE LOGS

- 2 (6-ounce) rolls garlic cheese, shredded
- 2 (5-ounce) jars Old English cheese spread
- 8 ounces cream cheese, softened
- 1/4 cup chili powder
- 1/2 cup ground walnuts

Combine the garlic cheese, Old English cheese spread and cream cheese in a bowl; mix well. Divide into 2 portions. Shape each portion into a log. Roll 1 log in chili powder to coat. Roll the remaining log in walnuts to coat. Refrigerate until serving time.

Yield: 24 servings.

Approx Per Serving: Cal 138; T Fat 12 g; 78% Calories from Fat; Prot 7 g; Carbo 2 g; Fiber <1 g; Chol 32 mg; Sod 382 mg

Conni Bales, Grand Island

CHEESE SPREAD

- 3 tablespoons flour
- 1 cup milk
- 1 tablespoon butter
- 1 teaspoon finely minced onion
- 2 tablespoons vinegar
- 1/2 teaspoon salt
- 1 cup shredded American cheese
- 4 hard-cooked eggs, chopped and refrigerated until used in recipe

Combine the flour and milk in a saucepan. Cook over low heat, stirring until smooth. Add the butter, onion, vinegar and salt. Cook until thickened, stirring constantly. Remove from the heat. Stir in the cheese until melted. Stir in the eggs. Store, covered, in refrigerator until serving time. Spread on wheat bread or crackers.

Makes a tasty snack.

Yield: 24 servings.

Approx Per Serving: Cal 45; T Fat 3 g; 64% Calories from Fat; Prot 3 g; Carbo 1 g; Fiber <1 g; Chol 43 mg; Sod 132 mg

Anita Keys, Elsmere

Buffalo Wings Original New York-Style

- **1/3 cup barbecue sauce**
- **1/3 cup white vinegar**
- **1/4 cup melted butter**
- **1/3 cup (more or less) hot sauce**
- **24 chicken wings**

Combine the barbecue sauce, vinegar, butter and hot sauce in a bowl. Refrigerate until ready to use. Rinse the chicken wings and pat dry. Deep-fry the chicken wings until well done; drain. Dip hot chicken in the barbecue sauce mixture. Serve with bleu cheese dressing.

This recipe came from friends who came to hunt with us.

Yield: 24 servings.

Approx Per Serving: Cal 119; T Fat 9 g; 66% Calories from Fat; Prot 9 g; Carbo 1 g; Fiber <1 g; Chol 34 mg; Sod 77 mg

Jane Dewey, Trenton

Mozzarella Sticks

- **2 eggs**
- **1 tablespoon water**
- **1 cup dry bread crumbs**
- **2 1/2 teaspoons Italian seasoning**
- **1/2 teaspoon garlic powder**
- **1/8 teaspoon pepper**
- **12 sticks string cheese or 1/2x4-inch sticks mozzarella cheese**
- **1/2 cup sifted flour**
- **3 tablespoons melted butter**
- **1 cup marinara or spaghetti sauce, heated**

Combine the eggs and water in a small bowl; beat well. Combine the bread crumbs, Italian seasoning, garlic powder and pepper in a plastic bag; mix well. Coat the cheese sticks in the flour; dip in the beaten eggs and coat with the bread crumb mixture. Repeat the egg and bread crumb coatings. Discard extra crumb mix. Refrigerate the coated cheese sticks, covered, for at least 4 hours. Place on an ungreased baking sheet; drizzle with melted butter. Bake at 400 degrees for 6 to 8 minutes. Let stand for 3 to 5 minutes before serving. Serve with sauce for dipping.

Yield: 12 servings.

Approx Per Serving: Cal 174; T Fat 9 g; 48% Calories from Fat; Prot 10 g; Carbo 13 g; Fiber <1 g; Chol 60 mg; Sod 375 mg

Sue and Bethany Babovec, Cedar Rapids

RUMAKI

- 2 pounds bacon
- 3 (8-ounce) cans whole water chestnuts, drained
- 1/2 cup sugar
- 1/2 cup packed brown sugar
- 1/2 cup catsup
- 1/2 cup vinegar
- 1/4 cup soy sauce

Cut the bacon slices into thirds. Wrap each piece of bacon around a water chestnut; secure with a wooden pick. Place on a rack in a nonstick baking pan. Bake at 400 degrees for 20 minutes. Remove to a 9x13-inch baking dish and cool slightly. May refrigerate for 8 to 10 hours. Combine the sugar, brown sugar, catsup, vinegar and soy sauce in a saucepan. Cook over medium heat until the sugar dissolves, stirring constantly. Pour over bacon-wrapped water chestnuts. Bake at 350 degrees for 30 minutes. Serve hot. May transfer to a hot slow cooker or chafing dish for serving.

Yield: 24 servings.

Approx Per Serving: Cal 117; T Fat 6 g; 46% Calories from Fat; Prot 4 g; Carbo 14 g; Fiber <1 g; Chol 10 mg; Sod 417 mg

Linda Raddatz, Sidney

CONFETTI BARS

- 2 (8-count) cans crescent rolls
- 16 ounces cream cheese, softened
- 1/2 cup mayonnaise
- 1/2 package ranch dressing mix
- 1 cup each chopped celery, carrots, broccoli florets, cauliflowerets and black olives
- 1 cup shredded Cheddar cheese

Unroll crescent roll dough. Line a jelly roll pan with the dough, pressing perforations to seal. Bake using package directions just until golden brown. Cool to room temperature. Combine the cream cheese, mayonnaise and ranch dressing mix in a bowl; mix well. Refrigerate until ready to use. Spread cream cheese mixture over cooled layer. Add chopped vegetables. Sprinkle with shredded cheese. Refrigerate until very cold. Cut into bars. May add any combination of your favorite chopped vegetables.

This recipe was used for nutrition bars and won best food and overall food exhibitor at the county fair.

Yield: 36 servings.

Approx Per Serving: Cal 125; T Fat 10 g; 69% Calories from Fat; Prot 3 g; Carbo 7 g; Fiber <1 g; Chol 20 mg; Sod 248 mg

Jill Arnold, Broken Bow
Julie Kehrli, Schuyler
Kristi Steffen, Hartington

TORTILLA ROLL-UPS

1 cup sour cream
8 ounces cream cheese, softened
1 (4-ounce) can chopped green chiles
1 (4-ounce) can chopped black olives
1 cup shredded Cheddar cheese
1/2 cup chopped green onions
Garlic powder to taste
5 flour tortillas
1 (8-ounce) jar salsa

Combine the sour cream, cream cheese, green chiles, olives, cheese, green onions and garlic powder in a bowl; mix well. Spread mixture on tortillas. Roll to enclose filling; wrap tightly in plastic wrap. Refrigerate for 2 to 3 hours. Cut into 1/4-inch thick slices. Place on a serving platter. Serve with salsa.

Yield: 50 servings.

Approx Per Serving: Cal 51; T Fat 4 g; 66% Calories from Fat; Prot 1 g; Carbo 3 g; Fiber <1 g; Chol 9 mg; Sod 109 mg

Linda Dannehl, Bertrand
Donna Rose, Blue Hill
Gina Splattstoesser, Franklin

HOT AND SWEET SNACK MIX

1 cup light corn syrup
1/2 cup sugar
1/2 cup butter
1 teaspoon cayenne
1 teaspoon Tabasco sauce
1 teaspoon baking soda
2 (9 1/2-ounce) packages traditional flavor Ritz Snack Mix
1 1/2 cups pecans
1 cup dry roasted peanuts

Combine the corn syrup, sugar and butter in a saucepan. Bring to a boil over medium heat, stirring frequently. Remove from heat. Stir in the cayenne, Tabasco sauce and baking soda. Combine the snack mix, pecans and peanuts in a large bowl; mix well. Pour the syrup over the mixture, tossing to coat. Spread in a nonstick baking pan. Bake at 250 degrees for 1 hour, stirring every 15 minutes. Pour onto waxed paper, breaking up the mixture. Let stand until cool. Store in an airtight food-graded container.

I received this recipe from friends and fellow 4-H Extension co-workers from Louisiana.

Yield: 16 servings.

Approx Per Serving: Cal 412; T Fat 25 g; 51% Calories from Fat; Prot 6 g; Carbo 48 g; Fiber 2 g; Chol 16 mg; Sod 590 mg

Tracy J. Behnken, Omaha

BANANA MILK SHAKE

- $^1/_2$ banana
- $^1/_2$ cup skim milk
- $^1/_4$ teaspoon almond extract
- 2 ice cubes
- 1 teaspoon sugar or equivalent in artificial sweetener

Process banana, skim milk, almond extract and ice cubes in a securely covered blender or food processor container until smooth. Stir in the sugar.

This is great for breakfast or after school!

Yield: 1 serving.

Approx Per Serving: Cal 111; T Fat <1 g; 4% Calories from Fat; Prot 5 g; Carbo 23 g; Fiber 1 g; Chol 2 mg; Sod 64 mg

Stephanie Scharf, Curtis

PURPLE COW SHAKES

- 1 (6-ounce) can frozen grape juice concentrate
- 1 cup milk
- 2 cups vanilla ice cream

Process grape juice concentrate, milk and ice cream in a securely covered blender container for 30 seconds. Serve immediately. May shake ingredients in a tightly covered 2-quart jar or beat with an egg beater in a large bowl.

My big brother, Taylor, used to make this for me a lot when I was little. Now I make it for my family.

Yield: 3 servings.

Approx Per Serving: Cal 329; T Fat 13 g; 34% Calories from Fat; Prot 6 g; Carbo 50 g; Fiber 1 g; Chol 50 mg; Sod 114 mg

Kelsey Cupp, Champion

SLUSH PUNCH

- 2 (3-ounce) packages fruit-flavored gelatin
- 2 cups boiling water
- 1 cup cold water
- 2 (46-ounce) cans unsweetened pineapple juice
- 2 cups sugar
- 3 quarts lemon-lime beverage or ginger ale

Dissolve the gelatin in boiling water in a bowl. Add the cold water, juice and sugar, stirring until the sugar dissolves. Pour the gelatin punch base into three $^1/_2$-gallon food-graded containers. Freeze, covered, until firm. Thaw in the refrigerator until slightly slushy before preparing punch. Place the punch base in a punch bowl. Add 1 quart lemon-lime beverage or ginger ale for each $^1/_2$ gallon base. Do not use ginger ale with lime gelatin because it changes the color.

Yield: 59 (4-ounce) servings.

Approx Per Serving: Cal 82; T Fat <1 g; <1% Calories from Fat; Prot <1 g; Carbo 21 g; Fiber <1 g; Chol 0 mg; Sod 13 mg

Barb Bierman Batie, Lexington
Janice Mehl, North Platte

PROM PUNCH

10 envelopes unsweetened raspberry drink mix
10 cups sugar
10 quarts water
3 (6-ounce) cans frozen lemon juice
1 (46-ounce) can each fruit punch and pineapple juice
2 (6-ounce) cans frozen orange juice concentrate
3 quart bottles ginger ale

Combine the drink mix, sugar, water, lemon juice, fruit punch, pineapple juice and orange juice concentrate in a food-graded container; mix well. Store, covered, in the refrigerator until serving time. Pour into a punch bowl. Add ginger ale, stirring gently to mix. Add an ice ring made from a mixture of these ingredients to avoid diluting the punch.

Yield: 36 (4-ounce) servings.

Approx Per Serving: Cal 298; T Fat <1 g; <1% Calories from Fat; Prot <1 g; Carbo 76 g; Fiber <1 g; Chol 0 mg; Sod 37 mg

Brandy Hansen, Hampton

ALMOND TEA

2 cups water
2 cups sugar
2 tablespoons instant tea
1 cup lemon juice
1 tablespoon vanilla extract
2 tablespoons almond extract

Combine the water and sugar in a glass container. Boil, uncovered, for 2 minutes in the microwave. Cool slightly. Add the tea powder, lemon juice, vanilla and almond extract; mix well. Store in the refrigerator if not using immediately. Mix 1 part tea mix to 3 parts water for each serving. Heat before serving.

Yield: 20 servings.

Approx Per Serving: Cal 91; T Fat <1 g; <1% Calories from Fat; Prot <1 g; Carbo 23 g; Fiber <1 g; Chol 0 mg; Sod <1 mg

Kim Mehl, North Platte
Ann Wiemann, Pierce

CAPPUCCINO MIX

1 cup each instant coffee creamer and instant hot chocolate mix
2/3 cup instant coffee
1/2 cup sugar
1/2 teaspoon cinnamon
1/4 teaspoon nutmeg

Combine the coffee creamer, hot chocolate mix, coffee powder, sugar, cinnamon and nutmeg in a bowl; mix well. Store in an airtight container. Stir 1 tablespoon of the mix into 6 ounces of hot water for each serving.

This is really delicious on cold winter days.

Yield: 45 servings.

Approx Per Serving: Cal 38; T Fat 1 g; 21% Calories from Fat; Prot 1 g; Carbo 7 g; Fiber <1 g; Chol <1 mg; Sod 26 mg

Vanessa Cole, Hayes Center

Soups, Salads and Vegetables

Cool and Crisp
Salad Luncheon Menu

Peaches and Cream Salad
page 43

Leprechaun Salad
page 45

Chicken Salad with Pecans
page 47
or
Ham and Mandarin Salad
page 48

Herbed Tomato Rolls
page 120

Lean and Luscious Cheesecake
page 145

PHOTOGRAPH BY KRIS EGGERS
Nemaha County

OLD-FASHIONED HAM AND BEAN SOUP

2 cups navy beans
3 quarts water
1 ham bone
1/2 cup chopped green bell pepper
1 cup chopped celery
2 cups chopped potatoes
1 medium onion, chopped
3 carrots, sliced
Salt and pepper to taste
1 cup tomato juice
1 bay leaf

Rinse and sort the beans. Soak the beans in the water in a bowl in the refrigerator overnight. Pour into a saucepan. Add the ham bone, green pepper, celery, potatoes, onion, carrots, salt, pepper, tomato juice and bay leaf. Bring to a boil; reduce heat. Simmer for 4 to 6 hours or until the beans are tender, stirring occasionally. Remove the bay leaf and ham bone before serving. May add ham if desired. May substitute any soup beans for the navy beans.

Yield: 10 servings.

Approx Per Serving: Cal 206; T Fat 2 g; 8% Calories from Fat; Prot 12 g; Carbo 37 g; Fiber 10 g; Chol 4 mg; Sod 196 mg

Dorothy Schultz, Wood River

VEGETABLE CHEESE SOUP

4 chicken bouillon cubes
1 quart water
1 1/2 cups chopped celery
1 medium onion, chopped
2 1/2 cups chopped potatoes
1 cup chopped carrots
1 (20-ounce) package frozen broccoli and cauliflower, thawed in refrigerator
2 (10-ounce) cans cream of chicken soup
8 to 16 ounces Velveeta cheese, cubed

Place the bouillon cubes in the water in a saucepan. Bring to a boil; reduce heat. Stir until the bouillon cubes are dissolved. Add the celery, onion, potatoes and carrots. Cook for 20 minutes, stirring occasionally. Add the broccoli and cauliflower. Cook until tender. Add the cream of chicken soup and cheese. Simmer until the cheese is melted and the cooking thermometer registers 165 degrees. May vary the amounts of vegetables to taste. May cook in a slow cooker.

Yield: 10 servings.

Approx Per Serving: Cal 283; T Fat 18 g; 56% Calories from Fat; Prot 14 g; Carbo 17 g; Fiber 3 g; Chol 48 mg; Sod 1621 mg

Conni Bales, Grand Island
Anita Keys, Elsmere
Lane Phillips, Beaver Crossing
Sara M. Wagnitz, Grand Island
Juli Wilcox, Bertrand

CHICKEN AND BROCCOLI SOUP

1 medium onion, chopped
1/4 cup margarine
8 ounces fresh mushrooms, sliced
1/2 cup sliced celery
1 (16-ounce) package frozen chopped broccoli
4 cups chicken broth
1/2 cup wild rice, cooked
1/2 teaspoon each salt, pepper and paprika
3 cups cubed cooked chicken
1/2 cup flour
2 cups milk

Sauté the onion in margarine in a 3-quart saucepan until golden. Add the mushrooms, celery and frozen broccoli. Sauté for 2 minutes, stirring constantly. Add 3 cups of the broth, rice, salt, pepper, paprika and chicken. Simmer for 5 minutes. Combine the remaining 1 cup broth and flour in a bowl, stirring until smooth. Blend into the soup mixture. Simmer for 8 to 10 minutes or until slightly thickened, stirring frequently. Stir in the milk; heat thoroughly or until a cooking thermometer registers 165 degrees.

Yield: 8 servings.

Approx Per Serving: Cal 301; T Fat 13 g; 38% Calories from Fat; Prot 25 g; Carbo 23 g; Fiber 3 g; Chol 55 mg; Sod 685 mg

Jane Munson, Columbus

CHEESY POTATO AND HAM CHOWDER

1 cup chopped onion
1 rib celery, thinly sliced
1 large carrot, thinly sliced
3 tablespoons butter or margarine
4 cups chopped peeled potatoes
2 cups water
2 chicken-flavored bouillon cubes
1/4 teaspoon salt
1/8 teaspoon pepper
2 tablespoons chopped fresh dill or 1/2 teaspoon dried dillweed
1 to 2 cups cubed ham
1 cup milk
1 cup half-and-half or milk
1/2 to 2 cups shredded Cheddar cheese

Sauté the onion, celery and carrot in the butter in a 3-quart saucepan over medium heat for 5 minutes or until tender. Add the potatoes, water, bouillon cubes, salt, pepper, dill and ham. Bring to a boil; reduce heat. Simmer for 10 minutes or until the potatoes are tender. Process 2 1/2 cups of the potato mixture in a securely covered blender container until smooth; return the processed mixture to the soup. Stir in the milk, half-and-half and Cheddar cheese. Cook over medium heat until heated through or until a cooking thermometer registers 165 degrees. May substitute 9 ounces cubed Velveeta cheese for the Cheddar cheese.

Yield: 6 servings.

Approx Per Serving: Cal 452; T Fat 27 g; 53% Calories from Fat; Prot 27 g; Carbo 27 g; Fiber 3 g; Chol 101 mg; Sod 1438 mg

Chris Bartak, Long Pine
Karen Niewohner, Albion
Cheri Werner, Petersburg

APPLESAUCE GELATIN SALAD

3/4 cup red hot cinnamon candies
2 cups boiling water
1 (3-ounce) package lemon gelatin
1 (3-ounce) package orange gelatin
2 cups applesauce
8 ounces cream cheese, softened
1 cup mayonnaise-type salad dressing
1 1/2 cups crushed pineapple, drained
1 cup chopped walnuts

Dissolve the cinnamon candies in boiling water in a saucepan. Remove from heat. Add the gelatins, stirring until dissolved. Stir in the applesauce. Pour half the gelatin mixture into an 8x8-inch glass dish. Chill in the refrigerator until set. Beat the cream cheese, mayonnaise-type salad dressing and pineapple in a mixer bowl until creamy. Stir in the walnuts. Spread the cream cheese mixture carefully over the prepared layer. Pour the remaining gelatin mixture over the top. Chill until set.

This makes a very festive and pretty holiday salad.

Yield: 9 servings.

Approx Per Serving: Cal 494; T Fat 26 g; 46% Calories from Fat; Prot 6 g; Carbo 64 g; Fiber 2 g; Chol 35 mg; Sod 315 mg

Linda K. Petersen, Hemingford

CRANBERRY SALAD

1 pound cranberries
3/4 cup sugar
1 cup miniature marshmallows
2 (3-ounce) packages cranberry gelatin
1/2 cup chopped apples
1/2 cup chopped walnuts
1 (8-ounce) can crushed pineapple
1 cup whipped cream

Grind the cranberries into a bowl. Add the sugar and marshmallows; mix well. Chill, covered, in the refrigerator overnight. Prepare gelatin in a bowl using package directions, substituting pineapple juice for some of the water, if desired. Stir in the cranberry mixture, apples, walnuts and pineapple. Spoon into a serving dish. Chill in the refrigerator until firm. Fold in the whipped cream. Chill in the refrigerator until serving time.

This salad is always served at Thanksgiving and Christmas at our family gatherings.

Yield: 10 servings.

Approx Per Serving: Cal 261; T Fat 8 g; 27% Calories from Fat; Prot 3 g; Carbo 47 g; Fiber 2 g; Chol 16 mg; Sod 51 mg

Susan Hansen, Schuyler

GARDEN GLOW SALAD

1 (3-ounce) package orange gelatin
1 cup boiling water
1 (8-ounce) can crushed pineapple
1 tablespoon lemon juice
1/4 teaspoon salt
3/4 cup finely shredded carrots

Dissolve the gelatin in boiling water in a bowl. Drain the pineapple, reserving the juice. Add the lemon juice to the reserved pineapple juice in a 2-cup measure; add enough water to the juices to measure 1 cup. Stir in the salt. Add the juice mixture to the gelatin; mix well. Chill until partially set. Stir in the pineapple and carrots. Spoon into an oiled 4-cup mold. Chill, covered, until set. Unmold onto a serving plate. May double the recipe.

Yield: 6 servings.

Approx Per Serving: Cal 90; T Fat <1 g; 1% Calories from Fat; Prot 1 g; Carbo 22 g; Fiber 1 g; Chol 0 mg; Sod 130 mg

Terri Shelton, Danbury

ORANGE PUDDING SALAD

1 (4-ounce) package vanilla instant pudding mix
1 (4-ounce) package tapioca instant pudding mix
1 (3-ounce) package orange gelatin
2 cups hot water
1 (11-ounce) can mandarin oranges, drained
12 ounces whipped topping

Combine the pudding mixes, gelatin and hot water in a saucepan. Bring to a boil; reduce heat. Cook until thickened, stirring constantly. Let stand until cool. Stir in the mandarin oranges and whipped topping. Spoon into a serving dish. Chill in the refrigerator until set.

Yield: 6 servings.

Approx Per Serving: Cal 374; T Fat 15 g; 34% Calories from Fat; Prot 2 g; Carbo 62 g; Fiber <1 g; Chol 0 mg; Sod 528 mg

Sue Finke, Cozad

PEACHES AND CREAM SALAD

- 1 (3-ounce) package orange gelatin
- 1 cup boiling water
- 3 ounces cream cheese, softened
- 8 ounces whipped topping
- 1 (3-ounce) package orange gelatin
- 1 cup boiling water
- 1 (21-ounce) can peach pie filling

Dissolve 1 package gelatin in 1 cup boiling water in a bowl. Let stand until cool. Add the cream cheese; mix well. Fold in the whipped topping. Spread into the bottom of a 9x13-inch dish. Chill in the refrigerator until set. Dissolve 1 package gelatin in 1 cup boiling water in a bowl. Stir in the pie filling; let stand until cool. Spread over the prepared layer. Chill in the refrigerator until serving time.

Yield: 12 servings.

Approx Per Serving: Cal 189; T Fat 7 g; 34% Calories from Fat; Prot 2 g; Carbo 30 g; Fiber <1 g; Chol 8 mg; Sod 84 mg

Sara Miller, Aurora

CLUB RASPBERRY SALAD

- 2 cups sour cream
- 4 cups miniature marshmallows
- 1 (6-ounce) package raspberry gelatin
- 2 cups boiling water
- 2 (10-ounce) packages frozen raspberries
- 2 cups applesauce

Mix the sour cream and marshmallows in a bowl. Chill, covered, in the refrigerator overnight. Dissolve the gelatin in boiling water in a bowl. Stir in the raspberries and applesauce. Spoon into a 9x13-inch dish. Chill in the refrigerator until set. Spread the marshmallow mixture over the top. Chill in the refrigerator until serving time.

Yield: 10 servings.

Approx Per Serving: Cal 318; T Fat 10 g; 27% Calories from Fat; Prot 4 g; Carbo 57 g; Fiber 3 g; Chol 20 mg; Sod 79 mg

Mary Schoenefeld, Butte

FRESH FRUIT SALAD

1 watermelon
1 pint fresh strawberries
1 (8-ounce) can juice-pack chunk pineapple
1 cantaloupe
1/2 cup maraschino cherries
1 cup seedless green grapes
1 banana, sliced
1/4 cup chopped pecans or walnuts

Cube or ball the watermelon. Cap the strawberries and cut into halves. Peel, seed and cube the cantaloupe. Cut the cherries into halves. Combine the watermelon, strawberries, pineapple, cantaloupe and cherries gently in a large serving bowl. Stir in the grapes, banana and walnuts. Chill until serving time.

This was my 1995 Cuming County Favorite Foods contest entry.

Yield: 24 servings.

Approx Per Serving: Cal 119; T Fat 2 g; 15% Calories from Fat; Prot 2 g; Carbo 26 g; Fiber 2 g; Chol 0 mg; Sod 7 mg

Katie Schroeder, West Point

FROG-EYE SALAD

3/4 cup sugar
1 tablespoon flour
1/2 teaspoon salt
2/3 cup pineapple juice
1 egg, beaten
1 teaspoon lemon juice
6 cups water
1 cup acini di pepe
1 (11-ounce) can mandarin oranges, drained
2 (16-ounce) cans fruit cocktail, drained
1 (16-ounce) can sliced peaches, drained
1 (20-ounce) can crushed pineapple, drained
8 ounces whipped topping

Combine the sugar, flour, salt, pineapple juice and egg in a saucepan; mix well. Cook over medium heat, stirring constantly until thickened. Stir in the lemon juice. Remove from heat; let stand until cool. Boil the water in a saucepan. Add the acini di pepe gradually, stirring until the water boils again. Boil for 2 minutes. Remove from heat. Let stand, covered, for 6 to 8 minutes; drain. Rinse in cold water; drain. Combine the acini di pepe with the pineapple juice mixture in a bowl; mix well. Spoon into a large serving dish. Chill, covered, in the refrigerator until cold. Stir in the mandarin oranges, fruit cocktail, peaches, pineapple and whipping topping. Chill in the refrigerator for 1 hour or longer before serving.

Yield: 8 servings.

Approx Per Serving: Cal 391; T Fat 8 g; 18% Calories from Fat; Prot 4 g; Carbo 80 g; Fiber 3 g; Chol 27 mg; Sod 162 mg

Danny Morrison, Elgin

LEPRECHAUN SALAD

- 1 cup thinly sliced green cabbage
- 1 cup halved seedless green grapes
- 1 cup chopped Granny Smith apple
- 1/2 cup raisins
- 1/2 cup nonfat or low-fat vanilla yogurt
- 1/2 cup miniature marshmallows

Combine the cabbage, grapes, apple, raisins and yogurt in a bowl; mix well. Chill in the refrigerator. Stir in the marshmallows just before serving. May spoon into cabbage leaves to serve.

Yield: 6 servings.

Approx Per Serving: Cal 125; T Fat 1 g; 3% Calories from Fat; Prot 2 g; Carbo 31 g; Fiber 2 g; Chol <1 mg; Sod 21 mg

Mary K. Warner, Arapahoe

LUNCHEON CHICKEN SALAD

- 2 cups chopped cooked chicken, chilled
- 1/2 cup sliced water chestnuts
- 3/4 cup slivered almonds
- 1/2 cup seedless green grapes
- 1/4 cup chopped celery
- 3/4 cup mayonnaise-type salad dressing
- 2 teaspoons vinegar
- 1 teaspoon curry powder
- 1 teaspoon soy sauce
- 1 teaspoon onion salt

Combine the chicken, water chestnuts, almonds, grapes and celery in a bowl, tossing to mix. Combine the mayonnaise-type salad dressing, vinegar, curry powder, soy sauce and onion salt in a bowl; mix well. Pour over the chicken mixture, tossing lightly to mix. Chill in the refrigerator until serving time.

Yield: 4 servings.

Approx Per Serving: Cal 480; T Fat 33 g; 61% Calories from Fat; Prot 26 g; Carbo 22 g; Fiber 4 g; Chol 74 mg; Sod 867 mg

Sandra Cole, Hayes Center

PASTA CHICKEN SALAD

8 ounces medium shell pasta
1 (6-ounce) can white chunk chicken, drained
2 cups fresh bite-size broccoli florets
1 medium red bell pepper, chopped
1/2 cup chopped celery
2 tablespoons chopped green onions
2 teaspoons prepared mustard
1/2 teaspoon dried dillweed
1 (8-ounce) bottle Italian salad dressing

Prepare the pasta using package directions; drain. Combine the chicken, broccoli, red pepper, celery, green onions and cooled pasta in a bowl; mix gently. Stir in the mustard, dillweed and Italian dressing, tossing to coat. Chill, covered, in the refrigerator. Stir just before serving. May double the recipe.

Yield: 4 servings.

Approx Per Serving: Cal 568; T Fat 32 g; 50% Calories from Fat; Prot 19 g; Carbo 53 g; Fiber 3 g; Chol 26 mg; Sod 722 mg

Mary Jane McReynolds, Lincoln

SUMMER CHICKEN SALAD

3/4 cup mayonnaise
3/4 cup whipped topping
15 ounces chopped cooked chicken, chilled
3/4 cup sliced celery
3/4 cup seedless grapes, halved
3/4 cup toasted slivered almonds
3/4 cup chopped peeled apples
6 lettuce leaves

Combine the mayonnaise and whipped topping in a bowl. Stir in the chicken, celery, grapes, almonds and apples. Chill in the refrigerator until serving time. Spoon onto lettuce leaves on individual salad plates. Garnish with fresh fruit.

Yield: 6 servings.

Approx Per Serving: Cal 490; T Fat 39 g; 70% Calories from Fat; Prot 25 g; Carbo 13 g; Fiber 3 g; Chol 79 mg; Sod 237 mg

Marlena Culver, Omaha

CHICKEN SALAD WITH PECANS

6 1/2 cups water
1 pound boneless skinless chicken breasts
1/2 cup chopped pecans or walnuts
1 3/4 cups spaetzle or orzo
1 (9-ounce) package frozen cut green beans
1 large red bell pepper, seeded, coarsely chopped
3 tablespoons oriental sesame oil
3 tablespoons vegetable oil
2 tablespoons rice wine vinegar or white vinegar
1 tablespoon orange juice
1 1/2 teaspoons ground sage
1/2 teaspoon salt
1/2 teaspoon pepper
1/8 teaspoon sugar

Simmer 6 cups of the water in a large saucepan over medium heat. Add the chicken and bring to a boil; reduce heat. Simmer for 10 minutes or until the chicken is no longer pink on the inside. Remove from heat; remove the chicken to a bowl. Chill the chicken in the refrigerator. Spread the pecans into a baking pan. Bake at 350 degrees for 8 to 10 minutes or until lightly toasted; set aside. Return the liquid to a boil over high heat. Add the spaetzle; reduce heat. Simmer, uncovered, over low heat for 10 minutes or until tender. Remove the spaetzle to a large bowl using a slotted spoon. Chill the spaetzle in the refrigerator. Add the remaining 1/2 cup water to the saucepan. Stir in the green beans. Bring to a boil again over high heat; reduce heat. Simmer, covered, for 3 to 5 minutes or until the beans are tender-crisp; drain. Add to the spaetzle; chill in the refrigerator. Chop the chicken. Stir the chicken, red pepper and pecans into the spaetzle mixture, tossing gently to mix. Chill in the refrigerator. Whisk the sesame oil, vegetable oil, vinegar and orange juice in a small bowl. Add the sage, salt, pepper and sugar, whisking until smooth. Pour over the chicken mixture, tossing to coat.

This recipe was a 1994 Poultry Cook Off Contest Entry.

Yield: 4 servings.

Approx Per Serving: Cal 616; T Fat 34 g; 50% Calories from Fat; Prot 35 g; Carbo 43 g; Fiber 4 g; Chol 72 mg; Sod 342 mg

Libby Conrad, West Point

HAM AND MANDARIN SALAD

1 clove of garlic
2 cups cubed cooked ham
1 cup chopped celery
1/3 cup chopped green bell pepper
1/2 cup chopped walnuts
1 (11-ounce) can mandarin oranges, drained
1/3 cup mayonnaise
2 tablespoons cream or half-and-half
1 tablespoon vinegar
6 lettuce leaves

Rub a bowl with the garlic; combine the ham, celery, green pepper, walnuts and mandarin oranges in the bowl. Chill in the bowl in the refrigerator. Pour a blended mixture of the mayonnaise, cream and vinegar over the top before serving, tossing to coat. Spoon onto lettuce leaves on individual salad plates. Serve with hot rolls and a beverage.

Yield: 6 servings.

Approx Per Serving: Cal 282; T Fat 21 g; 63% Calories from Fat; Prot 14 g; Carbo 13 g; Fiber 1 g; Chol 40 mg; Sod 714 mg

Kathryn Barger, Wauneta

TUNA MACARONI SALAD

8 ounces cooked macaroni
2 eggs, hard-cooked, chopped, refrigerated until used
1/2 (6-ounce) can tuna, drained
2 slices bacon, crisp-fried, crumbled
1 small onion, chopped
2 small carrots, chopped
1 rib celery, chopped
1/4 cup chopped black olives
1 1/4 cups mayonnaise
1/2 cup sugar
2 tablespoons mustard
1 teaspoon vinegar
1/3 to 1/2 cup milk

Combine the macaroni, eggs, tuna, bacon, onion, carrots, celery and black olives in a bowl; mix gently. Mix the mayonnaise, sugar, mustard, vinegar and milk in a small bowl. Pour over the macaroni mixture, tossing to coat. Chill in the refrigerator until serving time.

Yield: 8 servings.

Approx Per Serving: Cal 405; T Fat 31 g; 68% Calories from Fat; Prot 8 g; Carbo 25 g; Fiber 1 g; Chol 80 mg; Sod 373 mg

Sheryl Fellers, Lexington

LENTIL VEGETABLE SALAD

1 1/2 cups dry lentils
3 cups hot water
1 envelope Italian salad dressing mix
12 cherry tomatoes, halved
3/4 cup 1/2-inch slices green bell pepper
1/2 cup 1/2-inch slices red bell pepper
5 green onions, chopped
2 tablespoons pimento

Rinse and sort the lentils. Simmer the lentils in 3 cups hot water in a saucepan for 15 minutes; drain. Rinse in cold water; drain. Prepare Italian salad dressing using package directions; pour over the lentils in a bowl. Chill in the refrigerator. Stir in the tomatoes, green pepper, red pepper, green onions and pimento. Marinate, covered, in the refrigerator for 2 hours before serving.

Lentils have a good amount of protein. This is a new recipe for me that I have prepared for potluck dinners.

Yield: 8 servings.

Approx Per Serving: Cal 283; T Fat 17 g; 52% Calories from Fat; Prot 11 g; Carbo 24 g; Fiber 5 g; Chol 0 mg; Sod 274 mg

Maribeth Sall, Chappell

STRAWBERRY SPINACH SALAD

1 bunch fresh spinach, torn into bite-size pieces
1 quart fresh strawberries, sliced
1 cup mayonnaise
1/2 cup sugar
2 tablespoons vinegar
2 to 4 tablespoons half-and-half

Toss the spinach and strawberries gently in a glass serving bowl. Combine the mayonnaise, sugar and vinegar in a bowl; mix well. Add enough half-and-half to make of desired pourable consistency. Pour over the spinach mixture, tossing to coat. Garnish with additional whole fresh strawberries.

Yield: 6 servings.

Approx Per Serving: Cal 379; T Fat 31 g; 71% Calories from Fat; Prot 2 g; Carbo 26 g; Fiber 3 g; Chol 25 mg; Sod 244 mg

Dorothy Bremer, Lexington

SWEET-AND-SOUR SPINACH SALAD

1 1/2 pounds fresh spinach, torn into bite-size pieces, chilled
Sections of 2 oranges
1/4 red onion, thinly sliced
3 to 4 green onions, thinly sliced
2 tablespoons brown sugar
1/4 cup cider vinegar
1/2 teaspoon dry mustard
1/2 teaspoon paprika
1/2 teaspoon celery seeds
1/2 cup canola or olive oil

Combine the spinach, orange sections, red onion and green onions in a salad bowl, tossing gently to mix. Mix the brown sugar, vinegar, mustard, paprika and celery seeds in a bowl just before serving; mix well. Add the oil in a fine stream, stirring constantly. Pour half the dressing over the spinach mixture, tossing to coat. Serve the remaining dressing with the salad.

This healthy salad has a combination of ingredients that may become a family favorite.

Yield: 6 servings.

Approx Per Serving: Cal 225; T Fat 19 g; 70% Calories from Fat; Prot 4 g; Carbo 14 g; Fiber 4 g; Chol 0 mg; Sod 93 mg

Barbara Scharf, Curtis

CAMPFIRE BAKED BEANS

1 (16-ounce) can green beans, drained
1 (16-ounce) can kidney beans, drained
1 (8-ounce) can garbanzo beans, drained
1 (16-ounce) can lima beans, drained
1 (16-ounce) can navy beans, drained
1 (16-ounce) can black-eyed peas, drained
1 (16-ounce) can pork and beans
1/2 cup mustard
1/2 cup catsup
1/2 cup packed brown sugar
1 large onion, chopped

Combine the green beans, kidney beans, garbanzo beans, lima beans, navy beans, black-eyed peas and pork and beans in a large cast-iron pot. Add mixture of mustard, catsup, brown sugar and onion; mix well. Cook over an open fire until thick and bubbly and the cooking thermometer registers 165 degrees. May substitute salsa for the catsup for a spicier flavor. May add any cooked meat to the mixture.

This recipe was originated for overnight campouts for my son's 4-H club. The longer and slower it cooks, the better the flavor.

Yield: 20 servings.

Approx Per Serving: Cal 159; T Fat 1 g; 6% Calories from Fat; Prot 8 g; Carbo 31 g; Fiber 8 g; Chol 2 mg; Sod 520 mg

Jo Ann Sharpe, Pawnee City

ORIENTAL MUSHROOMS

- 1 pound fresh mushrooms, sliced
- 1/4 cup chopped onion
- 1/4 cup margarine
- 2 teaspoons flour
- 1/2 cup water
- 1 teaspoon instant beef bouillon or 1 beef bouillon cube
- 1 tablespoon soy sauce
- 1 tablespoon slivered almonds

Sauté the mushrooms and onion in the margarine in a skillet until tender. Sprinkle the flour over the top; stir gently. Add the water, instant bouillon, soy sauce and almonds; mix gently. Cook over low heat until slightly thickened, stirring constantly. Serve with beef. May substitute two 8-ounce cans sliced mushrooms, drained, for the fresh mushrooms.

Yield: 6 servings.

Approx Per Serving: Cal 103; T Fat 9 g; 71% Calories from Fat; Prot 2 g; Carbo 5 g; Fiber 1 g; Chol <1 mg; Sod 408 mg

Sharilyn Lemke, Osmond

STUFFED POTATOES

- 4 large potatoes
- 1 (10-ounce) package frozen California-blend vegetables
- 1 (10-ounce) can cream of mushroom soup
- 1 (8-ounce) jar Cheez Whiz
- 1 cup cubed cooked ham

Rinse and scrub the potatoes; pat dry. Pierce the potatoes with a fork and place on a microwave-safe plate. Cover with plastic wrap. Microwave on High for 15 minutes or until tender. Cook the frozen vegetables using package directions; drain. Mix the soup and Cheez Whiz in a microwave-safe bowl. Stir in the cooked vegetables and ham. Microwave on High for 3 minutes or until heated through. Cut the potatoes and squeeze open. Spoon the vegetable mixture over the top of each potato. Serve hot.

This was my 1995 Cuming County Favorite Foods entry.

Yield: 4 servings.

Approx Per Serving: Cal 544; T Fat 20 g; 33% Calories from Fat; Prot 26 g; Carbo 67 g; Fiber 4 g; Chol 51 mg; Sod 1890 mg

John Lase, Bancroft

SOUTH-OF-THE-BORDER SQUASH

- 1 1/2 pounds yellow crookneck squash, chopped
- 1 medium onion, chopped
- 2 tablespoons margarine
- 1 (4-ounce) can chopped green chiles, drained
- 2 tablespoons flour
- 1 teaspoon salt
- 1/2 teaspoon pepper
- 1 1/2 cups shredded Monterey Jack cheese
- 1 egg
- 8 ounces cottage cheese
- 2 tablespoons parsley flakes
- 1/2 cup grated Parmesan cheese

Sauté the squash and onion in margarine in a skillet until tender-crisp. Stir in the chiles, flour, salt and pepper. Spoon into a greased 2-quart baking dish. Sprinkle with the Monterey Jack cheese. Combine the egg, cottage cheese and parsley flakes in a small bowl; mix well. Spread over the top. Sprinkle with the Parmesan cheese. Bake at 400 degrees for 30 minutes.

Yield: 6 servings.

Approx Per Serving: Cal 273; T Fat 18 g; 57% Calories from Fat; Prot 18 g; Carbo 11 g; Fiber 2 g; Chol 73 mg; Sod 1095 mg

Curtis Johnson, Imperial

STIR-FRY VEGETABLES

- 1 teaspoon cornstarch
- 1/2 teaspoon ground ginger
- 1/8 teaspoon garlic powder
- 1 teaspoon soy sauce
- 1/3 cup water
- 2 tablespoons vegetable oil
- 2/3 cup thinly sliced carrots
- 1/3 cup thinly sliced onion
- 2/3 cup thinly sliced celery
- 2 cups broccoli florets and thinly sliced stems
- 1 cup bean sprouts

Mix the cornstarch, ginger, garlic powder, soy sauce and water in a glass measure until well blended; set aside. Heat the oil in a large frying pan. Add the carrots, onion and celery. Stir-fry for 1 minute. Add the broccoli. Stir-fry for 2 minutes. Add the soy sauce mixture. Stir-fry for 1 minute or until bubbly. Add the bean sprouts; reduce heat. Cook, covered, for 2 minutes longer. Serve over hot rice. Be careful when removing the cover from the frying pan because the steam could rise up and burn you. May substitute drained canned green beans for the bean sprouts.

Yield: 8 servings.

Approx Per Serving: Cal 48; T Fat 4 g; 62% Calories from Fat; Prot 1 g; Carbo 4 g; Fiber 1 g; Chol 0 mg; Sod 61 mg

Gerald Johnson, Whitney

FRUIT AND HERB TURKEY DRESSING

1 (11-ounce) package dried mixed fruit, cut into small pieces
1/2 cup raisins
2 1/2 cups water
1 cup chopped celery
1/4 cup parsley
1/2 onion, chopped
1 tablespoon sage
2 tablespoons margarine
1 (16-ounce) loaf dry bread, crumbled

Combine the dried fruit, raisins and water in a saucepan. Simmer for 20 minutes; remove from heat. Let stand until cool. Chill in the refrigerator. Sauté the celery, parsley, onion and sage in margarine in a skillet until the vegetables are tender. Mix with the bread crumbs in a bowl. Chill, covered, for 24 hours. Stir in the fruit mixture. Stuff into a turkey just before roasting. Bake until the stuffing reaches an internal temperature of 165 degrees.

Yield: Enough stuffing for 1 turkey.

Nutritional information for this recipe is not available.

Keith King, Kearney

FRUITED HAM AND RICE PILAF

1 (11-ounce) can mandarin oranges
1 (20-ounce) can pineapple chunks or tidbits
2 teaspoons margarine or butter
2/3 cup finely chopped celery
1 1/2 cups quick-cooking rice
1/4 teaspoon cinnamon
1 cup chopped cooked ham
1 cup shredded Cheddar cheese

Drain the mandarin oranges and pineapple, reserving 2/3 cup juice. Combine the mandarin oranges, pineapple, reserved juice, margarine, celery, rice and cinnamon in a 2-quart casserole sprayed with nonstick cooking spray. Bake, covered, at 350 degrees for 25 minutes or until the rice is tender, stirring once. Stir the ham and cheese into the hot mixture. Bake, covered, for 5 minutes longer or until a cooking thermometer registers 165 degrees. May microwave a mixture of the first 6 ingredients, covered, on High for 6 minutes or until the rice is tender. Add the ham and cheese. Microwave, covered, for 1 to 2 minutes longer or until the cheese melts.

This is a great way to use 2 or 3 leftover ham slices or substitute cooked chicken or turkey.

Yield: 6 servings.

Approx Per Serving: Cal 308; T Fat 9 g; 26% Calories from Fat; Prot 13 g; Carbo 45 g; Fiber 2 g; Chol 33 mg; Sod 458 mg

Kathy Hopp, Falls City

CHEESY RICE AND ZUCCHINI CASSEROLE

- 8 ounces bacon, cut into small pieces
- 1/2 cup each chopped onion and green bell pepper
- 1 teaspoon Italian seasonings
- 1/2 teaspoon garlic powder
- 3/4 teaspoon curry powder
- Salt and pepper to taste
- 2 teaspoons sugar
- 1 (8-ounce) can tomato sauce
- 2 cups shredded zucchini
- 4 ounces process cheese, shredded
- 2 cups cooked rice
- 1/2 cup dry bread crumbs
- 1/2 tablespoon melted butter

Sauté the bacon in a skillet until crisp. Add the onion and green pepper. Cook until tender; drain. Stir in the Italian seasonings, garlic powder, curry powder, salt, pepper and sugar. Add the tomato sauce, stirring to mix. Stir in the zucchini. Cook for 3 minutes, stirring frequently. Add the cheese and rice, stirring until the cheese melts. Spoon into a large greased casserole. Sprinkle with a mixture of the bread crumbs and butter. Bake at 350 degrees for 25 to 30 minutes.

Yield: 6 servings.

Approx Per Serving: Cal 302; T Fat 13 g; 39% Calories from Fat; Prot 12 g; Carbo 34 g; Fiber 3 g; Chol 30 mg; Sod 765 mg

Norma J. Meyer, Scotia

HARVEST CELEBRATION SAUSAGE AND RICE STUFFING

- 1 (6-ounce) package long grain and wild rice mix
- 1 cup chopped onion
- 1 cup chopped celery
- 8 ounces mild or hot pork sausage
- 1 1/2 cups dry bread crumbs
- 2 ounces mushroom pieces and stems
- 4 egg whites, lightly beaten
- 3 cups chicken broth, made from reduced-sodium instant bouillon
- 1/4 teaspoon seasoned pepper

Cook the rice using package directions with only 1/2 of the seasoning packet. Sauté the onion and celery in a skillet sprayed with nonstick cooking spray. Cook the sausage until brown and crumbly; drain. Combine the rice, onion mixture, sausage, bread crumbs and mushrooms in a bowl; mix well. Stir in the egg whites and broth. Sprinkle with the pepper. Spoon into a nonstick 9x13-inch baking pan. Bake at 350 degrees for 45 minutes or until a cooking thermometer registers 165 degrees. May use as stuffing in a 12-pound turkey. Stuff the turkey just before roasting and roast until the stuffing reaches an internal temperature of 165 degrees.

Yield: 8 servings.

Approx Per Serving: Cal 247; T Fat 7 g; 27% Calories from Fat; Prot 11 g; Carbo 34 g; Fiber 2 g; Chol 15 mg; Sod 807 mg

Debra Schroeder and David Schroeder, West Point

Meat Main Dishes

Go Big Red
Tailgate Party Menu

Go-Big-Red Popcorn
page 155

Confetti Bars
page 33

Hot and Sweet Snack Mix
page 34

Barbecued Beef Brisket
page 57

Honey Barbecue-Style Baked Beans
page 16

Homemade Breadsticks
page 121

Salted Peanut Chews
page 134

Photograph by Mandy Gale
Cherry County

BARBECUED BEEF BRISKET

2 tablespoons liquid smoke
1 (5-pound) beef brisket, trimmed
Celery salt, garlic salt and onion salt to taste
2 tablespoons Worcestershire sauce
2 cups barbecue sauce

Pour the liquid smoke over the brisket in a 9x13-inch baking pan. Sprinkle both sides generously with celery salt, garlic salt and onion salt. Cover lightly with plastic wrap or foil. Marinate in the refrigerator overnight. Pour the Worcestershire sauce over the brisket at baking time and cover tightly with foil. Bake at 325 degrees for 3 hours. Remove from the oven and pour off the liquid. Pour the barbecue sauce over the brisket and replace the foil. Bake for 1 hour longer. Carve diagonally cross grain into thin slices.

The brisket is easier to carve if allowed to stand for 10 to 20 minutes. Reheat the slices in the barbecue sauce.

Yield: 15 servings.

Approx Per Serving: Cal 223; T Fat 9 g; 38% Calories from Fat; Prot 29 g; Carbo 5 g; Fiber <1 g; Chol 86 mg; Sod 339 mg

Cheryl Griffith, Curtis

ITALIAN ROAST BEEF

1 (3-pound) rump roast
3 cups water
4 beef bouillon cubes
1 teaspoon salt, or to taste
1/2 teaspoon pepper
1 tablespoon oregano
1 large clove of garlic, or 3 small, crushed
3 green bell peppers, cut into strips
2 tablespoons margarine

Brown the roast in a Dutch oven. Mix the water, bouillon cubes, salt, pepper, oregano and garlic in a bowl. Pour over the roast. Bake, covered, at 350 degrees for 3 hours. Remove the roast from the Dutch oven and cut into slices. Place the slices in the pan drippings and maintain at or above 140 degrees until serving time. Sauté the green peppers in the margarine in a skillet until tender. Combine with the sliced roast. Simmer until serving time. If the roast is well done, it will fall apart when sliced. For neater slices, let the roast cool for 10 to 15 minutes.

I found this recipe on a calendar. It is very tasty and easy to prepare.

Yield: 12 servings.

Approx Per Serving: Cal 155; T Fat 7 g; 39% Calories from Fat; Prot 22 g; Carbo 2 g; Fiber <1 g; Chol 64 mg; Sod 523 mg

Linda K. Petersen, Hemingford

PEPSI POT ROAST

1 (3- to 4-pound) beef or pork roast
1 (10-ounce) can cream of mushroom soup
1 envelope onion soup mix
1 (10-ounce) can Pepsi

Place the roast in a roasting pan. Cover with the soup and soup mix. Pour the Pepsi over the roast. Bake at 350 degrees for 2 to 3 hours or until the beef roast is done to taste or the pork roast is cooked through. May cook vegetables with the roast to make a complete meal.

I got this recipe from my college roommate. It has become a favorite at our house because it tastes so good and is so easy to fix.

Yield: 8 servings.

Approx Per Serving: Cal 336; T Fat 14 g; 38% Calories from Fat; Prot 43 g; Carbo 7 g; Fiber <1 g; Chol 129 mg; Sod 458 mg

Crystal Fangmeier, Hebron

BARBECUED MINUTE STEAK

1 cup catsup
1 cup barbecue sauce
$^{1}/_{4}$ cup chopped onion
4 pounds minute steak

Simmer the catsup, barbecue sauce and onion in a saucepan for 5 minutes. Brown the steak in a skillet. Place the steak in a roasting pan. Pour the catsup mixture over the steak. Bake, covered, for $1^{1}/_{2}$ hours or until a meat thermometer registers 140 degrees for rare, 160 degrees for medium, or 170 degrees for well done.

Yield: 6 servings.

Approx Per Serving: Cal 398; T Fat 10 g; 22% Calories from Fat; Prot 58 g; Carbo 17 g; Fiber 1 g; Chol 150 mg; Sod 932 mg

Angie, Haley and Kelsey Johnson, Crawford

COMPANY ROUND STEAK

2 tablespoons prepared mustard
1 (3-pound) beef round steak
1 envelope onion soup mix
1 (4-ounce) can mushrooms, drained
1 (10-ounce) can cream of celery soup

Spread the mustard on the steak. Sprinkle with the soup mix and cover with the mushrooms. Roll the steak up as for a jelly roll. Place the steak on a large sheet of foil. Cover the steak with the soup. Seal the foil tightly and place in a roaster. Bake at 325 degrees for 5 hours or until a meat thermometer registers 160 degrees.

Yield: 8 servings.

Approx Per Serving: Cal 217; T Fat 7 g; 30% Calories from Fat; Prot 33 g; Carbo 4 g; Fiber 1 g; Chol 89 mg; Sod 538 mg

Amy Kastanek, Crete

ROUND STEAK MEAL-IN-ONE

2 pounds round steak
1 cup cream of mushroom soup
4 to 6 potatoes, sliced
4 to 6 carrots, sliced
2 cups coarsely chopped tomatoes
Salt and pepper to taste

Cut the round steak into strips; place in a slow cooker. Add the soup, potatoes, carrots, tomatoes, salt, pepper and enough water to cover all the ingredients; stir well. Cook on Low for 8 to 10 hours.

This recipe works well with wild game substituted for the round steak. It is easy to prepare for a busy family.

Yield: 4 servings.

Approx Per Serving: Cal 513; T Fat 9 g; 15% Calories from Fat; Prot 51 g; Carbo 58 g; Fiber 7 g; Chol 115 mg; Sod 608 mg

Tamara Eitel, Crawford

GREEN PEPPER STEAK

1/4 cup soy sauce
1 clove of garlic, minced
1 (1-pound) chuck steak, cut into thin strips
1/4 cup vegetable oil
1 cup chopped green onions
1 cup chopped mixed green and red bell peppers
2 ribs celery, chopped
2 tomatoes, cut into wedges
1 tablespoon cornstarch
1 cup water

Mix the soy sauce and garlic in a bowl. Add the beef strips, stirring to coat. Cook the beef in the oil in a skillet until tender. Add the green onions, bell peppers, celery and tomatoes. Cook until the vegetables are tender. Add a mixture of the cornstarch and water. Cook until thickened.

Yield: 4 servings.

Approx Per Serving: Cal 317; T Fat 20 g; 57% Calories from Fat; Prot 24 g; Carbo 11 g; Fiber 2 g; Chol 64 mg; Sod 1089 mg

Connie Carroll, Broken Bow

BEEF SHISH KABOBS

1 pound round steak
2 tablespoons vegetable oil
1 tablespoon lemon juice
1 tablespoon water
1 teaspoon honey
1 teaspoon oregano
12 large fresh mushrooms
1 yellow bell pepper, coarsely chopped
1 green bell pepper, coarsely chopped
1 red bell pepper, coarsely chopped
Salt to taste

Cut the round steak into 1-inch pieces. Combine the oil, lemon juice, water, honey and oregano in a bowl; mix well. Add the steak and vegetables, turning to coat with the oil mixture; drain. Thread on skewers, alternating beef and vegetables. Season with salt. Broil on a rack in a broiler pan 5 inches from heat source for 10 minutes or to desired doneness.

Yield: 6 servings.

Approx Per Serving: Cal 149; T Fat 7 g; 42% Calories from Fat; Prot 16 g; Carbo 6 g; Fiber 1 g; Chol 38 mg; Sod 30 mg

Julie Maddux, Wauneta

BEEF KABOBS IN LEMON MARINADE

3 to 4 ears sweet corn, cut into 1 1/2-inch wedges
1 1/2 pounds (1 1/2-inch) flank steak or top round steak
1 cup pearl onions
1 green bell pepper, chopped
1 pint cherry tomatoes
1 (8-ounce) can pineapple chunks
2 teaspoons grated lemon peel
1/2 cup lemon juice
1/2 cup vegetable oil
3 tablespoons honey
2 tablespoons Worcestershire sauce
1/2 teaspoon pepper
1/4 teaspoon garlic powder
2 tablespoons melted butter or margarine

Parboil the corn in a saucepan for 10 minutes. Cool with cold water. Cut the steak into 3/4x3-inch strips. Combine the steak, pearl onions, green pepper, tomatoes, pineapple and corn in a large sealable plastic bag or a covered large plastic bowl. Refrigerate until needed. Mix the lemon peel, lemon juice, oil, honey, Worcestershire sauce, pepper and garlic powder in a small bowl. Pour over the steak mixture and seal the bag or cover the bowl. Marinate in the refrigerator for 2 hours to overnight, turning once or twice. Remove the steak and vegetables from the marinade and thread onto 6 skewers. Brush with the melted butter. Grill for 8 to 12 minutes per side or until done to taste or broil for 5 to 8 minutes per side, brushing occasionally with the marinade. Discard unused marinade.

This was my 1995 Cuming County Beef Cook-Off Contest entry. I received Reserve Champion.

Yield: 6 servings.

Approx Per Serving: Cal 476; T Fat 30 g; 54% Calories from Fat; Prot 21 g; Carbo 36 g; Fiber 4 g; Chol 55 mg; Sod 164 mg

Kristin Leitow, Bancroft

PERFECT MARINATED STEAKS

1/3 cup soy sauce
1/3 cup vegetable oil
3 tablespoons vinegar
1/4 teaspoon red pepper
1/2 teaspoon ginger
2 tablespoons brown sugar
1/8 teaspoon garlic powder
1 tablespoon dried minced onion
4 (1-inch) T-bone steaks or Husker pork chops

Mix the soy sauce, oil, vinegar, red pepper, ginger, brown sugar, garlic powder and onion in a large bowl. Add the steaks. Marinate in the refrigerator for 8 hours to overnight; drain and discard the unused marinade. Grill or broil the steaks to the desired degree of doneness or the pork chops until cooked through. The marinade may be used to marinate thinly sliced chicken breast or to stir-fry meats.

We enjoy entertaining in our home, and we have countless requests for this recipe. After years of experimenting, we have set the ingredients and measurements to our liking.

Yield: 4 servings.

Approx Per Serving: Cal 587; T Fat 37 g; 58% Calories from Fat; Prot 53 g; Carbo 8 g; Fiber <1 g; Chol 147 mg; Sod 1491 mg

Sheryl J. Kastanek, Crete

PUMPKIN STEW

- 2 pounds stew beef, cut into bite-size pieces
- 2 tablespoons vegetable oil
- 1 cup water
- 3 potatoes, cubed
- 4 carrots, sliced
- 3 cloves of garlic, minced
- 1 onion, chopped
- 2 teaspoons salt
- 1/2 teaspoon pepper
- 1 beef bouillon cube
- 2 cups stewed tomatoes
- 1 (10- to 12-pound) pumpkin
- 1 tablespoon vegetable oil

Brown the beef in 2 tablespoons oil in a Dutch oven. Add the water, potatoes, carrots, garlic, onion, salt and pepper. Simmer, covered, for 2 hours. Stir in the bouillon cube and tomatoes. Rinse the pumpkin and cut out the top. Remove and discard the seeds and loose fibers. Place the pumpkin in a shallow baking dish. Spoon the stew into the pumpkin and replace the top. Brush the pumpkin with 1 tablespoon oil. Bake at 325 degrees for 2 hours or until a cooking thermometer registers 165 degrees; do not overbake. Scoop out a small amount of the baked pumpkin with each serving of stew.

Having a son with a Halloween birthday has always been fun! I'm always searching for fun food to serve as a birthday treat on that special day.

Yield: 10 servings.

Approx Per Serving: Cal 252; T Fat 10 g; 37% Calories from Fat; Prot 19 g; Carbo 21 g; Fiber 5 g; Chol 54 mg; Sod 815 mg

Arlys Cupp, Champion

REUBEN CASSEROLE

- 1 (27-ounce) can sauerkraut
- 1 (12-ounce) can corned beef, sliced
- 1/2 cup shredded Swiss cheese
- 1/2 cup shredded Cheddar cheese
- 1 (10-ounce) can cream of chicken soup
- 1 cup bread crumbs
- 1 tablespoon melted butter

Layer the sauerkraut, corned beef, Swiss cheese, Cheddar cheese and soup 1/2 at a time in a 2-quart casserole. Mix the bread crumbs with the butter. Sprinkle over the top. Bake at 350 degrees for 45 minutes or until a cooking thermometer registers 165 degrees.

Yield: 8 servings.

Approx Per Serving: Cal 275; T Fat 15 g; 49% Calories from Fat; Prot 19 g; Carbo 16 g; Fiber 3 g; Chol 57 mg; Sod 1543 mg

Sandra Cole, Hayes Center

WEDNESDAY, NOVEMBER 5, 2003

LIVING

Recipes to get some ba

Black Russian Bundt Cake

1 18.25-ounce yellow cake mix (without pudding)
½ cup sugar
6 ounces instant chocolate pudding
1 cup vegetable oil
4 eggs
¼ cup vodka
¼ cup coffee-flavored liqueur
¾ cup water

For glaze:

½ cup powdered sugar, unsifted
¼ cup coffee-flavored liqueur
Powdered sugar for sprinkling

Preheat oven to 350 degrees.

In large mixer bowl, combine cake ingredients. Mix at low speed about one minute; beat at medium speed four minutes. Pour into greased and floured 10- to 12-cup Bundt or other molded cake pan. Bake for 60 to 70 minutes. Cake is done if toothpick inserted into middle comes out clean.

Let cool in pan 10 minutes; invert onto rack or plate. Poke holes in cake with tines of fork; slowly pour glaze over. Cool completely; dust with powdered sugar.

For glaze: Combine powdered sugar and liqueur. Blend until smooth.

www.recipesource.com

Tunnel of Fudge Cake

1¾ cups (3½ sticks) butter or margarine, room temperature
1¾ cups granulated sugar
6 eggs
2¾ cups powdered sugar (divided)
2¼ cups flour
1 cup unsweetened cocoa powder (divided)
2 cups chopped walnuts (see note)
1½ to 2 tablespoons milk

Preheat oven to 350 degrees. Grease and flour a 12-cup fluted tube pan.

In large bowl, beat butter and granulated sugar until light and fluffy. Add eggs one at a time, beating well after each addition. Gradually add 2 cups powdered sugar; blend well. By hand, stir in flour, ¾ cup cocoa powder and nuts. Mix until well blended. Spoon batter into prepared pan, spread evenly.

Bake 58 to 62 minutes. Cool upright in pan on cooling rack one hour; then invert onto serving plate. Cool completely.

For glaze: In small bowl combine remaining ¾ cup powdered sugar, remaining ¼ cup cocoa powder and milk. Mix until smooth. Spoon over top of cake allowing some to run down sides. Store tightly covered.

Note: Nuts are essential for the success of the recipe. Because this cake has a soft tunnel of fudge, the ordinary doneness test cannot be used. Accurate oven temperature and baking time are critical.

www.bakeoff.com

ng out of your Bundt

hite Chocolate Bundt Cake

cup (2 sticks) unsalted butter, room temperature, plus 1 tablespoon to coat pan

cups sugar, plus 2 tablespoons for sugaring the pan

cups flour

teaspoon baking powder

teaspoon baking soda

teaspoon salt

/2 teaspoons vanilla extract

teaspoon almond extract

arge eggs, room temperature

ounces white chocolate, melted, still warm, plus 4 ounces white chocolate chunks or chips

cup sour cream

ounces semisweet chocolate, melted and still warm

hite Chocolate Ganache

ounces white chocolate, coarsely chopped

cup whipping cream

Preheat oven to 350 degrees. at a 10- to 12-cup fluted tube n with 1 tablespoon butter, en sprinkle with 2 tablespoons gar.

Into medium bowl, sift together flour, baking powder, king soda and salt.

Put remaining 1 cup butter and cups sugar in large bowl and at with electric mixer on meum speed until light and fluffy. d vanilla and almond extracts d eggs, one at a time, beating seconds after each addition. wly beat in the 4 ounces lted white chocolate. Scrape down bowl.

Add flour mixture to butter mixture in thirds, alternating with the sour cream. Beat 45 seconds after each addition. Place batter in prepared pan in three layers, separating each layer with some of the remaining 4 ounces white chocolate chunks or chips.

Bake in preheated oven 55 to 60 minutes, or until done. Top will be brown, and a cake tester inserted into center will come out with a few crumbs on it. Remove cake to a wire rack to cool for 15 minutes, then invert onto a wire rack and cool to room temperature.

While cake cools, make white chocolate ganache: In a glass bowl covered with plastic wrap, heat white chocolate with cream on high (100 percent power) in microwave oven in 30-second intervals, stirring after each interval, until smooth.

When ganache is done, let it cool about 10 minutes, then drizzle over cake in a decorative pattern.

Pour melted semisweet chocolate into a squeeze bottle and squeeze it over the white chocolate in a decorative pattern. Transfer cake to a serving platter.

"Debbi Fields' Great American Desserts"

Omaha World-Herald

TechBytes

PhotoSite helps you build album

Digital photographs are a great way to share your adventures with family and friends over the Internet, but not if your picture files are so enormous that they clog a dial-up connection, become scrambled in transit or are translated into a format that your relatives cannot open.

photosite by homestead

The New York Times reports that the new PhotoSite service from Homestead Technologies is designed to let digital photographers create and publish Web-based electronic photo albums in five minutes and just a few

LASAGNA ❀ *from The 4-H Friends' Cookbook*

- 8 ounces uncooked lasagna noodles
- 1 pound ground beef
- 1/2 teaspoon minced garlic or 2 cloves of garlic
- 1 (6-ounce) can tomato paste
- 2 1/2 cups chopped fresh or canned tomatoes
- 1 teaspoon salt
- 3/4 teaspoon pepper
- 1/2 teaspoon oregano
- 1 1/2 cups cottage cheese
- 1/2 cup grated Parmesan cheese

Simmer the lasagna noodles for 20 minutes using package directions; drain. Cook the ground beef in a large skillet until no pink remains, stirring until crumbly; drain. Add the garlic, tomato paste, tomatoes, salt, pepper and oregano; mix well. Remove from heat. Layer the noodles, cottage cheese and meat sauce 1/2 at a time in a greased 7x11-inch baking dish. Sprinkle with the Parmesan cheese. Bake at 350 degrees for 30 minutes or until a cooking thermometer registers 165 degrees. May substitute 8 ounces Swiss cheese for the cottage cheese.

Yield: 8 servings.

Approx Per Serving: Cal 324; T Fat 13 g; 35% Calories from Fat; Prot 25 g; Carbo 28 g; Fiber 3 g; Chol 53 mg; Sod 759 mg

Mrs. Harold Stevens

BARBECUED MEATBALLS

- 1 cup catsup
- 1 cup water
- 3/4 cup packed brown sugar
- 1 tablespoon chili powder
- 3 tablespoons vinegar
- 2 tablespoons Worcestershire sauce
- 2 pounds ground beef
- 1 pound seasoned pork sausage
- 1 egg
- 1 cup milk
- 2 cups saltine crumbs
- 1 tablespoon minced onion

Combine the catsup, water, brown sugar, chili powder, vinegar and Worcestershire sauce in a small saucepan; bring to a boil. Mix the ground beef, sausage, egg, milk, cracker crumbs and onion in a bowl. Shape into large meatballs. Place in a 9x13-inch baking pan; the pan will be full. Pour the sauce over the meatballs. Bake at 325 degrees for 2 hours or until the juices are no longer pink and a meat thermometer registers 160 degrees.

This is great as a one-dish casserole or to serve at picnics. It reheats well.

Yield: 15 servings.

Approx Per Serving: Cal 303; T Fat 15 g; 45% Calories from Fat; Prot 19 g; Carbo 23 g; Fiber 1 g; Chol 73 mg; Sod 598 mg

Kathy Lammers, Hartington

CHEESY PORCUPINE MEATBALLS

1 pound ground beef
2 eggs
8 ounces mozzarella cheese, shredded
$1\frac{1}{2}$ cups quick-cooking rice
1 teaspoon salt
$\frac{1}{4}$ teaspoon pepper
2 to 3 tablespoons Worcestershire sauce
2 tablespoons minced onion
1 (10-ounce) can tomato soup
$1\frac{1}{2}$ cups water

Mix the ground beef, eggs, cheese, rice, salt, pepper, Worcestershire sauce and onion in a bowl. Shape into 2-inch balls. Place in a large skillet or Dutch oven. Pour a mixture of the soup and water over the meatballs. Cook over medium or medium-high heat for 30 minutes or until the ground beef is cooked through and no pink remains in the center of the meatballs.

This is an easy family favorite that is the result of adapting several recipes to our tastes.

Yield: 5 servings.

Approx Per Serving: Cal 514; T Fat 25 g; 45% Calories from Fat; Prot 35 g; Carbo 35 g; Fiber 1 g; Chol 188 mg; Sod 1193 mg

Janet Latta, Stratton

SPICY MEATBALLS

2 cups catsup
$1\frac{1}{2}$ cups packed brown sugar
$\frac{1}{2}$ cup chopped onion
$\frac{1}{2}$ teaspoon garlic salt
3 pounds ground beef
2 eggs
2 cups rolled oats
1 cup chopped onion
$\frac{1}{2}$ teaspoon garlic powder
1 teaspoon salt
1 teaspoon pepper
1 teaspoon chili powder
1 (12-ounce) can evaporated milk

Mix the catsup, brown sugar, onion and garlic salt in a bowl. Combine the ground beef, eggs, oats, onion, garlic powder, salt, pepper, chili powder and evaporated milk in a bowl; mix well. Shape into 1-inch balls. Place in a 9x13-inch baking pan. Pour the sauce over the meatballs. Bake at 350 degrees for 1 to $1\frac{1}{2}$ hours or until the juices are no longer pink and a meat thermometer registers 160 degrees. May substitute one 14-ounce can sweetened condensed milk or 1 cup 2% milk for the evaporated milk. May add liquid smoke to taste to the catsup mixture.

This is a super meat dish for covered dish suppers. It may be made ahead and frozen.

Yield: 12 servings.

Approx Per Serving: Cal 667; T Fat 20 g; 26% Calories from Fat; Prot 31 g; Carbo 94 g; Fiber 2 g; Chol 128 mg; Sod 877 mg

Tyke Arnold, Broken Bow
Mary Finnegan, Bristow
Karen Hansen, Hemingford
Leanne Jurgens, Amherst
Joel Miller, Aurora
Susan Wattier, Randolph
Pat Zumbrum, St. Libory

POLYNESIAN MEATBALLS

- 1 (15-ounce) can juice-pack sliced pineapple
- 1 pound ground beef
- 1 egg
- 2 tablespoons chopped walnuts
- 2 tablespoons cracker crumbs
- 1/2 teaspoon salt
- 1/8 teaspoon pepper
- 1/8 teaspoon ginger
- 4 1/2 teaspoons low-sodium soy sauce
- 1 tablespoon molasses
- 2 tablespoons cornstarch
- 1/4 cup water
- 1 medium green bell pepper, cut into bite-size pieces
- 2 tablespoons vinegar

Drain the pineapple, reserving the juice. Combine the pineapple juice with enough water to measure 1 cup; set aside. Mix the ground beef, egg, walnuts, cracker crumbs, salt, pepper and ginger in a bowl. Shape into 8 to 12 meatballs. Cook at 350 degrees in an electric skillet for 7 minutes or until brown and no longer pink in the center. Remove the meatballs with a slotted spoon and set aside; drain the skillet. Pour a mixture of the pineapple juice mixture, soy sauce and molasses into the skillet. Bring to a boil. Mix the cornstarch and 1/4 cup water to make a paste. Stir into the boiling sauce. Cook until slightly thickened. Add the green pepper, pineapple and vinegar. Cook until heated through. Serve over hot fluffy rice.

My mother received this recipe from a college classmate. I revised it to reduce salt and fat. I presented this in the 1992 Nebraska Beef Ambassadors contest and won, and presented it at the 1992 National Beef Ambassadors Competition in Louisville, Kentucky.

Yield: 5 servings.

Approx Per Serving: Cal 324; T Fat 16 g; 44% Calories from Fat; Prot 23 g; Carbo 23 g; Fiber 1 g; Chol 110 mg; Sod 320 mg

Jennifer L. Hanson, Lexington

PORCUPINE MEATBALLS

- 1 (10-ounce) can tomato soup
- 1/2 teaspoon chili powder
- 1/2 cup water
- 1 pound ground beef
- 1/3 cup rice
- 1/4 cup chopped onion
- 1/4 cup water
- 1 teaspoon salt
- 1/8 teaspoon pepper, or to taste

Combine the soup and chili powder in a saucepan. Stir in 1/2 cup water. Bring to a boil. Mix the ground beef, rice, onion, 1/4 cup water, salt and pepper in a bowl. Shape into fifteen 1-inch balls. Add to the hot soup mixture. Simmer, covered, for 1 hour, or until the meatballs are cooked through, stirring several times while cooking.

Yield: 5 servings.

Approx Per Serving: Cal 288; T Fat 14 g; 43% Calories from Fat; Prot 22 g; Carbo 19 g; Fiber <1 g; Chol 67 mg; Sod 899 mg

Eileen Krumbach, Shelby

SWEDISH MEATBALLS

4 eggs
1 cup milk
8 slices white bread, torn into pieces
2 pounds ground beef
1/4 cup finely chopped onion
4 teaspoons baking powder
1 to 2 teaspoons salt
1 teaspoon pepper
2 tablespoons shortening
2 (10-ounce) cans cream of chicken soup
2 (10-ounce) cans cream of mushroom soup
1 (12-ounce) can evaporated milk
Minced fresh parsley to taste

Beat the eggs and milk in a bowl. Add the bread and mix gently. Let stand for 5 minutes. Add the ground beef, onion, baking powder, salt and pepper; mix well. Shape into 1-inch balls. Brown a few meatballs at a time in the shortening in a large skillet. Place the meatballs in a 3-quart baking dish. Mix the chicken soup, mushroom soup and evaporated milk in a bowl. Pour over the meatballs. Bake at 350 degrees for 1 hour or until the meatballs are cooked through and are no longer pink in the center. Sprinkle with the parsley. May serve over cooked noodles.

This is a recipe I have had since I was a teenager. I got it from a minister's wife from Wisconsin. It always gets rave reviews.

Yield: 10 servings.

Approx Per Serving: Cal 496; T Fat 29 g; 54% Calories from Fat; Prot 30 g; Carbo 26 g; Fiber 1 g; Chol 172 mg; Sod 1767 mg

Fran Obermire, Atkinson

BARBECUED MEAT LOAF

2 pounds ground beef
1 cup rolled oats
1 egg, beaten
4 tablespoons chopped onion
2 teaspoons salt
1/4 teaspoon pepper
3 tablespoons Worcestershire sauce
1 cup milk
1/2 cup catsup
2 drops of Tabasco sauce

Combine the ground beef, oats, egg, 2 tablespoons of the onion, salt, pepper, 2 tablespoons of the Worcestershire sauce and milk in a bowl; mix well. Shape into a loaf; place in a greased loaf pan. Combine the catsup, remaining 1 tablespoon Worcestershire sauce, remaining 2 tablespoons onion and Tabasco sauce in a saucepan. Cook until heated through. Pour over the meat loaf. Bake at 350 degrees for 1 hour or until the juices are no longer pink and a meat thermometer registers 160 degrees.

This recipe is everyone's favorite, so give it a try—you won't be sorry!

Yield: 8 servings.

Approx Per Serving: Cal 337; T Fat 18 g; 49% Calories from Fat; Prot 29 g; Carbo 14 g; Fiber 1 g; Chol 115 mg; Sod 861 mg

Danette Lillard, Lyman

CHEESE-FILLED MEAT LOAF

- $1\frac{1}{2}$ pounds lean ground beef
- 1 cup catsup
- $\frac{3}{4}$ cup quick-cooking oats
- $\frac{1}{2}$ cup chopped onion
- 1 egg
- 1 tablespoon Worcestershire sauce
- $1\frac{1}{2}$ teaspoons salt
- 1 teaspoon oregano
- $\frac{1}{4}$ teaspoon pepper
- 1 (6-ounce) package sliced mozzarella cheese

Combine the ground beef, catsup, oats, onion, egg, Worcestershire sauce, salt, oregano and pepper in a bowl; mix well. Pat $\frac{1}{3}$ of the ground beef mixture into a 5x9-inch loaf pan. Layer with half the cheese, $\frac{1}{3}$ of the ground beef mixture, remaining cheese and remaining ground beef mixture. Bake at 350 degrees for 1 hour or until the juices are no longer pink and a meat thermometer registers 160 degrees. May add $1\frac{1}{2}$ teaspoons MSG.

This has been a family recipe for over 25 years. We've served it for years to men working cattle.

Yield: 6 servings.

Approx Per Serving: Cal 429; T Fat 23 g; 49% Calories from Fat; Prot 34 g; Carbo 20 g; Fiber 2 g; Chol 142 mg; Sod 1221 mg

Laurine Huston, Emmet

MINIATURE CHEESE PATTIES

- 2 pounds ground beef
- $2\frac{3}{4}$ cups fresh bread crumbs
- $\frac{3}{4}$ cup chopped onion
- 1 teaspoon salt
- $\frac{1}{4}$ teaspoon pepper
- 1 (10-ounce) can vegetarian vegetable soup
- $\frac{1}{4}$ cup milk
- $\frac{1}{2}$ cup chopped Swiss cheese
- 1 (16-ounce) jar spaghetti sauce

Combine the ground beef, bread crumbs, onion, salt, pepper, soup and milk in a bowl; mix well. Shape into 16 patties and place on a baking sheet. Press a few pieces of cheese into each patty. Cover with the spaghetti sauce. Bake at 400 degrees for 35 minutes or until the juices are no longer pink and a meat thermometer registers 160 degrees.

Yield: 16 servings.

Approx Per Serving: Cal 205; T Fat 11 g; 48% Calories from Fat; Prot 16 g; Carbo 11 g; Fiber <1 g; Chol 46 mg; Sod 479 mg

Susan Ott, Osceola

BACON BEAN GROUND BEEF CASSEROLE

1 pound ground beef
1 pound bacon, cut into bite-size pieces
$^1/_2$ cup chopped onion
1 (15-ounce) can kidney beans, drained
2 (15-ounce) cans pork and beans, drained
1 (15-ounce) can butter beans, drained
1 cup packed brown sugar
$^1/_2$ cup sugar
1 cup catsup
2 teaspoons dry mustard
1 teaspoon salt
1 tablespoon vinegar

Combine the ground beef, bacon and onion in a skillet. Cook until the ground beef is crumbly and no pink remains and the bacon is cooked through, stirring constantly; drain well. Add all the beans; mix well. Add the brown sugar, sugar, catsup, dry mustard, salt and vinegar; mix well. Pour into a slow cooker. Cook on Low for several hours.

Yield: 6 servings.

Approx Per Serving: Cal 795; T Fat 25 g; 27% Calories from Fat; Prot 39 g; Carbo 109 g; Fiber 13 g; Chol 85 mg; Sod 2206 mg

Chris Bacon, Valentine

QUICK-AND-EASY CHINESE CASSEROLE

1 pound ground beef
1 cup chopped celery
1 cup chopped onion
$1^1/_4$ cups quick-cooking rice
1 (10-ounce) can cream of mushroom soup
1 (10-ounce) can cream of chicken soup
$1^1/_3$ soup cans water
2 tablespoons soy sauce
1 (5-ounce) can chow mein noodles

Cook the ground beef in a skillet until no pink remains, stirring until crumbly; drain. Combine the ground beef, celery, onion, rice, mushroom soup, chicken soup, water and soy sauce in a bowl; mix well. Spoon into a lightly greased 9x13-inch baking pan or a $2^1/_2$-quart baking dish. Bake at 350 degrees for 45 minutes or until a cooking thermometer registers 165 degrees. Spread the noodles evenly over the top of the casserole. Bake for 15 minutes longer.

I heard this recipe on a recipe-swap radio show more than 15 years ago. It has been a family favorite ever since.

Yield: 6 servings.

Approx Per Serving: Cal 481; T Fat 25 g; 46% Calories from Fat; Prot 23 g; Carbo 41 g; Fiber 2 g; Chol 61 mg; Sod 1317 mg

Fran Obermire, Atkinson

FRENCH BEEF

8 ounces flat egg noodles
2 cups sour cream
8 ounces cream cheese, softened
2 pounds ground beef
3 (8-ounce) cans tomato sauce
1 small onion, chopped
1 1/2 cups shredded Cheddar cheese
1/2 cup grated Parmesan cheese, or to taste
1/2 cup herb-flavor bread cubes
1/2 cup shredded Cheddar cheese

Cook the noodles using package directions; drain. Combine the noodles, sour cream and cream cheese in a bowl, stirring until the noodles are well coated. Cook the ground beef in a skillet until no pink remains, stirring until crumbly; drain. Combine the ground beef, tomato sauce and onion in the skillet; mix well. Place the noodle mixture in a 9x13-inch casserole. Cover with the ground beef mixture. Top with 1 1/2 cups Cheddar cheese. Sprinkle with the Parmesan cheese and top with the bread cubes. Bake at 350 degrees for 30 minutes or until a cooking thermometer registers 165 degrees. Top with 1/2 cup Cheddar cheese. Bake until the cheese is melted. Let stand for several minutes before slicing.

Yield: 8 servings.

Approx Per Serving: Cal 650; T Fat 51 g; 60% Calories from Fat; Prot 44 g; Carbo 32 g; Fiber 2 g; Chol 225 mg; Sod 998 mg

Bill Lux, Whitney

QUICK CHEESEBURGER PIE

1 1/3 cups flour
1/2 teaspoon salt
1/2 cup shortening
3 to 4 tablespoons cold water
1 pound ground beef
1/2 to 3/4 cup finely chopped onion
1 clove of garlic, minced
1/2 teaspoon salt
1/4 cup flour
1/3 cup dill pickle liquid
1/3 cup milk
1/2 cup chopped dill pickles
2 cups shredded Cheddar cheese

Mix 1 1/3 cups flour and 1/2 teaspoon salt in a bowl. Cut in the shortening until crumbly. Sprinkle in the water 1 tablespoon at a time. Mix lightly until the flour is moistened, adding an additional 1 to 2 teaspoons water if needed. Line an 8-inch quiche dish with the dough. Bake at 425 degrees for 15 minutes. Combine the ground beef, onion and garlic in a skillet. Cook until the ground beef is cooked through and no pink remains, stirring until crumbly; drain. Sprinkle with 1/2 teaspoon salt and 1/4 cup flour. Stir in the pickle liquid, milk, pickles and half the cheese. Spoon into the crust. Bake for 15 minutes longer. Sprinkle with the remaining cheese. Bake for 5 minutes or until the crust is brown.

Yield: 6 servings.

Approx Per Serving: Cal 607; T Fat 41 g; 61% Calories from Fat; Prot 30 g; Carbo 29 g; Fiber 1 g; Chol 98 mg; Sod 842 mg

Kathryn Valasek, Comstock

SMOTHERED BURRITOS

2 pounds ground beef
1 onion, chopped
1 (16-ounce) can refried beans
2 (12-ounce) cans green chile sauce
8 tortillas
1 cup sliced black olives
1 cup sour cream
4 cups shredded Cheddar cheese

Combine the ground beef with the onion in a skillet. Cook until no pink remains in the ground beef, stirring constantly; drain. Add the beans and chile sauce; mix well. Fill the tortillas with the ground beef mixture, olives, sour cream and 3 cups of the cheese. Place in a baking pan. Top with the remaining 1 cup cheese. Bake at 350 degrees for 30 minutes or until the cheese is melted.

Yield: 8 servings.

Approx Per Serving: Cal 806; T Fat 150 g; 56% Calories from Fat; Prot 49 g; Carbo 41 g; Fiber 7 g; Chol 170 mg; Sod 1106 mg

Jennifer Maddux, Wauneta

BEEFY ENCHILADA CASSEROLE

2 pounds ground beef
1/2 cup chopped onion
9 (8-inch) flour tortillas
2 (10-ounce) cans mild enchilada sauce
2 cups shredded Cheddar cheese

Cook the ground beef in a skillet until no pink remains, stirring until crumbly; drain. Sauté the onion in a nonstick skillet. Stir into the ground beef. Dip the tortillas in the enchilada sauce in a bowl, coating each side. Overlap 3 tortillas in a 9x13-inch baking dish. Layer 1/3 of the ground beef mixture and 1/3 of the cheese over the tortillas. Repeat the layers twice. Pour the remaining enchilada sauce over the top. Bake at 350 degrees for 30 to 40 minutes or until a cooking thermometer registers 165 degrees. Let stand for 10 minutes before cutting and serving. May serve on a bed of shredded lettuce, topped with sour cream and chopped black olives.

This was given as a 4-H presentation and is a favorite with my family and at carry-in dinners. It was also popular when I served it at a Methodist Youth Fellowship dinner.

Yield: 8 servings.

Approx Per Serving: Cal 582; T Fat 36 g; 56% Calories from Fat; Prot 37 g; Carbo 27 g; Fiber 2 g; Chol 137 mg; Sod 508 mg

Kayla Kudena, Valentine

ENCHILADAS

3 tablespoons vegetable oil
1 1/2 tablespoons flour
1 1/2 teaspoons chili powder
1 1/2 cups water
1 teaspoon vinegar
1/2 teaspoon garlic powder
1/2 teaspoon onion powder
1/4 teaspoon oregano
1 1/2 pounds ground beef
1 (16-ounce) can chili beans, mashed or puréed
1 medium onion, chopped
2 tablespoons picante sauce
1 envelope taco seasoning mix
1/2 cup water
8 to 10 flour tortillas
2 cups shredded Monterey Jack, Cheddar or mozzarella cheese

Combine the oil, flour, chili powder, 1 1/2 cups water, vinegar, garlic powder, onion powder and oregano in a saucepan. Cook until heated through. Cook the ground beef in a skillet until no pink remains, stirring until crumbly; drain. Combine the ground beef, beans, onion, picante sauce, taco seasoning and 1/2 cup water in a bowl; mix well. Fill the tortillas with the ground beef mixture and most of the cheese, reserving a small amount for the topping. Roll up and place seam side down in a 9x13-inch baking pan. Pour the heated sauce over the tortillas. Top with the reserved cheese. Bake at 350 degrees for 20 to 30 minutes or until a cooking thermometer registers 165 degrees.

Yield: 10 servings.

Approx Per Serving: Cal 461; T Fat 26 g; 50% Calories from Fat; Prot 27 g; Carbo 31 g; Fiber 3 g; Chol 79 mg; Sod 928 mg

Amber and Jami Talbott, Norfolk

SUPER NACHOS

1 pound ground beef
1 onion, chopped
Salt to taste
Liquid hot pepper to taste
Cumin to taste
1 (30-ounce) can refried beans
1 (4-ounce) can whole green chiles
3 cups shredded Cheddar cheese
3/4 cup taco sauce
1 cup chopped black olives
6 ounces avocado dip
2 cups sour cream

Cook the ground beef with the onion in a skillet until no pink remains in the ground beef, stirring constantly. Season with the salt, hot pepper and cumin; drain. Spread the beans in a 9x13-inch baking pan. Rinse, drain and chop the green chiles and stir into the ground beef mixture. Spread the mixture over the beans. Cover with the cheese and drizzle with the taco sauce. Cover and refrigerate until baking time. Bake, uncovered, at 400 degrees for 20 to 25 minutes or until heated through. Top with the olives, avocado dip and sour cream. Serve with tortilla chips.

This family favorite is a tradition during the televised Nebraska football games.

Yield: 10 servings.

Approx Per Serving: Cal 492; T Fat 33 g; 60% Calories from Fat; Prot 26 g; Carbo 23 g; Fiber 7 g; Chol 101 mg; Sod 1002 mg

Terri Uden, Lexington

TACO BEEF QUICHE

1 or 2 large flour tortillas
1 (4-ounce) can chopped green chiles
4 green onions, chopped
1/2 cup chopped fresh tomato
1 cup sour cream
1/4 teaspoon salt
1 pound ground beef
1/2 cup chopped onion
2 eggs
1 envelope taco seasoning mix
1 (5-ounce) can evaporated milk
1/3 cup beef bouillon
1 cup shredded Cheddar cheese

Warm the tortillas in a microwave for 10 seconds. Place in a lightly greased 9-inch pie plate. Mix the chiles, green onions, tomato, sour cream and salt in a bowl. Refrigerate until serving time. Crumble the ground beef and onion in a microwave-safe dish. Microwave on High for 5 minutes or until no pink remains, stirring once; drain. Spoon the ground beef mixture over the tortillas. Blend the next 4 ingredients in a bowl. Pour half the custard mixture over the ground beef mixture. Microwave on Medium for 5 minutes. Top with the cheese and remaining custard mixture. Microwave on Medium for 8 to 10 minutes or until the custard mixture is set and a knife inserted near the center comes out clean, turning at least once during cooking. Let stand for 5 minutes. Cut into slices. Top each slice with 2 tablespoons of the tomato mixture. Garnish with chopped lettuce, chopped black olives and/or crushed tortilla chips.

Yield: 6 servings.

Approx Per Serving: Cal 485; T Fat 30 g; 56% Calories from Fat; Prot 29 g; Carbo 24 g; Fiber 1 g; Chol 171 mg; Sod 1284 mg

Cristine Minneman, Wichita, KS

TACO BAKE

1 1/2 pounds ground beef
1 1/2 cups chopped onion
1 1/2 teaspoons salt
1/2 teaspoon pepper
1 teaspoon chili powder
2 (15-ounce) cans chili beans
2 cups shredded Cheddar cheese
1 (15-ounce) can tomato sauce
1 (10-ounce) package taco shells, broken

Cook the ground beef with the onion in a skillet until no pink remains in the ground beef, stirring constantly; drain. Season with the salt, pepper and chili powder. Add the beans, 1 cup of the cheese and tomato sauce. Line an 11x15-inch baking pan with the broken taco shells. Spoon the ground beef mixture over the shells. Top with the remaining 1 cup cheese. Bake at 350 degrees for 20 minutes or until a cooking thermometer registers 165 degrees.

Yield: 10 servings.

Approx Per Serving: Cal 485; T Fat 27 g; 49% Calories from Fat; Prot 29 g; Carbo 34 g; Fiber 5 g; Chol 89 mg; Sod 1248 mg

Judy Bausch, Pawnee City

TOSTADO CASSEROLE

1 pound ground beef
1 envelope taco seasoning mix
1 (15-ounce) can tomato sauce
2 cups crushed corn chips
1 (15-ounce) can refried beans
1 cup shredded Cheddar cheese
1/2 cup crushed corn chips

Cook the ground beef in a skillet until no pink remains, stirring until crumbly; drain. Add the taco seasoning and 3/4 cup of the tomato sauce. Line a 9x13-inch baking pan with 2 cups crushed chips. Add the ground beef mixture. Spread a mixture of the beans and remaining tomato sauce over the ground beef. Top with the cheese and 1/2 cup crushed chips. Bake, covered with foil, at 350 degrees for 35 minutes or until a cooking thermometer registers 165 degrees. Garnish with chopped lettuce, tomatoes, black olives or sour cream.

One of our good friends, who insists she "can't cook," shared this recipe with us. It's one of our family's favorites.

Yield: 8 servings.

Approx Per Serving: Cal 476; T Fat 26 g; 48% Calories from Fat; Prot 23 g; Carbo 39 g; Fiber 6 g; Chol 57 mg; Sod 1337 mg

Sue Babovec, Cedar Rapids
Carissa Sauer, Ogallala

CRUSTY GROUND BEEF NOODLE CASSEROLE

8 ounces Klusky noodles
1 pound ground beef
1 onion, finely chopped
1 tablespoon Worcestershire sauce
1 tablespoon soy sauce
2 (10-ounce) cans cream of chicken soup
3/4 cup milk
1 cup shredded Cheddar cheese
1 (3-ounce) can French-fried onions

Cook the noodles using the package directions; drain. Cook the ground beef in a skillet until no pink remains, stirring until crumbly; drain. Place the noodles in a 9x13-inch baking dish. Top with the ground beef and onion. Mix the Worcestershire sauce, soy sauce, soup and milk in a bowl and pour over the ground beef. Top with the cheese. Bake at 350 degrees for 45 minutes or until the cheese is melted, the soup is bubbly and a cooking thermometer registers 165 degrees. Sprinkle French-fried onions over the top. Bake for about 5 minutes longer. Serve immediately.

This is a recipe my grandmother shared with me. She won a cooking contest with it. I used it for my 4-H Food Revue entry a year ago and won first place. My family loves it!

Yield: 8 servings.

Approx Per Serving: Cal 340; T Fat 24 g; 49% Calories from Fat; Prot 24 g; Carbo 33 g; Fiber <1 g; Chol 116 mg; Sod 952 mg

Lori Buethe, Tecumseh

BEEF NOODLE CASSEROLE

1 1/2 pounds ground beef
1/2 cup chopped onion
1 tablespoon butter
8 ounces noodles
1 cup cottage cheese
8 ounces cream cheese, softened
1/4 cup sour cream
1/4 cup chopped green onions
1/4 cup chopped green bell pepper
1 teaspoon salt
1/4 teaspoon pepper
1/8 teaspoon garlic powder
1 (16-ounce) can tomato sauce
1 teaspoon brown sugar
2 tablespoons melted butter
1/3 cup grated Parmesan cheese

Combine the ground beef and onion in 1 tablespoon butter in a skillet. Cook until no pink remains in the ground beef, stirring constantly; drain. Cook the noodles using the package directions; drain. Mix the cottage cheese, cream cheese, sour cream, green onions, green pepper, salt, pepper and garlic powder in a bowl. Stir in the tomato sauce and brown sugar. Layer half the ground beef mixture, half the noodles, all the sour cream mixture and remaining noodles in a buttered 3-quart casserole. Pour 2 tablespoons melted butter over the casserole. Top with the remaining ground beef mixture. Sprinkle with the Parmesan cheese. Bake at 350 degrees for 30 minutes or until a cooking thermometer registers 165 degrees.

Yield: 10 servings.

Approx Per Serving: Cal 328; T Fat 25 g; 55% Calories from Fat; Prot 25 g; Carbo 22 g; Fiber 1 g; Chol 133 mg; Sod 780 mg

Jeannette Taubenheim, Amherst

YUM-A-SETTA

2 pounds ground beef
2 tablespoons brown sugar
1/4 cup chopped onion, or to taste
Salt and pepper to taste
1 (10-ounce) can tomato soup
16 ounces egg noodles, cooked, drained
2 (10-ounce) cans cream of chicken soup
1 cup shredded American cheese

Cook the ground beef in a skillet until no pink remains, stirring constantly; drain. Add the brown sugar, onion, salt and pepper. Stir in the tomato soup. Mix the noodles with the chicken soup in a bowl. Layer the ground beef mixture, noodles mixture and cheese in a 3-quart casserole. Bake at 350 degrees for 30 minutes or until a cooking thermometer registers 165 degrees.

This is an Amish dish.

Yield: 8 servings.

Approx Per Serving: Cal 410; T Fat 28 g; 41% Calories from Fat; Prot 39 g; Carbo 53 g; Fiber <1 g; Chol 203 mg; Sod 1137 mg

Kathryn Valasek, Comstock

SLOPPY JOE PIZZA

1 pound ground chuck
3/4 cup frozen corn, thawed
3/4 cup barbecue sauce
1/2 cup sliced green onions
1/2 teaspoon salt, or to taste
1 (12-inch) Italian bread shell or prepared pizza crust
1 1/2 cups shredded Co-Jack or mozzarella cheese

Cook the ground beef in a large nonstick skillet over medium heat for 8 to 10 minutes or until no pink remains, stirring constantly; drain. Add the corn, barbecue sauce, green onions and salt. Cook until heated through or until a cooking thermometer registers 165 degrees. Place the bread shell on a baking sheet. Spoon the ground beef mixture over the top. Sprinkle with the cheese. Bake at 425 degrees for 12 to 15 minutes or until the cheese is melted. Cut into 8 wedges.

Yield: 4 servings.

Approx Per Serving: Cal 739; T Fat 30 g; 36% Calories from Fat; Prot 45 g; Carbo 71 g; Fiber 5 g; Chol 118 mg; Sod 1531 mg

Denise Barry, Valparaiso

UPSIDE-DOWN PIZZA

2 pounds ground beef
1/4 cup chopped onion
1 envelope spaghetti sauce mix
1 (6-ounce) can tomato sauce
1 1/2 cups shredded mozzarella cheese
1/2 cup sour cream
1 (8-count) can crescent rolls
2 tablespoons melted butter
1/3 cup grated Parmesan cheese

Cook the ground beef and onion in a skillet until no pink remains in the ground beef, stirring constantly; drain. Add the spaghetti sauce and tomato sauce. Simmer gently to allow the flavors to combine. Spread in a 9x13-inch baking pan. Add the mozzarella cheese and sour cream. Unroll the roll dough; do not separate into triangles. Place over the top of the prepared layers in 1 large rectangle. Brush with the butter and sprinkle with the Parmesan cheese. Bake at 375 degrees for 20 to 30 minutes or until the top is golden brown. Cool slightly before serving.

Yield: 10 servings.

Approx Per Serving: Cal 393; T Fat 24 g; 56% Calories from Fat; Prot 27 g; Carbo 16 g; Fiber <1 g; Chol 97 mg; Sod 862 mg

Kelly Penke, Craig

HEARTY BEEF AND POTATO CASSEROLE

1 (15-ounce) package frozen potato rounds
1 pound ground beef
1 (10-ounce) package frozen chopped broccoli, thawed
1 (3-ounce) can French-fried onions
1 medium tomato, chopped
1/3 cup milk
1 (10-ounce) can cream of celery soup
1/2 cup shredded Cheddar cheese
1/4 teaspoon garlic powder
1/8 teaspoon pepper
1/2 cup shredded Cheddar cheese

Arrange the potatoes over the bottom and up the sides of a greased 8x12-inch casserole. Bake at 400 degrees for 10 minutes. Cook the ground beef in a skillet until no pink remains, stirring constantly; drain. Spoon a mixture of the ground beef, broccoli, half the French-fried onions and tomato over the potatoes. Mix the milk, soup, 1/2 cup cheese, garlic powder and pepper in a bowl. Pour over the ground beef mixture. Bake, covered, at 400 degrees for 20 minutes or until a cooking thermometer registers 165 degrees. Top with 1/2 cup cheese and the remaining French-fried onions. Bake, uncovered, for 2 to 3 minutes longer or until the cheese is melted. Serve hot.

This is a family favorite.

Yield: 6 servings.

Approx Per Serving: Cal 449; T Fat 27 g; 53% Calories from Fat; Prot 27 g; Carbo 26 g; Fiber 2 g; Chol 84 mg; Sod 670 mg

Gail Mooter, Omaha

HAMBURGER SPUD CASSEROLE

1 (10-ounce) can cream of celery soup
1/2 cup milk
4 cups shredded potatoes
1 tablespoon chopped onion
Salt and pepper to taste
1 1/2 pounds ground beef
1/2 cup quick-cooking oats
1/4 cup chopped onion
1/4 cup catsup
1 (5-ounce) can evaporated milk

Combine the soup with the milk. Combine with the potatoes, 1 tablespoon onion, salt and pepper in a bowl. Spoon into a greased 8x11-inch casserole. Mix the ground beef, oats, 1/4 cup onion, catsup and evaporated milk in a bowl. Spoon over the potato mixture. Bake at 350 degrees for 1 1/4 hours or until bubbly and heated through and no pink remains in the ground beef. May substitute cream of mushroom soup for cream of celery soup and frozen hash brown potatoes for the shredded potatoes.

Yield: 8 servings.

Approx Per Serving: Cal 395; T Fat 16 g; 36% Calories from Fat; Prot 25 g; Carbo 38 g; Fiber 3 g; Chol 75 mg; Sod 460 mg

Carol Thomsen, St. Paul

RUNZAS

1 envelope fast-rising yeast
2 cups lukewarm water
1/2 cup sugar
1 teaspoon salt
3 tablespoons melted shortening
2 eggs, beaten
5 cups flour
4 cups shredded cabbage
2 cups chopped onions
1 teaspoon shortening
2 tablespoons water
2 pounds ground beef
1 tablespoon Worcestershire sauce
1/8 teaspoon pepper
1/4 teaspoon oregano
1/4 teaspoon seasoned salt

Dissolve the yeast in 2 cups lukewarm water in a bowl. Add the sugar, salt and 3 tablespoons shortening; beat until smooth. Beat in the eggs. Add the flour 1 cup at a time, beating well after each addition. Cover with a damp cloth and let rise until doubled in bulk. Combine the cabbage, onions, 1 teaspoon shortening and 2 tablespoons water in a steamer or saucepan. Cook, tightly covered, until the vegetables are tender. Cook the ground beef in a skillet until no pink remains, stirring constantly; drain. Combine with the cabbage mixture. Stir in the remaining ingredients. Refrigerate until needed. Roll the dough 1/8 inch thick on a lightly floured surface. Cut the dough into squares. Place a spoonful of the ground beef mixture in the center of 1 square. Top with another square; pinch the sides to seal. Repeat the process until all ingredients are used. Place on a greased baking sheet. Let rise until doubled in bulk. Bake at 400 degrees for 20 to 25 minutes or until golden brown and a cooking thermometer registers 165 degrees.

Yield: 15 servings.

Approx Per Serving: Cal 361; T Fat 13 g; 32% Calories from Fat; Prot 19 g; Carbo 42 g; Fiber 2 g; Chol 73 mg; Sod 221 mg

Susan Stevenson, Petersburg
Beth Wendland, Arapahoe

MARY'S MIRACLE

- 2 (8-count) cans crescent rolls
- 1 1/2 pounds ground beef
- 1/4 cup chopped onion
- 2 tablespoons flour
- 3/4 teaspoon salt
- 1/4 teaspoon garlic salt
- 3 ounces cream cheese, softened
- 1 1/2 cups milk
- 1 egg, beaten
- 1 (10-ounce) package frozen broccoli, cooked, drained
- 4 ounces Monterey Jack cheese, shredded

Unroll 1 can of the roll dough on a floured surface, pressing perforations to seal. Roll to fit a 9x13-inch baking dish; place in the baking dish. Cook the ground beef and onion in a skillet until no pink remains in the ground beef, stirring constantly; drain. Add the flour, salt, garlic salt, cream cheese, milk and egg. Cook until thickened, stirring occasionally. Stir in the broccoli. Spread over the dough in the baking dish. Sprinkle with the cheese. Roll the remaining dough, sealing the edges. Place over the top of the cheese; cut vents. Bake at 350 degrees for 1 hour or until golden brown and a cooking thermometer registers 165 degrees. Let stand for 10 minutes before serving.

This recipe was supposedly entitled Mary's Miracle because the originator prepared this casserole and served it to her granddaughter, who would never eat ground beef, but loved this. This was also served at the 1987 FCE (formerly, Home Extension Club) convention in Valentine. Requests for this recipe were received for the next two years!

Yield: 10 servings.

Approx Per Serving: Cal 402; T Fat 22 g; 24% Calories from Fat; Prot 24 g; Carbo 26 g; Fiber 1 g; Chol 100 mg; Sod 764 mg

Lynda Radant, Valentine

HUNGRY MAN CASSEROLE

- 1 pound ground beef
- 1 teaspoon salt
- 1 (16-ounce) can pork and beans
- 1/4 cup barbecue sauce
- 3/4 cup catsup
- 2 tablespoons brown sugar
- 1 tablespoon dried minced onion
- 1 (10-count) can biscuits
- 1 cup shredded Cheddar cheese

Cook the ground beef in a skillet until no pink remains, stirring constantly; drain. Mix the ground beef, salt, pork and beans, barbecue sauce, catsup, brown sugar and onion in a bowl. Spoon into a 9x9-inch baking pan. Cut the biscuit dough pieces into halves horizontally. Place cut side down 1/2 to 1 inch apart over the ground beef mixture. Sprinkle with the cheese. Bake at 375 degrees for 30 minutes or until a cooking thermometer registers 165 degrees.

Yield: 6 servings.

Approx Per Serving: Cal 511; T Fat 25 g; 41% Calories from Fat; Prot 30 g; Carbo 49 g; Fiber 5 g; Chol 81 mg; Sod 1715 mg

Mrs. Tim Wills, Hemingford

RANCH BURGERS

1 pound ground beef
1 teaspoon prepared mustard
$^{1}/_{2}$ cup chopped black olives
1 cup shredded American cheese
8 hamburger buns
2 to 3 tablespoons margarine, softened

Place the ground beef in a microwave-safe dish. Microwave on High for 5 to 6 minutes or until no pink remains. Stir until crumbly; drain. Add the mustard and olives. Microwave, covered, on High for 45 to 60 seconds or until heated through. Stir in the cheese and cover the dish. Let stand for 5 to 10 minutes. Split the buns into halves and spread both sides with margarine. Spoon the ground beef mixture onto the bottom halves; cover with the tops. Wrap each sandwich in a paper napkin. Microwave 4 sandwiches at a time on Medium-High for 45 to 60 seconds or until heated through. May prepare the ground beef mixture in a skillet, wrap the sandwiches in foil and bake at 350 degrees for 20 minutes.

I adapted this recipe for the microwave when I taught a community college class on microwave cookery. Our daughter, Jennifer, won a beef award at the state fair 4-H presentation contest in 1991, using this recipe.

Yield: 8 servings.

Approx Per Serving: Cal 357; T Fat 20 g; 51% Calories from Fat; Prot 20 g; Carbo 24 g; Fiber 1 g; Chol 56 mg; Sod 612 mg

Cathy Biehl Hanson, Lexington

SLOPPY JOES

1 pound ground beef
$^{2}/_{3}$ cup chopped onion
$^{1}/_{2}$ teaspoon salt
$^{1}/_{4}$ teaspoon pepper
$^{1}/_{4}$ cup water
1 (10-ounce) can chicken gumbo
1 tablespoon catsup
1 tablespoon prepared mustard
8 hamburger buns

Cook the ground beef and onion in a skillet until no pink remains in the ground beef, stirring constantly. Add the salt, pepper, water, soup, catsup and mustard. Simmer, covered, for 30 minutes; drain. Fill the buns with the cooked mixture.

This recipe comes from one of my 4-H foods project books that I used as a 4-H'er in Indiana, where I grew up.

Yield: 8 servings.

Approx Per Serving: Cal 278; T Fat 11 g; 35% Calories from Fat; Prot 17 g; Carbo 27 g; Fiber 1 g; Chol 43 mg; Sod 733 mg

Barbara Schmidt, Fairbury

BAKED SPAGHETTI

- 12 ounces spaghetti, broken into 3-inch pieces
- 1 teaspoon salt, or to taste
- 1 pound ground beef
- 1 (30-ounce) jar spaghetti sauce
- 1 (10-ounce) can cream of mushroom soup
- 1/2 cup grated Parmesan cheese
- 2 cups shredded Cheddar or mozzarella cheese, or a mixture of both

Combine the spaghetti and salt with water to cover in a saucepan. Cook using package directions; drain. Cook the ground beef in a skillet until no pink remains, stirring constantly; drain. Add the spaghetti sauce, soup, Parmesan cheese and 1 cup of the Cheddar cheese; mix well. Combine the spaghetti and ground beef mixture in a 9x13-inch baking dish. Sprinkle with the remaining 1 cup Cheddar cheese. Bake at 350 degrees for 30 to 45 minutes or until heated through and a cooking thermometer registers 165 degrees.

This is an easy way to serve baked spaghetti to a large group.

Yield: 12 servings.

Approx Per Serving: Cal 386; T Fat 19 g; 43% Calories from Fat; Prot 20 g; Carbo 35 g; Fiber 2 g; Chol 52 mg; Sod 951 mg

Michelle Lemke, Osmond

SPAGHETTI PIE

- 7 ounces spaghetti
- 2 tablespoons butter
- 1/3 cup grated Parmesan cheese
- 2 eggs, beaten
- 1 pound lean ground beef
- 1/2 cup chopped onion
- 1 (15-ounce) jar spaghetti sauce
- 1 cup cottage cheese
- 1/2 cup shredded mozzarella cheese

Cook the spaghetti using the package directions; drain. Add the butter, Parmesan cheese and eggs; mix well. Press into a 10-inch pie plate. Cook the ground beef and onion in a skillet until no pink remains in the ground beef, stirring constantly; drain. Stir in the spaghetti sauce. Spread the cottage cheese over the spaghetti mixture. Top with the ground beef mixture. Bake at 350 degrees for 20 minutes. Sprinkle with the mozzarella cheese. Bake for 5 minutes longer. May add 1/4 cup chopped green bell pepper to the ground beef mixture before cooking.

Yield: 6 servings.

Approx Per Serving: Cal 517; T Fat 25 g; 44% Calories from Fat; Prot 33 g; Carbo 39 g; Fiber 2 g; Chol 154 mg; Sod 735 mg

Connie Larrington, Springview

WESTERN CASSEROLE

1 pound ground beef
1/2 cup shredded American cheese
1 teaspoon salt
3/4 cup uncooked rice
1 medium onion, chopped
1 (10-ounce) can tomato soup
1 soup can water
1/2 teaspoon salt
1/2 teaspoon oregano
1/4 teaspoon dry mustard
1 (16-ounce) can cut green beans, drained
1 (16-ounce) can whole kernel corn, drained

Mix the ground beef, cheese and 1 teaspoon salt in a bowl. Shape into 12 balls. Brown in a hot skillet; drain. Place the meatballs in a 2-quart casserole. Add the rice. Combine the onion, soup, water, 1/2 teaspoon salt, oregano and dry mustard in a saucepan. Bring to a boil. Pour over the meatballs. Arrange the green beans and corn around the edges. Bake, covered, at 350 degrees for 1 1/4 hours or until no pink remains in the meatballs and a cooking thermometer registers 165 degrees.

Yield: 6 servings.

Approx Per Serving: Cal 403; T Fat 15 g; 33% Calories from Fat; Prot 24 g; Carbo 44 g; Fiber 4 g; Chol 65 mg; Sod 1496 mg

Lucille Wynegar, Ulysses

ZUCCHINI CASSEROLE

2 pounds ground beef
1 medium onion, finely chopped
2 to 3 cups shredded zucchini
1 (6-ounce) package stuffing mix
1 (10-ounce) can cream of mushroom soup

Cook the ground beef, onion and zucchini in a skillet until no pink remains in the ground beef, stirring constantly; drain. Prepare the stuffing using the package directions. Mix the stuffing and soup in a large bowl. Add the ground beef mixture; mix well. Spoon into a baking dish. Bake at 350 degrees for 30 minutes or until the top is golden brown and a cooking thermometer registers 165 degrees.

Yield: 8 servings.

Approx Per Serving: Cal 385; T Fat 19 g; 45% Calories from Fat; Prot 29 g; Carbo 23 g; Fiber 2 g; Chol 85 mg; Sod 711 mg

Alice Morrison, Elgin

BARBECUE BISON MEATBALLS

2 pounds ground bison
1 1/2 sleeves crackers, finely crushed
2 eggs
1/2 cup milk
1/2 medium onion, chopped
1/2 medium green bell pepper, chopped
2 teaspoons Worcestershire sauce
1 teaspoon salt
1/4 teaspoon pepper
1/4 teaspoon garlic salt
1 (12-ounce) can ginger ale
1 1/2 cups barbecue sauce

Combine the ground bison, cracker crumbs, eggs, milk, onion, green pepper, Worcestershire sauce, salt, pepper and garlic salt in a bowl; mix well. Shape into 1-inch balls. Place on a baking sheet. Bake at 325 degrees for 15 minutes. Simmer the meatballs in a mixture of the ginger ale and barbecue sauce in a skillet for 15 minutes or until no pink remains in the meatballs, stirring constantly. Serve with hot cooked rice.

Bison is a good red meat choice for people who need to reduce dietary fat and cholesterol.

Yield: 12 servings.

Approx Per Serving: Cal 183; T Fat 5 g; 23% Calories from Fat; Prot 16 g; Carbo 19 g; Fiber 1 g; Chol 73 mg; Sod 722 mg

Karen Bredthauer, Broken Bow

BISON STEW

2 pounds cubed bison
2 tablespoons vegetable oil
2 onions, chopped
2 (6-ounce) cans tomato sauce
6 carrots, peeled, sliced
1 (8-ounce) can peeled tomatoes
2 teaspoons salt
1/2 teaspoon pepper
3 medium potatoes, cubed
1/2 cup water

Brown the bison in the oil in a large kettle or Dutch oven. Add the onions. Cook until the onions are golden brown. Add the tomato sauce, carrots, tomatoes, salt and pepper. Cook, covered, over low heat for 1 to 1 1/2 hours or until a cooking thermometer registers 165 degrees. Add the potatoes and 1/2 cup water if needed. Cook, covered, for 30 minutes longer or until the potatoes and bison are tender. Serve with corn bread or biscuits. May cook in a slow cooker on High for 3 to 4 hours.

Bison is low in fat and cholesterol and high in protein. It is tasty, tender and easy to digest.

Yield: 12 servings.

Approx Per Serving: Cal 146; T Fat 4 g; 22% Calories from Fat; Prot 15 g; Carbo 15 g; Fiber 3 g; Chol 37 mg; Sod 598 mg

Karen Bredthauer, Broken Bow

"CHICKEN LICKIN' GOOD" PORK CHOPS

8 (1-inch) lean pork chops
1/2 cup flour
1 tablespoon salt
1 1/2 teaspoons dry mustard
1/2 teaspoon garlic powder
2 tablespoons vegetable oil
1 (10-ounce) can chicken and rice soup

Dredge the pork chops in a mixture of the flour, salt, mustard and garlic powder. Brown in the oil in a large skillet. Place the pork chops in a slow cooker. Add the soup. Cook, covered, on Medium for 6 to 8 hours or until a cooking thermometer registers 170 degrees.

Yield: 8 servings.

Approx Per Serving: Cal 245; T Fat 12 g; 44% Calories from Fat; Prot 25 g; Carbo 8 g; Fiber 1 g; Chol 73 mg; Sod 1103 mg

Conni Bales, Grand Island

MARINATED PORK CHOPS

2 tablespoons brown sugar
1/4 cup soy sauce
1/2 teaspoon garlic salt
1/4 teaspoon pepper
3 tablespoons vegetable oil
3 tablespoons water
4 pork chops

Mix the brown sugar, soy sauce, garlic salt, pepper, oil and water in a bowl. Add the pork chops, turning several times to coat. Marinate in the refrigerator for 9 hours to overnight, turning occasionally. Drain, reserving the marinade. Grill over medium heat for 15 minutes or until a meat thermometer registers 170 degrees. Turn and grill for 15 minutes longer, brushing with the reserved marinade occasionally. Discard unused marinade.

Yield: 4 servings.

Approx Per Serving: Cal 283; T Fat 18 g; 57% Calories from Fat; Prot 24 g; Carbo 6 g; Fiber 0 g; Chol 71 mg; Sod 1341 mg

Dana Reppert, West Point

PORK CHOPS AND POTATOES ✤ *from The 4-H Friends' Cookbook*

4 pork chops
2 tablespoons vegetable oil
6 medium potatoes, peeled, sliced
1 (10-ounce) can cream of mushroom soup
1 cup (or more) milk
Salt and pepper to taste

Brown the pork chops in hot oil in a skillet; drain. Place the potatoes in a shallow baking dish. Pour the soup and enough milk to cover over the potatoes. Add salt and pepper. Place the pork chops on top of the potatoes. Bake at 350 degrees for 1 1/2 hours or until a meat thermometer registers 170 degrees.

Yield: 4 servings.

Approx Per Serving: Cal 511; T Fat 22 g; 39% Calories from Fat; Prot 30 g; Carbo 48 g; Fiber 3 g; Chol 80 mg; Sod 713 mg

Mrs. Richard Fuchser

FRUITED PORK

- 2 pounds lean pork, cut into cubes
- 2 to 4 tablespoons flour
- 3 tablespoons vegetable oil
- 1 cup orange juice
- 2 tablespoons lemon juice
- 1 tablespoon Worcestershire sauce
- 3 tablespoons brown sugar
- 1 teaspoon salt
- 1/4 teaspoon pepper
- 1 tablespoon cornstarch
- 1/4 cup water
- 1/3 cup raisins
- 1 (10-ounce) can mandarin oranges

Coat the pork with the flour. Brown in hot oil in a skillet. Remove to a 2-quart casserole. Drain the pan drippings from the skillet; pour the orange juice and lemon juice into the skillet. Add the Worcestershire sauce, brown sugar, salt and pepper. Stir the cornstarch into the water. Add the juice mixture while bringing it to a boil, stirring constantly. Pour the juice mixture over the pork. Add the raisins and drained oranges, stirring lightly. Bake, covered, at 325 degrees for 1 1/2 hours or until a meat thermometer registers 170 degrees.

This was a 1995 Pork Cook-Off entry.

Yield: 6 servings.

Approx Per Serving: Cal 395; T Fat 17 g; 38% Calories from Fat; Prot 31 g; Carbo 30 g; Fiber 1 g; Chol 92 mg; Sod 463 mg

Ginny Franzluebbers, West Point

SWEET-AND-SOUR PORK

- 1 egg, beaten
- 1/4 cup cornstarch
- 1/4 cup flour
- 1/4 cup chicken broth
- 1/2 teaspoon salt
- 1 pound boneless pork, cut into 1-inch cubes
- Vegetable oil for deep-frying
- 1 large green bell pepper, chopped
- 1/2 cup chopped carrot
- 1 clove of garlic, minced
- 2 tablespoons vegetable oil
- 1 1/4 cups chicken broth
- 1/2 cup sugar
- 1/3 cup red vinegar
- 2 teaspoons soy sauce
- 2 tablespoons cornstarch
- 1/4 cup cold water

Combine the egg, 1/4 cup cornstarch, flour, 1/4 cup broth and salt in a bowl; beat until smooth. Dip the pork into the batter. Place in hot oil in a skillet or deep fryer. Cook for 5 to 6 minutes or until golden brown; drain and keep warm. Cook the green pepper, carrot and garlic in 2 tablespoons oil in a skillet until the vegetables are tender but not brown. Stir in 1 1/4 cups broth, sugar, vinegar and soy sauce. Bring to a boil. Boil rapidly for 1 minute. Blend 2 tablespoons cornstarch with the water. Stir into the vegetable mixture. Cook until thickened and bubbly, stirring constantly. Stir in the pork. Serve with hot cooked rice.

This recipe is one that I have used for 4-H suppers and leader demonstrations. It is a dish most people enjoy.

Yield: 6 servings.

Approx Per Serving: Cal 295; T Fat 11 g; 33% Calories from Fat; Prot 18 g; Carbo 31 g; Fiber 1 g; Chol 81 mg; Sod 536 mg
Nutritional information does not include oil for deep-frying.

Bill Hawthorne, Chadron

HAM BALLS

1 pound ground ham
$1\frac{1}{2}$ pounds ground fresh pork
$\frac{1}{2}$ teaspoon pepper
1 cup cracker crumbs
1 cup milk
2 eggs
$1\frac{1}{2}$ cups packed brown sugar
1 teaspoon dry mustard
$\frac{1}{2}$ cup vinegar
$\frac{1}{2}$ cup water

Mix the ham, ground pork, pepper, cracker crumbs, milk and eggs in a bowl. Shape into balls. Place in a greased casserole. Mix the brown sugar, mustard, vinegar and water in a saucepan. Bring to a boil. Pour over the ham balls. Bake at 350 degrees for 1 hour or until a meat thermometer registers 170 degrees, basting frequently with the pan drippings. Turn the balls and return to the oven. Bake for 30 minutes longer, basting frequently.

I could live on ham—and this is the best way.

Yield: 10 servings.

Approx Per Serving: Cal 394; T Fat 16 g; 37% Calories from Fat; Prot 27 g; Carbo 35 g; Fiber <1 g; Chol 119 mg; Sod 783 mg

Kinsey DeBoer, Smithfield

GLAZED HAM BALLS

3 pounds ground ham
2 pounds ground beef
2 pounds ground fresh pork
3 eggs
2 cups milk
3 cups graham cracker crumbs
2 (10-ounce) cans cream of tomato soup
$\frac{3}{4}$ cup cider vinegar
$2\frac{1}{4}$ cups packed brown sugar
2 tablespoons dry mustard

Mix the ham, ground beef, ground pork, eggs, milk and graham cracker crumbs in a bowl. Shape into eighty $1\frac{1}{2}$-inch meatballs. Arrange in a single layer in 2 large shallow roasting pans. Mix the soup, vinegar, brown sugar and mustard in a bowl. Pour over the meatballs. Bake at 350 degrees for 1 hour or until a cooking thermometer registers 170 degrees. Remove the meatballs to a serving dish. Skim the fat from the sauce. Pour the sauce over the meatballs. May bake meatballs first without the brown sugar mixture poured over them, then pour the heated brown sugar mixture over the meatballs and bake for 30 minutes longer.

Yield: 20 servings.

Approx Per Serving: Cal 512; T Fat 21 g; 38% Calories from Fat; Prot 40 g; Carbo 40 g; Fiber 1 g; Chol 138 mg; Sod 1301 mg

Jason Bartak, Long Pine
Anita Keys, Elsmere
Michelle Lemke, Osmond
Marcia Swan, Grant

PARTY PRIDE HAM LOAF

- 1 pound ground smoked ham
- 1 pound ground fresh pork
- 2 eggs
- 3/4 cup bread crumbs
- 3/4 cup milk
- 2 tablespoons catsup
- 9 pineapple rings
- 1 cup packed brown sugar
- 1/4 cup pineapple juice
- 1 teaspoon prepared mustard
- 2 tablespoons vinegar

Mix the ham, ground pork, eggs, bread crumbs, milk and catsup in a bowl. Shape into 9 patties. Stand the patties and pineapple rings on edge alternately around a deep 9x13-inch baking pan. Bake at 325 degrees for 25 to 30 minutes or until a meat thermometer registers 170 degrees. Bring the brown sugar, pineapple juice, mustard and vinegar to a boil in a saucepan; remove from the heat. Remove the ham loaf from the oven and baste with some of the brown sugar mixture. Bake for 1 hour longer, basting every 20 minutes during the last hour of the baking time. Garnish with spiced apple rings or maraschino cherries.

I found this recipe years ago and use it often. It is so easy to serve and looks very festive on each plate.

Yield: 9 servings.

Approx Per Serving: Cal 378; T Fat 13 g; 31% Calories from Fat; Prot 26 g; Carbo 39 g; Fiber 1 g; Chol 113 mg; Sod 848 mg

Vivian Hall, Falls City

NOODLE AND HAM CASSEROLE

- 8 ounces noodles
- 2 cups chopped ham
- 1 1/2 cups shredded sharp Cheddar cheese
- 1/2 cup chopped green bell pepper
- 2 cups frozen peas, cooked
- 1 (10-ounce) can cream of chicken soup
- 1/2 cup milk
- 1/2 cup shredded sharp Cheddar cheese
- 1 cup fine bread crumbs
- 1 tablespoon melted butter

Cook the noodles using the package directions; drain. Mix the ham, 1 1/2 cups cheese and green pepper in a bowl. Layer the noodles, ham mixture and peas in a greased 8x13-inch baking pan or 2-quart baking dish. Pour a mixture of the soup and milk over the top. Sprinkle with 1/2 cup cheese. Mix the bread crumbs and butter in a bowl. Sprinkle over the casserole. Bake at 300 degrees for 45 to 60 minutes or until a cooking thermometer registers 165 degrees. May substitute 1 cup sliced mushrooms for peas.

This is a great dish to take to a potluck supper or dinner.

Yield: 15 servings.

Approx Per Serving: Cal 163; T Fat 9 g; 39% Calories from Fat; Prot 13 g; Carbo 20 g; Fiber 1 g; Chol 57 mg; Sod 594 mg

Dorothy Bremer, Lexington
Stephanie Hudson, Belvidere

BARBECUED RIBS

- 3 to 4 pounds ribs, cut into serving-size pieces
- 1 lemon, sliced
- 1 large onion, sliced
- 1 cup catsup
- 3 tablespoons Worcestershire sauce
- 1/4 teaspoon Tabasco sauce, or to taste
- 1 cup water
- 1 teaspoon salt

Place the ribs meat side up in a baking pan. Place a lemon slice and onion slice on each piece. Bake at 450 degrees for 30 minutes. Mix the catsup, Worcestershire sauce, Tabasco sauce, water and salt in a bowl. Pour over the ribs. Reduce the oven temperature to 350 degrees. Bake for 1 1/2 hours or until a meat thermometer registers 160 degrees, basting 2 or 3 times.

Yield: 8 servings.

Approx Per Serving: Cal 388; T Fat 26 g; 61% Calories from Fat; Prot 26 g; Carbo 12 g; Fiber 1 g; Chol 104 mg; Sod 773 mg

Janet Classen, Spencer

ITALIAN RICE BAKE

- 1 (5-ounce) package chicken-flavor Rice-A-Roni
- 1 pound Italian sausage
- 2 cups spaghetti sauce
- 3 cups shredded mozzarella cheese

Prepare the Rice-A-Roni using the package directions. Brown the sausage in a skillet; drain. Stir in the spaghetti sauce. Cook until heated through. Stir in the Rice-A-Roni and half the cheese. Pour into a greased 9x13-inch glass baking dish. Top with the remaining 1 1/2 cups cheese. Bake at 350 degrees for 25 to 30 minutes or until a cooking thermometer registers 165 degrees. May bake in two 8x8-inch pans for separate meals; this freezes well.

Yield: 8 servings.

Approx Per Serving: Cal 308; T Fat 21 g; 62% Calories from Fat; Prot 15 g; Carbo 15 g; Fiber 1 g; Chol 54 mg; Sod 908 mg

Cheryl Goehring, Lincoln

GERMAN SAUERKRAUT CASSEROLE

1 medium onion, chopped
1/2 cup margarine
1 quart sauerkraut
1 quart hot water
2 pounds Polish sausage, cut into pieces
1 cup rice
Salt and pepper to taste

Sauté the onion in the margarine in a skillet until transparent. Add the sauerkraut, hot water, sausage and rice; mix well. Season with salt and pepper. Pour into a 9x13-inch baking pan or large casserole. Bake at 350 degrees for 1 1/2 hours or until a cooking thermometer registers 165 degrees, stirring several times.

Yield: 20 servings.

Approx Per Serving: Cal 155; T Fat 11 g; 63% Calories from Fat; Prot 4 g; Carbo 10 g; Fiber 1 g; Chol 15 mg; Sod 552 mg

Sue Finke, Cozad

SAUSAGE-STUFFED ACORN SQUASH

2 medium to large acorn squash, cut into halves, seeded
1 pound sausage
1 1/2 cups sliced carrots

Place the squash cut side down in a 9x13-inch baking pan. Add 1/2 inch boiling water. Bake at 350 degrees for 40 minutes. Brown the sausage in a skillet until cooked through, stirring constantly; drain. Cook the carrots in a small amount of water in a saucepan or microwave in a microwave-safe bowl just until tender; drain. Mix the carrots and sausage in a bowl. Drain the squash and set the squash upright. Fill with the sausage mixture. Bake for 20 minutes longer or until a cooking thermometer registers 165 degrees. May add 4 to 8 ounces chopped canned mushrooms to the sausage mixture.

I created this recipe for dinner October 14, 1995, when Mom was gone for the morning. She said it was nice to come home to a prepared meal!

Yield: 4 servings.

Approx Per Serving: Cal 351; T Fat 17 g; 41% Calories from Fat; Prot 14 g; Carbo 41 g; Fiber 12 g; Chol 44 mg; Sod 709 mg

Adele Phillips, Beaver Crossing

More Main Dishes
(Poultry, Seafood, Egg and Vegetarian)

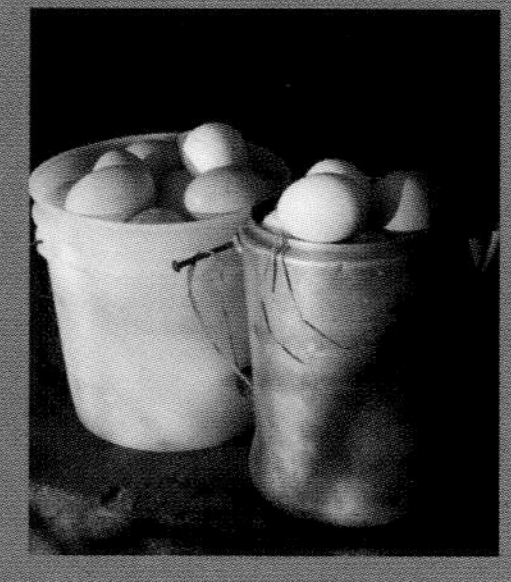

Coming Home
Sunday Brunch Menu

Fresh Fruit Salad
page 44

Breakfast Strata
page 104
or
Breakfast Casserole
page 104

Texas Potatoes
page 19

Kiwifruit Danish
page 124
or
Cinnamon Rolls
page 122

Banana Milk Shake
page 35

PHOTOGRAPH BY JIM RAHRS
Hamilton County

OVEN-BAKED CHICKEN

1 (3-pound) chicken, cut up
1/2 cup evaporated milk
2 cups crushed cornflakes
1 1/2 teaspoons salt
1/4 teaspoon pepper
2 tablespoons melted margarine

Line a baking sheet with foil; spray with nonstick cooking spray. Rinse the chicken and pat dry. Dip the chicken in the evaporated milk. Coat with a mixture of the cornflakes, salt and pepper. Arrange the chicken skin side up on the prepared baking sheet. Combine the remaining evaporated milk with the margarine in a bowl and mix well. Drizzle over the chicken. Bake at 350 degrees for 1 hour or until tender and a meat thermometer registers 170 degrees.

Yield: 5 servings.

Approx Per Serving: Cal 449; T Fat 17 g; 34% Calories from Fat; Prot 44 g; Carbo 29 g; Fiber 1 g; Chol 128 mg; Sod 1142 mg

Megan, Melissa and Sarah Loftis, Craig

POLYNESIAN HONEY PINEAPPLE CHICKEN

1/2 cup pineapple juice
1/4 cup honey
2 to 4 cloves of garlic, minced
1 to 3 tablespoons Worcestershire sauce
1 teaspoon ginger
1 teaspoon salt
3 pounds chicken legs or thighs

Bring the pineapple juice, honey, garlic, Worcestershire sauce, ginger and salt to a boil in a saucepan; reduce heat. Simmer for 15 minutes or until the mixture is reduced to 1/2 cup, stirring occasionally. Cool to room temperature. Rinse the chicken and pat dry. Place in a sealable plastic bag. Pour the pineapple juice mixture over the chicken, turning to coat. Marinate in the refrigerator for 6 to 24 hours, turning occasionally. Drain the chicken, reserving the marinade. Arrange medium-hot coals around a drip pan. Place the chicken on the grill rack; close the lid. Grill for 40 to 45 minutes or until juices run clear and a meat thermometer registers 170 degrees, brushing with reserved marinade during the first 30 minutes of the grilling process. Discard the leftover marinade.

Yield: 12 servings.

Approx Per Serving: Cal 129; T Fat 3 g; 23% Calories from Fat; Prot 16 g; Carbo 8 g; Fiber <1 g; Chol 53 mg; Sod 274 mg

Cheryl Goehring, Lincoln

BAKED CHICKEN BREASTS SUPREME

- 8 boneless skinless chicken breast halves
- 1 1/2 cups nonfat plain yogurt
- 1/4 cup lemon juice
- 1/2 teaspoon celery seeds
- 1/2 teaspoon paprika
- 1 clove of garlic, minced
- 2 cups fine dry bread crumbs

Rinse the chicken and pat dry. Coat the chicken with a mixture of the yogurt, lemon juice, celery seeds, paprika and garlic. Place in a dish. Marinate, covered, in the refrigerator overnight. Remove the chicken from the marinade, discarding the marinade. Coat the chicken with the bread crumbs. Arrange in a shallow baking pan. Bake at 350 degrees for 45 minutes or until juices run clear and a meat thermometer registers 170 degrees.

Yield: 8 servings.

Approx Per Serving: Cal 268; T Fat 5 g; 16% Calories from Fat; Prot 33 g; Carbo 22 g; Fiber 1 g; Chol 74 mg; Sod 314 mg

Linda Fitzke, Glenvil

CASHEW CHICKEN

- 2 whole chicken breasts, boned, skinned, cubed
- 2 tablespoons vegetable oil
- 2 chicken bouillon cubes
- 1 1/4 cups boiling water
- 5 teaspoons cornstarch
- 2 tablespoons soy sauce
- 2 teaspoons light brown sugar
- 1/4 teaspoon ginger
- 2 cups sliced fresh mushrooms
- 2 cups broccoli florets
- 1 (8-ounce) can sliced water chestnuts, drained
- 1/2 cup coarsely chopped onion
- 1 small green bell pepper, sliced
- 1/2 cup cashews
- 1 cup rice, cooked

Rinse the chicken and pat dry. Cook the chicken in the oil in a skillet until the chicken is brown and cooked through. Dissolve the bouillon cubes in the boiling water in a bowl. Stir in a mixture of the cornstarch, soy sauce, brown sugar and ginger. Pour over the chicken and mix well. Cook until slightly thickened, stirring constantly. Stir in the mushrooms, broccoli, water chestnuts, onion and green pepper. Simmer for 5 to 8 minutes or until of the desired consistency, stirring occasionally. Remove from heat. Stir in the cashews. Serve over hot cooked rice. May substitute canned mushrooms for fresh mushrooms and sliced carrots for water chestnuts.

Mom took a combination of several cashew chicken recipes and came up with this one. We love Mom's version.

Yield: 4 servings.

Approx Per Serving: Cal 554; T Fat 19 g; 30% Calories from Fat; Prot 37 g; Carbo 61 g; Fiber 5 g; Chol 73 mg; Sod 1178 mg

Christopher, Kelly and Nicholas Holeka, Brainard

CHICKEN AND CHIPPED BEEF

6 whole chicken breasts, cut into halves, boned, skinned
12 slices bacon
6 to 8 ounces chipped beef, cut into strips
1 (10-ounce) can cream of mushroom soup
1 cup sour cream
1 tablespoon dried minced onion
Paprika to taste

Rinse the chicken and pat dry. Wrap each chicken piece with 1 slice of bacon. Line a 9x13-inch baking dish with the chipped beef. Arrange the chicken on top. Spread with a mixture of the soup, sour cream and minced onion; sprinkle with paprika. Bake at 325 degrees for 2 1/2 to 3 hours or until juices run clear and a meat thermometer registers 170 degrees. May omit bacon to reduce fat grams. May use reduced-fat and low-sodium cream of mushroom soup.

Yield: 12 servings.

Approx Per Serving: Cal 277; T Fat 13 g; 43% Calories from Fat; Prot 35 g; Carbo 3 g; Fiber <1 g; Chol 95 mg; Sod 1036 mg

Marilyn Criswell, Oshkosh
Marian Wiemann, Howells

HAWAIIAN CHICKEN

1 (20-ounce) can juice-pack pineapple slices
3/4 cup sugar
1/2 cup cider vinegar
2 tablespoons cornstarch
1 tablespoon low-sodium soy sauce
1 teaspoon grated gingerroot
1 teaspoon chicken bouillon granules
4 boneless skinless chicken breast halves
1/4 cup flour
1 large green bell pepper, cut into 1/4-inch rings

Drain the pineapple, reserving the juice. Combine the reserved juice with enough water to measure 1 1/4 cups. Bring the juice mixture, sugar, vinegar, cornstarch, soy sauce, gingerroot and bouillon granules to a boil in a saucepan over medium heat; reduce heat. Simmer for 4 minutes, stirring frequently. Rinse the chicken and pat dry; coat with the flour. Brown the chicken on both sides in a skillet sprayed with nonstick cooking spray. Arrange in an 8x8-inch baking dish. Pour half of the pineapple juice mixture over the chicken; top with the pineapple slices and green pepper rings. Pour the remaining pineapple juice mixture over the prepared layers. Bake at 350 degrees for 40 minutes or until the chicken is cooked through and a meat thermometer registers 170 degrees.

Yield: 4 servings.

Approx Per Serving: Cal 430; T Fat 3 g; 7% Calories from Fat; Prot 29 g; Carbo 73 g; Fiber 2 g; Chol 73 mg; Sod 367 mg

Kelly Steffen, West Point

CHICKEN ROLL-UPS WITH NOODLES

- 4 whole boneless skinless chicken breast halves
- 4 thin slices ham
- 4 slices Swiss cheese
- 2 tablespoons butter
- 1 cup sliced fresh mushrooms
- 2 cloves of garlic, minced
- 1/2 cup plain yogurt
- 1/2 cup milk
- 2 tablespoons flour
- 1/4 teaspoon paprika
- 1/8 teaspoon salt
- 1/8 teaspoon pepper
- 2 cups hot cooked noodles

Rinse the chicken and pat dry. Pound 1/8 inch thick between sheets of plastic wrap with a meat mallet. Layer each chicken piece with 1 slice ham and 1 slice cheese. Roll to enclose the filling; secure with a wooden pick. Place in a microwave-safe dish. Microwave, covered, on High for 4 minutes; turn the dish. Microwave for 2 to 4 minutes longer or until juices run clear. Melt the butter in a saucepan. Add the mushrooms and garlic and mix well. Cook until the mushrooms are tender, stirring frequently. Stir in the yogurt, milk, flour, paprika, salt and pepper. Cook until thickened, stirring constantly. Spoon the noodles onto a serving platter. Top with the chicken; drizzle with the mushroom sauce. May reduce fat grams by using low-fat ingredients.

Yield: 4 servings.

Approx Per Serving: Cal 506; T Fat 22 g; 39% Calories from Fat; Prot 49 g; Carbo 28 g; Fiber 2 g; Chol 165 mg; Sod 674 mg

Hale Dooley, York

STIR-FRIED CHICKEN AND ZUCCHINI

- 3 whole boneless skinless chicken breasts
- 1 clove of garlic, coarsely chopped
- 1 tablespoon vegetable oil
- 2 tablespoons soy sauce
- 1 1/2 cups sliced zucchini
- 1 (4-ounce) can sliced mushrooms, drained
- 1/2 cup thinly sliced celery
- 1 tablespoon cornstarch
- 1/4 cup water

Rinse the chicken and pat dry. Cut into 1x1-inch pieces. Sauté the chicken and garlic in the oil in a skillet for 5 to 10 minutes or until the chicken is no longer pink in the center. Remove the garlic pieces. Stir in the soy sauce. Add the zucchini, mushrooms and celery and mix well. Cook for 4 to 5 minutes or until the vegetables are tender, stirring frequently. Add a mixture of the cornstarch and water gradually, stirring constantly. Cook for 1 minute or until the ingredients are coated with a thin glaze. Serve over hot cooked rice.

Yield: 6 servings.

Approx Per Serving: Cal 181; T Fat 5 g; 28% Calories from Fat; Prot 28 g; Carbo 4 g; Fiber 1 g; Chol 73 mg; Sod 496 mg

Janice Mehl, North Platte

SOUTHERN CORN BREAD CHICKEN SANDWICHES

2 cups cornmeal
1 teaspoon baking powder
1 teaspoon salt
1/2 teaspoon baking soda
1 cup buttermilk
2 eggs, beaten
6 tablespoons melted shortening
2 tablespoons each minced onion and celery
1/2 cup butter
1/4 cup flour
3 cups chicken broth
3/4 cup cream
Salt and pepper to taste
8 baked chicken breasts, sliced

Combine the cornmeal, baking powder, 1 teaspoon salt and baking soda in a bowl and mix well. Stir in the buttermilk, eggs and shortening until blended. Spoon into a greased square cast-iron skillet or greased 9x13-inch baking pan. Bake at 400 degrees for 20 minutes. Cut into 8 squares. Sauté the onion and celery in the butter in a saucepan until light brown. Stir in the flour until mixed. Add the broth, cream, salt to taste and pepper and mix well. Cook until thickened, stirring constantly. Split each corn bread square into halves. Place the bottom halves on a serving platter; top each with 1 piece sliced chicken breast. Top with the remaining corn bread halves. Spoon the sauce over the sandwiches.

Yield: 8 servings.

Approx Per Serving: Cal 593; T Fat 35 g; 54% Calories from Fat; Prot 35 g; Carbo 33 g; Fiber 2 g; Chol 189 mg; Sod 890 mg

Norma J. Meyer, Scotia

ALTA'S CHICKEN CASSEROLE

1/2 cup (or more) butter or margarine
1/2 cup flour
2 cups chicken broth
1 cup milk
16 ounces Cheddar cheese, shredded
1 (4-ounce) can mushrooms
1 (2-ounce) jar chopped pimento, drained
16 ounces medium egg noodles, cooked, drained
3 cups chopped cooked chicken

Heat the butter in a saucepan until melted. Stir in the flour until blended. Cook until bubbly, stirring constantly. Add the broth and milk and mix well. Bring to a boil, stirring constantly. Boil for 1 minute. Stir in the cheese, undrained mushrooms and pimento. Remove from heat. Layer the noodles and chicken 1/2 at a time in a greased 9x13-inch baking pan, ending with the chicken. Pour the mushroom mixture over the prepared layers; push the sauce through the layers with a fork. Bake at 350 degrees for 45 to 60 minutes or until brown and bubbly and a cooking thermometer registers 165 degrees. May substitute chopped cooked turkey for chicken.

Alta Krasser led a 4-H Club in Seward County for over fifty years. This recipe is prepared every year at the church guest day.

Yield: 12 servings.

Approx Per Serving: Cal 329; T Fat 26 g; 49% Calories from Fat; Prot 27 g; Carbo 33 g; Fiber <1 g; Chol 161 mg; Sod 529 mg

Adele, Eliot and Lane Phillips, Beaver Crossing

CHICKEN CASSEROLE

3 cups chopped cooked chicken
2 (10-ounce) cans cream of chicken soup
2 cups chopped celery
2 cups uncooked instant rice
2 cups chicken broth
$1\frac{1}{2}$ cups mayonnaise
1 (8-ounce) can water chestnuts, drained, chopped
1 tablespoon dried minced onion
2 teaspoons lemon juice
1 teaspoon salt
$\frac{1}{2}$ teaspoon pepper
Chopped pimento to taste
$1\frac{1}{2}$ cups crushed potato chips

Combine the chicken, soup, celery, rice, broth, mayonnaise, water chestnuts, minced onion, lemon juice, salt, pepper and pimento in a bowl and mix well. Spoon into a 9x13-inch baking pan. Sprinkle with the potato chips. Bake at 350 degrees for 1 hour and 10 minutes or until the casserole is brown and bubbly and a cooking thermometer registers 165 degrees. May be prepared in advance and frozen for future use. May substitute chopped cooked turkey for chicken.

Yield: 12 servings.

Approx Per Serving: Cal 430; T Fat 30 g; 63% Calories from Fat; Prot 15 g; Carbo 25 g; Fiber 1 g; Chol 51 mg; Sod 955 mg

Sue Finke, Cozad

HOT AND SPICY CASSEROLE

1 (10-ounce) can cream of chicken soup
1 (10-ounce) can cream of mushroom soup
1 pound chicken, cooked, boned, chopped
1 small onion, chopped
1 green bell pepper, chopped
Garlic salt to taste
1 (15-ounce) package tortilla chips, crushed
$1\frac{1}{2}$ cups shredded Cheddar cheese
1 (16-ounce) jar mild, medium or hot salsa

Combine the soups in a bowl and mix well. Layer the chicken, onion, green pepper, garlic salt, soup mixture, tortilla chips, cheese and salsa $\frac{1}{2}$ at a time in a 9x13-inch baking dish. Bake at 350 degrees for 20 to 30 minutes or until the casserole is bubbly and a cooking thermometer registers 165 degrees. May be prepared in advance, refrigerated and baked just before serving. May substitute 1 pound browned and drained ground beef for chicken.

Yield: 6 servings.

Approx Per Serving: Cal 672; T Fat 38 g; 50% Calories from Fat; Prot 25 g; Carbo 59 g; Fiber 5 g; Chol 68 mg; Sod 1746 mg

Marcia Mortensen, Curtis

CHICKEN AND RICE BALLS

1/2 cup chopped celery
1/4 cup sliced green onions
2 tablespoons margarine
2 tablespoons flour
1/4 cup chicken broth
2 cups cooked rice
1 1/2 cups chopped cooked chicken
1/2 cup shredded Cheddar cheese
1 egg, beaten
1/2 teaspoon salt
1/2 teaspoon chili powder
1/4 teaspoon poultry seasoning
1/2 cup crushed cornflakes
1 cup cream of mushroom soup
1/4 cup milk
2 teaspoons sliced green onions

Sauté the celery and 1/4 cup green onions in the margarine in a saucepan until tender. Stir in the flour. Add the broth and mix well. Cook until thickened, stirring constantly. Stir in the rice, chicken, cheese, egg, salt, chili powder and poultry seasoning. Shape into small balls. Roll in the crushed cornflakes. Arrange in a greased 9x13-inch baking pan. Bake at 350 degrees for 25 to 30 minutes or until brown and a cooking thermometer registers 165 degrees. Combine the soup, milk and 2 teaspoons green onions in a saucepan. Cook just until heated through, stirring constantly. Spoon over the chicken and rice balls. May be prepared in advance, frozen and baked just before serving.

Yield: 4 servings.

Approx Per Serving: Cal 491; T Fat 21 g; 40% Calories from Fat; Prot 26 g; Carbo 47 g; Fiber 2 g; Chol 117 mg; Sod 1157 mg

Bethany and Sue Babovec, Cedar Rapids

CHICKEN POCKETS

- 3 (8-count) cans crescent rolls
- 8 ounces cream cheese, softened
- 1/4 cup milk
- 1 teaspoon dillweed
- 1/2 teaspoon salt
- 1/2 teaspoon pepper
- 4 cups chopped cooked chicken
- 1/2 cup finely chopped celery
- 4 green onions with tops, thinly sliced
- 1/4 cup melted butter or margarine

Unroll the crescent roll dough; separate into 12 rectangles. Arrange the rectangles on a greased baking sheet; press the perforations to seal. Beat the cream cheese, milk, dillweed, salt and pepper in a mixer bowl until blended. Stir in the chicken, celery and green onions. Spoon 1/3 cup of the chicken mixture into the center of each rectangle. Bring the edges up to the center; pinch to seal. Brush with the melted butter. Bake for 15 to 20 minutes or until brown and a cooking thermometer registers an external temperature of 165 degrees. May sprinkle the chicken pockets with seasoned bread crumbs before baking.

Yield: 12 servings.

Approx Per Serving: Cal 364; T Fat 20 g; 50% Calories from Fat; Prot 18 g; Carbo 27 g; Fiber <1 g; Chol 78 mg; Sod 731 mg

Elizabeth Norris, Omaha

SCALLOPED CHICKEN

- 1 (3-pound) chicken, cooked
- 4 cups cracker crumbs
- 2 cups chicken broth
- 1 (16-ounce) can cream-style corn
- 1 1/2 cups chopped celery
- 1 1/2 cups cubed Cheddar cheese
- 1 (10-ounce) can cream of chicken soup
- 1 onion, chopped
- 2 eggs, beaten

Chop the chicken, discarding the skin and bones. Combine the chicken, cracker crumbs, broth, corn, celery, cheese, soup, onion and eggs in a bowl and mix well. Spoon into a 9x13-inch baking pan. Bake at 350 degrees for 1 hour or until bubbly and a cooking thermometer registers 165 degrees.

Yield: 12 servings.

Approx Per Serving: Cal 371; T Fat 16 g; 38% Calories from Fat; Prot 27 g; Carbo 31 g; Fiber 2 g; Chol 105 mg; Sod 976 mg

The Wes Grube Family, Franklin

CHICKEN SPAGHETTI

1 (3-pound) chicken, cooked
1 green bell pepper, chopped
1 small onion, chopped
1 cup chopped celery
1 teaspoon garlic powder
1 (16-ounce) can tomatoes and green chiles
1 (10-ounce) can cream of chicken soup
1 (10-ounce) can cream of mushroom soup
1 (6-ounce) can sliced mushrooms, drained
16 ounces Velveeta cheese, shredded
16 ounces spaghetti, cooked, drained
1/3 cup shredded Cheddar cheese

Chop the chicken, discarding the skin and bones. Refrigerate, covered, until needed. Sauté the green pepper, onion, celery and garlic powder in a nonstick saucepan. Add the tomatoes, soups, mushrooms and Velveeta cheese. Cook over low heat until the cheese melts, stirring constantly. Stir in the chicken and spaghetti. Spoon into a 9x13-inch baking pan. Sprinkle with the Cheddar cheese. Bake at 350 degrees for 45 to 60 minutes or until brown and bubbly. May add 1 small jar pimentos to mixture. May substitute Parmesan cheese for Cheddar cheese.

Yield: 15 servings.

Approx Per Serving: Cal 372; T Fat 17 g; 41% Calories from Fat; Prot 26 g; Carbo 29 g; Fiber 2 g; Chol 73 mg; Sod 990 mg

Louann, Joshua and Shane Reiss, Minden
Sandra K. Stockall, Hershey
Lisa Wilson, Gothenburg

PHEASANT POTPIE

1 recipe (2-crust) pie pastry
1 1/2 cups chopped cooked pheasant
1 cup chopped cooked potatoes
1 cup chopped cooked carrots
1 cup chopped celery
1 cup white sauce
1/2 cup peas
1 tablespoon chopped onion
Salt and pepper to taste
1 to 2 tablespoons milk

Line a pie plate with half the pastry. Combine the pheasant, potatoes, carrots, celery, white sauce, peas, onion, salt and pepper in a bowl and mix well. Spoon into the pastry-lined pie plate. Top with the remaining pastry, sealing the edge and cutting vents. Brush with the milk; sprinkle with salt to taste. Bake at 400 degrees until brown and a cooking thermometer registers 165 degrees. May substitute 1 1/4 cups cream of mushroom soup diluted with a small amount of milk for white sauce.

Yield: 6 servings.

Approx Per Serving: Cal 418; T Fat 22 g; 48% Calories from Fat; Prot 15 g; Carbo 40 g; Fiber 3 g; Chol 30 mg; Sod 474 mg

Kelley Watkins, Benkelman

POLYNESIAN TURKEY

1/2 cup pineapple juice
1/4 cup catsup
1/4 cup minced onion
1 tablespoon molasses
1 tablespoon red wine vinegar
1 tablespoon rosemary
1 tablespoon margarine
1 teaspoon soy sauce
1 clove of garlic, minced
1/2 teaspoon dry mustard
1/8 teaspoon pepper
7 pounds boneless turkey breast, cut into 4 equal portions
1 cup pineapple juice
1/2 cup margarine
1 teaspoon rosemary
1/4 teaspoon salt
1/8 teaspoon pepper

Combine 1/2 cup pineapple juice, catsup, onion, molasses, vinegar, 1 tablespoon rosemary, 1 tablespoon margarine, soy sauce, garlic, dry mustard and 1/8 teaspoon pepper in a microwave-safe dish and mix well. Microwave on High for 5 minutes; stir. Reserve for basting sauce. Rinse the turkey and pat dry. Place each portion of turkey on a sheet of heavy-duty foil. Combine 1 cup pineapple juice, 1/2 cup margarine, 1 teaspoon rosemary, salt and 1/8 teaspoon pepper in a microwave-safe dish and mix well. Microwave for 2 minutes or until the margarine melts; stir. Pour over the turkey; wrap the turkey in the foil. Place on a grill rack. Grill at 325 to 400 degrees for 20 minutes; turn. Grill for 20 minutes longer; remove the foil. Grill the turkey until a meat thermometer registers 170 degrees, basting with the reserved sauce during the last 10 minutes of grilling.

Yield: 12 servings.

Approx Per Serving: Cal 493; T Fat 24 g; 46% Calories from Fat; Prot 58 g; Carbo 8 g; Fiber <1 g; Chol 143 mg; Sod 350 mg

Kelli Seeman, Aurora

TEX-MEX TURKEY ENCHILADAS

1 1/2 cups shredded or cubed cooked turkey
1/2 cup chopped onion
1/4 cup picante sauce
3 ounces cream cheese, softened
3/4 teaspoon cumin
1/4 teaspoon oregano
1/2 cup shredded Cheddar cheese
8 flour tortillas
3/4 cup picante sauce
1 cup shredded Cheddar cheese

Combine the turkey, onion, 1/4 cup picante sauce, cream cheese, cumin and oregano in a skillet. Cook over low heat until the cream cheese melts, stirring frequently. Stir in 1/2 cup Cheddar cheese. Spoon 1/3 cup of the turkey mixture down the center of each tortilla; roll to enclose the filling. Place seam side down in a lightly greased 7x12-inch baking dish. Spoon 3/4 cup picante sauce over the enchiladas; sprinkle with 1 cup Cheddar cheese. Bake at 350 degrees for 15 minutes or until a cooking thermometer registers 165 degrees. Garnish with shredded lettuce.

Yield: 8 servings.

Approx Per Serving: Cal 299; T Fat 15 g; 45% Calories from Fat; Prot 17 g; Carbo 24 g; Fiber 2 g; Chol 54 mg; Sod 510 mg

Susan Hansen, Schuyler

Any Way You Want It

$9.99 Medium

OR

$12.99 Large

Choose Up to 3-Toppings, Supreme or any Lover's® Pizza

Offer expires July 15, 2003. Valid only on Pan, Thin 'n Crispy® or Hand Tossed pizzas. Stuffed Crust extra. Valid at participating locations. A delivery charge will apply where delivery is available. Limited delivery area. Not valid with any other coupon or offer. One discount honored per guest check. Additional charge for Super Supreme.

$3.00 OFF A Large Pizza

OR

$2.00 OFF A Medium Pizza

Add an order of Breadsticks for $2.99! Add 4 20oz. Pepsi®s for $3.99!

Offer expires July 15, 2003. Valid only on Pan, Thin 'n Crispy® or Hand Tossed pizzas. Stuffed Crust extra. Valid at participating locations. A delivery charge will apply where delivery is available. Limited delivery area. Not valid with any other coupon or offer. One discount honored per guest check.

1-Topping Pizza

$7.99 Medium

OR

$9.99 Large

Add an order of Buffalo Wings for $5.99!

Offer expires July 15, 2003. Valid only on Pan, Thin 'n Crispy® or Hand Tossed pizzas. Valid at participating locations. A delivery charge will apply where delivery is available. Limited delivery area. Not valid with any other coupon or offer. One discount honored per guest check. Additional charge for each additional topping and all specialty flavors.

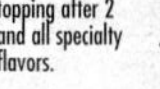

Two 2-Topping Pizzas

$14.99 Mediums

OR

$18.99 Larges

Add 12 Hot Wings for $5.99! Add an order of Breadsticks for $2.99!

Offer expires July 15, 2003. Valid only on Pan, Thin 'n Crispy® or Hand Tossed pizzas. Stuffed Crust extra. Valid at participating locations. A delivery charge will apply where delivery is available. Limited delivery area. Not valid with any other coupon or offer. One discount honored per guest check. Additional charge for each additional topping after 2 and all specialty flavors.

Large for Medium Charge

Get up to 5 pizzas with this coupon!

Offer expires July 15, 2003. Valid only on Pan, Thin 'n Crispy® or Hand Tossed pizzas. Stuffed Crust extra. Valid at participating locations. A delivery charge will apply where delivery is available. Limited delivery area. Not valid with any other coupon or offer. One discount honored per guest check.

$14.99

One Large 2-Topping Pizza & 12 Hot Wings

Offer expires July 15, 2003. Valid only on Pan, Thin 'n Crispy® or Hand Tossed pizzas. Stuffed Crust extra. Valid at participating locations. A delivery charge will apply where delivery is available. Limited delivery area. Not valid with any other coupon or offer. One discount honored per guest check. Additional charge for each additional topping after 2 and all specialty flavors.

THE FAMILY FEAST

One Pizza Any Way You Want It
(Up to 3 Toppings, Supreme or any Lover's® Pizza)
One 1-Topping Pizza
Your choice of Cheese Breadsticks or Cinnamon Breadsticks

$17.99 Medium Family Feast

$20.99 Large Family Feast

Add a 2-Liter of Pepsi® for only $1.99!

Offer expires July 15, 2003. 2-liters may not be available at all locations. Two 20 oz. Bottles will be substituted for $1.99 where 2-liters are not available. Valid only on Pan, Thin 'n Crispy® or Hand Tossed pizzas. Stuffed Crust extra. Valid at participating locations. A delivery charge will apply where delivery is available. Limited delivery area. Not valid with any other coupon or offer. One discount honored per guest check. Additional charge for each additional topping and all specialty flavors.

$18.99

Sports Fan Special

Two Medium 1-Topping Pizzas, 5 Breadsticks and 12 Buffalo Wings

Upgrade to Two Large Pizzas for $5 more!

Offer expires July 15, 2003. Valid only on Pan, Thin 'n Crispy® or Hand Tossed pizzas. Stuffed Crust extra. Valid at participating locations. A delivery charge will apply where delivery is available. Limited delivery area. Not valid with any other coupon or offer. One discount honored per guest check. Additional charge for each additional topping and all specialty flavors.

P'ZONE
PIZZA
TM
Choose from P'zone Meat Lover's®, P'zone Pepperoni Lover's®, or P'zone Classic!
Savory Toppings and Cheese Sealed Inside a 12" Folded Pizza Crust!
Big Enough for Any Appetite!

TURKEY TETRAZZINI *from The 4-H Friends' Cookbook*

8 ounces spaghetti
6 cups water
Salt to taste
1 (4-ounce) can sliced mushrooms
2 cups chopped cooked turkey
2 tablespoons chopped pimento
3 tablespoons chopped onion
1/4 cup butter
1/2 teaspoon celery salt
1/4 teaspoon marjoram
Cayenne to taste
1 (10-ounce) can cream of chicken soup
1 2/3 cups evaporated milk
1/2 cup shredded sharp Cheddar cheese
1/4 cup grated Parmesan cheese

Break the spaghetti into 2-inch lengths. Cook the spaghetti in 6 cups salted boiling water in a saucepan until tender. Drain and rinse with hot water. Drain the mushrooms, reserving the liquid. Combine the spaghetti, mushrooms, turkey and pimento in a bowl and mix well. Sauté the onion in the butter in a skillet until tender. Stir in the reserved mushroom liquid, celery salt, marjoram and cayenne. Add the soup, stirring until mixed. Add the evaporated milk gradually. Cook until thickened, stirring constantly. Add to the spaghetti mixture and mix well. Spoon into a buttered baking dish. Sprinkle with the Cheddar cheese and Parmesan cheese. Bake at 350 degrees for 30 minutes or until light brown and an oven thermometer registers 165 degrees.

Yield: 10 servings.

Approx Per Serving: Cal 295; T Fat 14 g; 43% Calories from Fat; Prot 18 g; Carbo 25 g; Fiber 1 g; Chol 56 mg; Sod 557 mg

Bobbie Sward

BARBECUED TROUT

6 pan-dressed trout
2/3 cup soy sauce
1/2 cup catsup
2 tablespoons lemon juice
2 tablespoons vegetable oil
1 teaspoon rosemary

Arrange the trout in a single layer in a glass dish. Pour a mixture of the soy sauce, catsup, lemon juice, oil and rosemary over the fish, turning to coat. Marinate, covered, in the refrigerator for 1 hour, turning once. Drain, reserving the marinade. Arrange the fish in a greased hinged wire grill basket. Place the wire basket on the grill rack; close the lid. Grill over medium-hot coals for 8 to 10 minutes or until the trout is brown on the bottom; turn and baste with the reserved marinade. Grill for 5 to 7 minutes longer or until the fish flakes easily. Serve with lemon wedges.

Yield: 6 servings.

Approx Per Serving: Cal 266; T Fat 12 g; 41% Calories from Fat; Prot 30 g; Carbo 9 g; Fiber <1 g; Chol 86 mg; Sod 2138 mg

Linda Raddatz, Sidney

TUNA BURGERS

6 hamburger buns
3 tablespoons butter
1 (7-ounce) can tuna, drained
1 cup chopped celery
1/2 cup chopped yellow process cheese
1/4 cup mayonnaise
1 small onion, minced
Salt and pepper to taste

Spread both sides of the buns with the butter. Combine the tuna, celery, cheese, mayonnaise, onion, salt and pepper in a bowl and mix well. Spread the tuna mixture on the bottom half of each bun; top with the remaining half. Wrap the buns in foil. Bake at 350 degrees for 15 minutes or until the tuna mixture is heated through and a cooking thermometer registers 165 degrees.

This recipe is from a 4-H cookbook and was a favorite with our kids. The burgers are quick and easy to make.

Yield: 6 servings.

Approx Per Serving: Cal 335; T Fat 19 g; 52% Calories from Fat; Prot 15 g; Carbo 25 g; Fiber 1 g; Chol 42 mg; Sod 659 mg

Edee Lindstrom, Holdrege

CHEESE AND TUNA CRESCENTS

- 1 (8-count) can crescent rolls
- 1 (7-ounce) can tuna, drained
- 1 (10-ounce) can cream of mushroom soup
- 1 tablespoon minced onion
- 1/2 cup shredded Cheddar cheese
- 1/2 cup milk
- 1/4 cup shredded Cheddar cheese

Unroll the crescent roll dough; separate into 8 triangles. Combine the tuna, 5 tablespoons of the soup, onion and 1/2 cup cheese in a bowl and mix well. Spoon 2 tablespoons of the tuna mixture onto each triangle; roll up from wide end. Arrange in an 8x8-inch baking pan. Spoon a mixture of the remaining soup, milk and 1/4 cup cheese over the top. Bake at 375 degrees for 25 to 30 minutes or until the crescents are golden brown and a cooking thermometer registers 165 degrees.

Yield: 8 servings.

Approx Per Serving: Cal 205; T Fat 10 g; 44% Calories from Fat; Prot 12 g; Carbo 17 g; Fiber <1 g; Chol 24 mg; Sod 716 mg

Conni Bales, Grand Island

CHILI AND CHEESE BAKE

- 3 English muffins, split
- 2 tablespoons margarine, softened
- 1 pound sausage
- 1 (4-ounce) can chopped green chiles
- 3 cups shredded Cheddar cheese
- 12 eggs, beaten
- 1 1/2 cups sour cream

Spread the cut sides of the muffins with the margarine. Arrange cut side down in a greased 9x13-inch baking dish. Brown the sausage in a skillet, stirring until crumbly; drain. Layer 1/2 of the sausage, 1/2 of the chiles and 1/2 of the cheese in the prepared baking dish. Spread with a mixture of the eggs and sour cream. Layer with the remaining sausage, chiles and cheese in the order listed. Refrigerate, covered, for 8 hours or longer. Let stand at room temperature for 30 minutes. Bake, uncovered, at 350 degrees for 35 to 40 minutes or until brown and bubbly and a cooking thermometer registers 165 degrees.

Yield: 6 servings.

Approx Per Serving: Cal 735; T Fat 57 g; 57% Calories from Fat; Prot 38 g; Carbo 18 g; Fiber 2 g; Chol 538 mg; Sod 1365 mg

Clint Johnson, Imperial

BREAKFAST STRATA

12 slices bread, crusts trimmed
$^1/_4$ cup butter, softened
$1^1/_2$ cups chopped ham
2 cups shredded Cheddar cheese
3 cups milk
6 eggs
$^1/_2$ teaspoon dry mustard

Spread both sides of the bread with butter; cut into quarters. Layer the bread, ham and cheese $^1/_2$ at a time in a 9x13-inch baking pan. Beat the milk, eggs and dry mustard in a mixer bowl until blended. Pour over the prepared layers. Refrigerate, covered, overnight. Bake at 325 degrees for 1 hour or until set and a cooking thermometer registers 165 degrees.

Yield: 12 servings.

Approx Per Serving: Cal 265; T Fat 16 g; 56% Calories from Fat; Prot 16 g; Carbo 13 g; Fiber <1 g; Chol 154 mg; Sod 550 mg

Joan Wolfe, Hartington

BREAKFAST CASSEROLE

1 pound cured pork chops or ham
6 eggs, beaten
2 cups milk
2 cups shredded Cheddar cheese
1 teaspoon dry mustard
6 slices bread, torn into bite-size pieces

Brown the pork chops in a skillet; drain. Cut into bite-size pieces. Mix the pork, eggs, milk, cheese and dry mustard in a bowl. Stir in the bread. Spoon into a 9x13-inch baking pan. Refrigerate, covered, overnight. Bake at 350 degrees for 1 hour and until a cooking thermometer registers 165 degrees.

Yield: 4 servings.

Approx Per Serving: Cal 693; T Fat 39 g; 52% Calories from Fat; Prot 54 g; Carbo 29 g; Fiber 1 g; Chol 464 mg; Sod 774 mg

Kim Ryland, Stapleton

SAUSAGE AND POTATO BREAKFAST CASSEROLE

1 pound seasoned sausage
16 ounces frozen hash brown potatoes
1 (10-ounce) can cream of mushroom soup
1 cup milk
6 eggs, beaten
1 teaspoon salt
$^1/_8$ teaspoon pepper
1 cup shredded Cheddar cheese

Brown the sausage in a skillet, stirring until crumbly; drain. Spread the potatoes in a 10x13-inch baking pan. Sprinkle with the sausage. Spread with a mixture of the soup and milk. Top with a mixture of the eggs, salt and pepper. Bake at 350 degrees for 1 hour or until set and a cooking thermometer registers 165 degrees. Sprinkle with the cheese. Bake just until the cheese melts.

Yield: 8 servings.

Approx Per Serving: Cal 315; T Fat 21 g; 60% Calories from Fat; Prot 16 g; Carbo 15 g; Fiber <1 g; Chol 201 mg; Sod 1082 mg

Nicole Busboom, Pickrell

ANGEL HAIR PASTA WITH TOMATOES AND BASIL

1 pound angel hair pasta
1 tablespoon minced onion
1 tablespoon olive oil
5 cups chopped fresh tomatoes
1/2 teaspoon chopped fresh basil
Salt and pepper to taste
3/4 cup chicken broth, skimmed
1/4 cup grated Parmesan cheese

Cook the pasta using package directions; drain. Sauté the onion in the olive oil in a nonstick skillet for 1 minute. Add the tomatoes, basil, salt and pepper. Cook for 3 minutes, stirring frequently. Stir in the hot pasta and heat to 165 degrees. Add the broth and mix well. Add the cheese, tossing to coat. Serve immediately.

Yield: 8 servings.

Approx Per Serving: Cal 265; T Fat 4 g; 14% Calories from Fat; Prot 10 g; Carbo 48 g; Fiber 3 g; Chol 3 mg; Sod 151 mg

Mary Jane McReynolds, Lincoln

THREE-CHEESE ENCHILADAS

1 cup shredded Monterey Jack cheese
1 cup shredded Cheddar cheese
3 ounces cream cheese, softened
1/4 cup picante sauce
1 medium red or green bell pepper, chopped
1/2 cup sliced green onions
1 teaspoon cumin
8 (7- to 8-inch) flour tortillas
3/4 cup picante sauce
1/2 cup shredded Monterey Jack cheese
1/2 cup shredded Cheddar cheese
1 cup shredded lettuce
1 tomato, chopped
1/4 cup sliced black olives

Combine 1 cup Monterey Jack cheese, 1 cup Cheddar cheese and cream cheese in a mixer bowl and beat until blended. Stir in 1/4 cup picante sauce, red pepper, green onions and cumin. Spoon 1/4 cup of the cheese mixture down the center of each tortilla; roll to enclose the filling. Place seam side down in a greased 9x13-inch baking dish. Spoon 3/4 cup picante sauce over the top; sprinkle with 1/2 cup Monterey Jack cheese and 1/2 cup Cheddar cheese. Bake at 350 degrees for 20 minutes or until bubbly. Top with the lettuce, tomato and olives. Serve with additional picante sauce.

I have often used the Three-Cheese Enchiladas for Cooperative Mexican meals and potlucks.

Yield: 8 servings.

Approx Per Serving: Cal 344; T Fat 21 g; 53% Calories from Fat; Prot 15 g; Carbo 25 g; Fiber 2 g; Chol 53 mg; Sod 643 mg

Janet Latta, Stratton

CHILES RELLENOS CASSEROLE

2 (4-ounce) cans green chiles, drained, seeded, rinsed
10 ounces shredded Cheddar cheese
2 cups milk
1/2 cup flour
2 eggs
1/2 teaspoon salt

Line the bottom of a greased 9x13-inch baking dish with the green chiles. Sprinkle with the cheese. Blend the milk, flour, eggs and salt in a securely covered blender. Pour over the chiles. Bake at 350 degrees for 45 to 50 minutes or until bubbly and a cooking thermometer registers 165 degrees.

Yield: 8 servings.

Approx Per Serving: Cal 233; T Fat 15 g; 58% Calories from Fat; Prot 13 g; Carbo 11 g; Fiber 1 g; Chol 99 mg; Sod 731 mg

Erin-Louise Jones, Omaha

CHEESE ENCHILADAS WITH CHILI POWDER SAUCE

3 tablespoons vegetable oil
2 tablespoons flour
1/4 cup mild red chili powder
2 cups beef broth
1 (10-ounce) can tomato purée
1/2 teaspoon oregano
1/4 teaspoon cumin
1/4 teaspoon garlic powder
1/4 cup vegetable oil
12 corn tortillas
8 ounces Cheddar cheese, shredded
8 ounces Monterey Jack cheese, shredded
2 small onions, chopped
4 green onions, chopped
Green chiles to taste

Heat 3 tablespoons oil in a saucepan. Stir in the flour. Cook for 1 minute. Add the chili powder and mix well. Stir in the broth, tomato purée, oregano, cumin and garlic powder. Simmer for 15 minutes, stirring occasionally. Keep the sauce hot. Heat 1/4 cup oil in a skillet. Place 1 tortilla in the hot oil for 3 to 5 seconds or until softened, using tongs; turn the tortilla. Soften for 3 to 5 seconds; drain on a paper towel. Dip the tortilla in the hot sauce; do not soak. Place the tortilla on a plate. Reserve 1/3 of the Cheddar and Monterey Jack cheeses. Spread some of the remaining cheese down the center of the tortilla; sprinkle with some of the onions, green onions and chiles; roll to enclose the filling. Place seam side down in an 8x8-inch baking dish. Repeat the process with the remaining tortillas. Spoon the remaining sauce over the enchiladas; sprinkle with the reserved cheeses. Bake at 350 degrees for 15 to 20 minutes or until the cheese melts and a cooking thermometer registers 165 degrees.

Yield: 12 servings.

Approx Per Serving: Cal 314; T Fat 21 g; 59% Calories from Fat; Prot 13 g; Carbo 20 g; Fiber 3 g; Chol 37 mg; Sod 518 mg

Barbara A. Meister, Washington, D.C.

Breads and Rolls

Sharing and Caring
Coffee with Friends Menu

Lemon Poppy Seed Muffins
page 110

Pumpkin Biscuits with Maple Butter
page 109

Sour Cream Twists
page 124

Poppy Seed Tea Cake
page 129

Peaches and Cream Coffee Cake
page 115

Almond Tea
page 36

PHOTOGRAPH BY JENNY HEFTI
Jefferson County

PUMPKIN BISCUITS WITH MAPLE BUTTER

2 cups flour
1/3 cup nonfat dry milk powder
1/4 cup sugar
4 teaspoons baking powder
3/4 teaspoon pumpkin pie spice
1/4 teaspoon salt
1/4 cup shortening
3/4 cup solid-pack canned pumpkin
2 tablespoons water
Maple Butter

Combine the flour, dry milk powder, sugar, baking powder, pumpkin pie spice and salt in a bowl; mix well. Cut in the shortening until crumbly. Stir in the pumpkin and water just until all ingredients are moistened. The dough may be sticky. Knead 10 times on a lightly floured surface. Pat into an 8 inch square. Cut into sixteen 2-inch biscuits. Place the biscuits 2 inches apart on a nonstick baking sheet. Bake at 425 degrees for 8 to 10 minutes or until golden brown. Serve hot with Maple Butter.

MAPLE BUTTER

1/2 cup butter or margarine, softened
1/4 cup maple syrup

Cream the butter in a small mixer bowl just until smooth. Add the maple syrup gradually, beating until smooth.

Yield: 16 servings.

Approx Per Serving: Cal 172; T Fat 9 g; 48% Calories from Fat; Prot 2 g; Carbo 20 g; Fiber 1 g; Chol 16 mg; Sod 183 mg

Vera Bankson, Hordville

CARROT BREAD

1 cup sugar
3/4 cup vegetable oil
2 eggs
1 1/2 cups flour
1 teaspoon baking soda
1 teaspoon cinnamon
Pinch of salt
1 1/2 to 2 cups grated carrots
1/2 cup chopped pecans

Combine the sugar, oil and eggs in a bowl; mix well. Sift the flour, baking soda, cinnamon and salt together. Stir into the sugar mixture. Add the carrots and pecans; mix well. Spoon into 2 greased and lightly floured loaf pans. Bake at 350 degrees for 1 hour or until a wooden pick inserted in the center of the loaves comes out clean. Remove to a wire rack to cool.

This carrot bread recipe earned the trophy of the 1975 Red Willow County Fair Middle Division Foods Champion.

Yield: 24 servings.

Approx Per Serving: Cal 148; T Fat 9 g; 54% Calories from Fat; Prot 2 g; Carbo 16 g; Fiber 1 g; Chol 18 mg; Sod 43 mg

Ann Hofman Fornoff, Hayes Center

MONKEY BREAD

3/4 cup sugar
1 1/2 teaspoons cinnamon
4 (10-count) cans biscuits
1 cup sugar
1 1/2 teaspoons cinnamon
1/4 cup packed brown sugar
1/2 cup margarine
1/4 cup evaporated milk

Combine 3/4 cup sugar and 1 1/2 teaspoons cinnamon in a sealable plastic bag; mix well. Separate the biscuits, cutting each biscuit into quarters. Shake several biscuit pieces at a time in the sugar mixture; place in a greased 9x13-inch baking pan. Combine 1 cup sugar, 1 1/2 teaspoons cinnamon and brown sugar in a bowl; mix well. Sprinkle over the biscuits in the baking pan. Combine the margarine and evaporated milk in a saucepan. Heat just to the boiling point over medium heat, stirring frequently. Pour over the biscuits. Bake at 350 degrees for 35 minutes.

This is very easy for children to learn to make and is delicious.

Yield: 15 servings.

Approx Per Serving: Cal 376; T Fat 17 g; 37% Calories from Fat; Prot 6 g; Carbo 59 g; Fiber <1 g; Chol 1 mg; Sod 877 mg

Brandon and Brittany Kresha, David City
Stacy Ott, Osceola

LEMON POPPY SEED MUFFINS

1 egg
1 cup milk
1/4 cup vegetable oil
2 cups flour
1/3 cup sugar
1 tablespoon baking powder
1 teaspoon salt
1 tablespoon grated lemon peel
2 teaspoons poppy seeds

Beat the egg in a mixer bowl. Add the milk and oil; beat well. Add the flour, sugar, baking powder and salt, mixing just until the flour is moistened. Stir in lemon peel and poppy seeds. Fill 12 greased muffin cups 2/3 full. Bake at 400 degrees for 15 to 20 minutes or until golden brown. Remove from the pan immediately and cool on a wire rack.

Yield: 12 servings.

Approx Per Serving: Cal 160; T Fat 6 g; 34% Calories from Fat; Prot 3 g; Carbo 23 g; Fiber 1 g; Chol 20 mg; Sod 276 mg

Breanne Chamberlain, Craig

ORANGEY CRANBERRY MUFFINS

2 cups flour
1 cup sugar
1/2 teaspoon baking powder
1 teaspoon nutmeg
1 teaspoon cinnamon
1/2 teaspoon baking soda
1/2 teaspoon ginger
1/2 teaspoon salt
2 tablespoons grated orange peel
1/2 cup shortening
3/4 cup orange juice
2 eggs, beaten
1 tablespoon vanilla extract
1 1/2 cups coarsely chopped cranberries
3/4 cup chopped walnuts

Combine the flour, sugar, baking powder, nutmeg, cinnamon, baking soda, ginger, salt and orange peel in a bowl; mix well. Cut in the shortening until crumbly. Add the orange juice, eggs and vanilla, beating just until all the ingredients are moistened. Fold in the cranberries and walnuts. Fill 18 foil-lined muffin cups 2/3 full. Bake at 375 degrees for 15 minutes. Serve warm.

This recipe received the 1995 Thayer County Junior Foods Champ Trophy and a purple ribbon at the 1995 Nebraska State Fair.

Yield: 18 servings.

Approx Per Serving: Cal 200; T Fat 10 g; 42% Calories from Fat; Prot 3 g; Carbo 26 g; Fiber 1 g; Chol 24 mg; Sod 99 mg

Tyler Harms, Deshler

STRAWBERRY MUFFINS

2 cups flour
1/2 cup sugar
1 tablespoon baking powder
1/2 teaspoon salt
1 cup milk
1 egg
1/4 cup melted butter or margarine, cooled
3/4 cup fresh strawberries, sliced

Sift the flour, sugar, baking powder and salt into a bowl. Make a well in the center. Mix the milk, egg and butter in a small bowl. Add to the well in the flour mixture all at once, stirring 12 to 15 times or just until the dry ingredients are moistened. Fold in the strawberries. Fill paper-lined muffin cups 2/3 full. Bake at 425 degrees for 20 to 25 minutes or until the tops are light brown. Remove to a wire rack immediately.

This was my 1995 Cuming County Favorite Foods entry.

Yield: 12 servings.

Approx Per Serving: Cal 165; T Fat 5 g; 28% Calories from Fat; Prot 3 g; Carbo 26 g; Fiber 1 g; Chol 31 mg; Sod 226 mg

Desireé Luebbert, West Point

BULGUR BREAD

3 cups boiling water
1 cup bulgur
1/2 cup honey
2 tablespoons vegetable oil
1 tablespoon salt
2 envelopes dry yeast
6 to 7 cups flour

Combine the boiling water, bulgur, honey, oil and salt in a bowl; mix well. Let stand until lukewarm, 110 to 115 degrees on a cooking thermometer. Add the yeast. Stir in enough flour to make a soft dough. Place the dough in a greased bowl, turning to coat. Let rise, covered, in a warm place until doubled in bulk. Punch the dough down. Shape into 2 regular or 4 small loaves. Place on a greased baking sheet. Let rise until doubled in bulk. Bake at 350 degrees for 40 minutes or until the bread tests done.

Yield: 24 servings.

Approx Per Serving: Cal 186; T Fat 2 g; 8% Calories from Fat; Prot 5 g; Carbo 38 g; Fiber 2 g; Chol 0 mg; Sod 269 mg

Darcy Gengenbach, Smithfield

COLONIAL YEAST BREAD

1/2 cup cornmeal
1/2 cup packed brown sugar or honey
1 tablespoon salt
2 cups boiling water
1/2 cup vegetable oil
2 envelopes dry yeast
1/2 cup warm (110 to 115 degrees) water
3/4 cup whole wheat flour
1/2 cup rye flour
4 1/2 to 5 1/2 cups all-purpose flour

Combine the cornmeal, brown sugar, salt, boiling water and oil in a large bowl; mix well. Let stand until lukewarm, 110 to 115 degrees on a cooking thermometer. Dissolve the yeast in 1/2 cup warm water. Let stand for 5 minutes. Stir into the cornmeal mixture. Add the whole wheat flour, rye flour and enough all-purpose flour to make a stiff dough. Knead on a floured surface for 6 to 8 minutes or until smooth and elastic. Place the dough in a greased bowl, turning to grease all sides. Let rise, covered, in a warm place for 1 to 1 1/2 hours or until doubled in bulk. Punch the dough down. Divide into 2 equal portions. Let rise, covered, for 10 minutes. Shape into 2 loaves. Place in 2 greased 4x8-inch loaf pans. Let rise, covered, for 1 1/2 hours or until doubled in bulk. Bake at 375 degrees for 35 to 40 minutes or until brown, covering loosely with foil if the top browns too quickly.

Yield: 24 servings.

Approx Per Serving: Cal 191; T Fat 5 g; 24% Calories from Fat; Prot 4 g; Carbo 32 g; Fiber 2 g; Chol 0 mg; Sod 269 mg

Janet Hanna, Burwell

MULTIGRAIN BREAD

- 1 cup water
- 1 cup plain yogurt
- 1/4 cup vegetable oil
- 1/2 cup rolled or quick-cooking oats
- 1/3 cup wheat germ
- 1/3 cup unprocessed bran
- 5 to 5 1/2 cups all-purpose flour
- 1/4 cup packed light brown sugar
- 2 envelopes rapid-rise yeast
- 2 teaspoons salt
- 2 eggs
- 1/4 cup wheat germ or rolled oats

Combine the water, yogurt and oil in a saucepan. Bring to a boil. Stir in 1/2 cup oats, wheat germ and bran. Refrigerate, covered, until cooled to 120 to 130 degrees on a cooking thermometer. Combine 1 cup of the flour, brown sugar, yeast and salt in a large bowl. Mix in the bran mixture, 1 of the eggs and enough of the remaining flour to make a soft dough. Knead for 6 to 8 minutes on a lightly floured surface or until smooth and elastic. Let rest, covered, for 10 minutes. Divide the dough into 2 portions. Roll each into a 7x12-inch rectangle. Roll as for a jelly roll from the short end, sealing the edge and ends. Place each loaf seam side down in a greased 4x8-inch loaf pan. Let rise, covered, in a warm place for 30 to 45 minutes or until doubled in bulk. Cut 3 diagonal slashes 1/4-inch deep in the top of each loaf. Beat the remaining egg lightly; brush on top of the loaves. Sprinkle with the wheat germ. Bake at 375 degrees for 25 to 30 minutes or until the bread tests done. Remove to a wire rack to cool.

Yield: 24 servings.

Approx Per Serving: Cal 163; T Fat 4 g; 20% Calories from Fat; Prot 5 g; Carbo 27 g; Fiber 2 g; Chol 19 mg; Sod 190 mg

Jenny Hefti, Daykin

ONION BREAD

- 1 loaf frozen bread dough, thawed in refrigerator
- 1 cube beef bouillon
- 1/4 cup melted margarine, slightly cooled
- 1 tablespoon dried minced onion

Cut the bread dough into 4 strips lengthwise. Cut each strip into bite-size pieces; place in a greased bundt pan or large loaf pan. Dissolve the beef bouillon in the melted margarine. Stir in the dried onion. Pour over the bread pieces. Let rise, covered, in a warm place until the dough is at the top of the pan. Bake at 350 degrees for 20 to 25 minutes or until the bread tests done.

Yield: 12 servings.

Approx Per Serving: Cal 136; T Fat 5 g; 35% Calories from Fat; Prot 3 g; Carbo 19 g; Fiber 1 g; Chol <1 mg; Sod 294 mg

Tom Morrison, Elgin

ONION DILL BREAD

1 envelope dry yeast
$3^{1}/_{2}$ cups flour
$^{1}/_{4}$ teaspoon baking soda
$1^{1}/_{2}$ teaspoons salt
1 egg
$^{1}/_{4}$ cup water
$^{3}/_{4}$ cup cottage cheese
$^{3}/_{4}$ cup sour cream
3 tablespoons sugar
3 tablespoons dried minced onion
2 tablespoons whole dillseeds
$1^{1}/_{2}$ tablespoons butter

Combine the yeast, flour, baking soda, salt and egg in the inner pan of a bread machine. Combine the water, cottage cheese, sour cream, sugar, dried onion, dillseeds and butter in a saucepan; mix well. Heat over medium heat until the butter is melted, stirring frequently. Add to the inner pan of the bread machine. Bake using the manufacturer's directions. May brush the top with additional melted butter at baking time.

Yield: 12 servings.

Approx Per Serving: Cal 216; T Fat 6 g; 25% Calories from Fat; Prot 7 g; Carbo 34 g; Fiber 2 g; Chol 30 mg; Sod 366 mg

Kendre Linder, Loomis

SWEDISH RYE BREAD ❀ *from The 4-H Friends' Cookbook*

1 envelope yeast
$^{1}/_{4}$ cup lukewarm (110 to 115 degrees) water
$1^{1}/_{2}$ cups hot water
$^{1}/_{4}$ cup packed brown sugar
$^{1}/_{4}$ cup light molasses
2 tablespoons shortening
1 tablespoon salt
$2^{1}/_{2}$ cups medium rye flour
3 tablespoons caraway seeds
$3^{1}/_{2}$ to 4 cups all-purpose flour
2 tablespoons melted butter

Dissolve the yeast in the lukewarm water and mix well. Combine $1^{1}/_{2}$ cups hot water, brown sugar, molasses, shortening and salt in a bowl, stirring until the brown sugar dissolves. Stir in the rye flour until blended. Add the yeast mixture and caraway seeds and mix well. Add enough all-purpose flour to make a soft dough and mix well. Let rest, covered, for 10 minutes. Knead on a lightly floured surface for 10 minutes or until smooth. Place the dough in a greased bowl, turning to coat the surface. Let rise, covered, in a warm place for $1^{1}/_{2}$ hours or until doubled in bulk. Punch the dough down. Divide the dough into 2 equal portions. Shape into 2 round loaves. Place on a greased baking sheet. Let rise, covered, for $1^{1}/_{2}$ hours or until doubled in bulk. Bake at 375 degrees for 25 to 35 minutes or until brown. Brush with the melted butter. Remove to a wire rack to cool.

Yield: 24 servings.

Approx Per Serving: Cal 151; T Fat 3 g; 15% Calories from Fat; Prot 3 g; Carbo 29 g; Fiber 2 g; Chol 3 mg; Sod 279 mg

Mrs. Merill Baier; Mrs. Harvey Finke
Mrs. Harold G. Richard; Mrs. Ray Sall

PEACHES AND CREAM COFFEE CAKE

1 envelope dry yeast
1 teaspoon sugar
1/4 cup warm (110 to 115 degrees) water
1/2 cup (1 large) puréed peeled peach
1/2 cup half-and-half
1/2 cup sugar
2 eggs
1/2 cup melted butter
1 tablespoon vanilla extract
1 1/2 teaspoons salt
1/2 teaspoon nutmeg
1/2 teaspoon cinnamon
3 3/4 to 4 1/4 cups flour
1/2 cup chopped pecans, toasted
Topping
1/4 cup melted butter
2 ripe medium peaches, peeled
2 to 3 tablespoons chopped pecans

Dissolve the yeast and 1 teaspoon sugar in the warm water in a large mixer bowl. Let stand for 5 to 10 minutes or until foamy. Add the peach purée, half-and-half, 1/2 cup sugar, eggs, 1/2 cup melted butter, vanilla, salt, nutmeg, cinnamon, and 2 1/3 to 3 cups of the flour. Beat at medium speed for 4 minutes. Stir in the toasted pecans and enough of the remaining flour to make a stiff batter. Let rise, covered with a slightly damp towel, in a warm place for 1 to 1 1/2 hours or until doubled in bulk. Sprinkle the Topping in the bottom of a buttered 10-inch bundt pan. Drizzle with 1/4 cup melted butter. Cut the peaches into 1/4-inch slices; arrange over the Topping. Stir the batter down. Spoon into the pan over the peaches. Smooth the top of the batter; sprinkle with the remaining pecans. Let rise, covered with buttered waxed paper, for 45 minutes or until doubled in bulk. Bake at 350 degrees for 40 to 45 minutes or until a metal skewer inserted in the center comes out clean. Invert carefully onto a serving plate. Spoon any remaining Topping from the pan onto the coffee cake.

TOPPING

1/2 cup packed brown sugar
1/2 teaspoon cinnamon
1/4 teaspoon nutmeg

Combine the brown sugar, cinnamon and nutmeg in a bowl; mix well.

While I was in high school, I prepared this for the Pawnee County Fair and received a purple ribbon. It was then exhibited at the Nebraska State Fair.

Yield: 16 servings.

Approx Per Serving: Cal 308; T Fat 14 g; 40% Calories from Fat; Prot 5 g; Carbo 41 g; Fiber 2 g; Chol 53 mg; Sod 302 mg

Merri Wright, Kearney

HERBED SOUR CREAM BATTER BREAD

- 4 3/4 cups sifted flour
- 2 tablespoons sugar
- 2 teaspoons salt
- 2 envelopes dry yeast
- 1 cup warm (110 to 115 degrees) sour cream
- 6 tablespoons butter, softened
- 1/2 teaspoon marjoram
- 1/2 teaspoon oregano
- 1/2 teaspoon parsley flakes
- 1/2 cup very warm (120 to 130 degrees) water
- 2 eggs

Combine 1 cup of the flour, sugar, salt, yeast, sour cream, butter, marjoram, oregano, parsley and the very warm water in a mixer bowl; beat at medium speed for 2 minutes. Add the eggs and 1/2 cup of the flour; beat at high speed for 2 minutes longer. Stir in enough of the remaining flour to make a soft dough. Let rise, covered, for 35 minutes or until doubled in bulk. Stir the dough down. Divide the dough into 2 equal portions. Place each portion in a greased 1-quart baking dish. Let rise, covered, for 50 minutes or until doubled in bulk. Bake at 375 degrees for 35 minutes or until golden brown. Remove to a wire rack to cool.

I used this recipe for several years in my 4-H bread project. It was always a hit with the judge because of its unusual herb flavor and its ability to be served with most meats.

Yield: 24 servings.

Approx Per Serving: Cal 141; T Fat 6 g; 36% Calories from Fat; Prot 3 g; Carbo 19 g; Fiber 1 g; Chol 30 mg; Sod 218 mg

Dana Lueth, Curtis

SOUR CREAM POPPY SEED BREAD

- 2 cups bread flour
- 3/4 teaspoon salt
- 1 tablespoon sugar
- 1 teaspoon poppy seeds
- 1 1/2 teaspoons dry yeast
- 1 large egg
- 1/3 cup sour cream or yogurt
- 3 tablespoons water

Add all ingredients to a bread machine in the order suggested by the manufacturer, adding the sour cream with the water. The recommended cycle is 1 basic white bread cycle, medium or normal color setting.

Yield: 12 servings.

Approx Per Serving: Cal 102; T Fat 2 g; 19% Calories from Fat; Prot 3 g; Carbo 17 g; Fiber 1 g; Chol 21 mg; Sod 142 mg

Eileen Krumbach, Shelby

AWARD-WINNING HONEY WHOLE WHEAT LOAVES

1 cup milk, scalded
$^{1}/_{4}$ cup butter or margarine
2 tablespoons sugar
$^{1}/_{2}$ cup honey
1 teaspoon salt
2 envelopes dry yeast
$1^{1}/_{2}$ cups warm (110 to 115 degrees) water
$2^{1}/_{2}$ cups sifted all-purpose flour
5 cups whole wheat flour
2 tablespoons melted butter or margarine

Combine scalded milk, $^{1}/_{4}$ cup butter, sugar, honey and salt in a mixer bowl; mix well. Cool to lukewarm (110 to 115 degrees). Dissolve the yeast in the warm water. Add yeast, all-purpose flour and $2^{1}/_{2}$ cups of the whole wheat flour to the milk mixture. Beat at medium speed for 2 minutes or until smooth, scraping the bowl occasionally. Stir in enough of the remaining flour to make a soft dough. Place the dough on a floured surface. Let rest for 10 minutes. Knead for 10 minutes or until smooth and elastic. Place in a greased bowl, turning to grease all sides. Let rise, covered, in a warm place for $1^{1}/_{2}$ hours or until doubled in bulk. Divide the dough into 2 equal portions. Shape each portion into a loaf and place in a greased 5x9-inch loaf pan. Let rise, covered, for 35 minutes or until doubled in bulk. Bake at 375 degrees for 40 minutes or until the loaves sound hollow when tapped. Remove to a wire rack to cool.

Yield: 24 servings.

Approx Per Serving: Cal 187; T Fat 4 g; 18% Calories from Fat; Prot 5 g; Carbo 35 g; Fiber 4 g; Chol 9 mg; Sod 125 mg

Danielle Harris, Pawnee City

PURPLE RIBBON THREE-WHEAT BATTER BREAD

2 cups all-purpose flour
1 envelope rapid-rise yeast
$^{1}/_{8}$ teaspoon ginger
2 cups warm (110 to 115 degrees) milk
3 tablespoons honey
2 tablespoons vegetable oil
1 teaspoon salt
$^{1}/_{2}$ cup all-purpose flour
$1^{1}/_{4}$ cups whole wheat flour
$^{1}/_{2}$ cup wheat germ
$^{1}/_{4}$ cup cracked wheat

Combine 2 cups all-purpose flour, yeast and ginger in a large bowl. Stir in the warm milk. Add the honey, oil and salt. Combine $^{1}/_{2}$ cup all-purpose flour, whole wheat flour, wheat germ and cracked wheat in a bowl; mix well. Add to yeast mixture 1 cup at a time, stirring well after each addition. Spoon into 2 greased 1-pound coffee cans. Place a greased plastic lid over each can. Let rise in a warm place until lids are lifted from cans. Remove the lids. Place coffee cans on lowest rack in 350-degree oven. Bake for 45 minutes. Cool in cans for 5 minutes. Remove to a wire rack.

Yield: 24 servings.

Approx Per Serving: Cal 100; T Fat 2 g; 14% Calories from Fat; Prot 3 g; Carbo 19 g; Fiber 2 g; Chol 0 mg; Sod 90 mg

Sean Rapier, Harrison

STUFFED VIENNA BREAD

- 1 loaf French bread
- 10 ounces Swiss cheese, shredded
- 1 (4-ounce) can chopped mushrooms, drained
- 1 cup margarine
- 2 tablespoons minced onion
- 2 tablespoons poppy seeds
- 1 teaspoon dry mustard
- 1 teaspoon seasoned salt
- 1/8 teaspoon lemon juice

Slice the French bread thickly to but not through the bottom crust. Cut lengthwise down the center of the loaf to but not through the bottom crust. Combine the cheese and mushrooms in a bowl; mix well. Stuff the mixture into the slits in the bread. Place on a large sheet of heavy foil on a baking sheet. Combine the margarine, onion, poppy seeds, mustard, seasoned salt and lemon juice in a small saucepan. Heat over medium heat until the margarine is melted, stirring constantly. Pour over the bread. Pull up the sides of the foil to cover the bread. Bake at 350 degrees for 30 to 40 minutes. Open the foil slightly and place in a bread basket to serve.

I always take this to our church potluck dinners and I have yet to bring any back home.

Yield: 12 servings.

Approx Per Serving: Cal 340; T Fat 24 g; 62% Calories from Fat; Prot 11 g; Carbo 22 g; Fiber 1 g; Chol 22 mg; Sod 619 mg

Jolene DeBoer, Smithfield

BROCCOLI ROLLS

- 1 (10-ounce) package frozen chopped broccoli, thawed, drained
- 1 cup shredded Cheddar cheese
- 1 egg, beaten
- 2 tablespoons dried minced onion
- 1 pound loaf homemade or frozen bread dough, thawed in refrigerator

Combine the broccoli, cheese, egg and onion in a bowl; mix well. Roll the dough into a 1/2-inch thick rectangle on a lightly floured surface. Spread the broccoli mixture over the top of the dough. Roll as for a jelly roll, sealing the edge and ends. Cut into 1-inch slices. Place in greased baking pans. Let rise for 45 minutes. Bake at 375 degrees for 25 minutes. May be served with cheese sauce.

These broccoli rolls freeze well.

Yield: 10 servings.

Approx Per Serving: Cal 184; T Fat 6 g; 29% Calories from Fat; Prot 8 g; Carbo 24 g; Fiber 2 g; Chol 33 mg; Sod 296 mg

Adele, Eliot and Lane Phillips, Beaver Crossing

"BEST OF SHOW" DINNER ROLLS

1 (12-ounce) can evaporated milk
3 cups hot water
1 cup vegetable oil
1 tablespoon salt
1/2 cup sugar
3 envelopes dry yeast
3 tablespoons sugar
1/2 cup warm (110 to 115 degrees) water
3 eggs, beaten
11 cups (or more) flour

Combine the evaporated milk, hot water, oil, salt and 1/2 cup sugar in a large mixer bowl; mix well. Dissolve the yeast and 3 tablespoons sugar in the warm water. Add to the sugar mixture with the eggs and 3 cups of the flour; beat well. Add the remaining flour 2 cups at a time, kneading lightly on a floured surface until a soft dough forms. Place the dough in a greased bowl, turning to grease the sides. Let rise, covered, until doubled in bulk. Punch the dough down. Shape into rolls; place on greased baking pans. Let rise until doubled in bulk. Bake at 350 degrees for 20 minutes or until brown.

Yield: 96 servings.

Approx Per Serving: Cal 86; T Fat 3 g; 30% Calories from Fat; Prot 2 g; Carbo 13 g; Fiber <1 g; Chol 8 mg; Sod 73 mg

Sue Finke, Cozad

BUTTERHORN ROLLS

1 envelope dry yeast
1/4 cup warm (110 to 115 degrees) water
1/2 cup margarine
1/2 cup sugar
1 teaspoon salt
1 cup milk, scalded
3 eggs, beaten
4 1/2 cups flour
1/2 cup melted margarine
1/2 cup milk or 1 egg
1/2 cup poppy seeds

Dissolve yeast in warm water. Mix margarine, sugar, salt and scalded milk in a large bowl. Cool to lukewarm, 110 to 115 degrees. Stir in yeast and eggs. Add flour gradually until a stiff dough forms. Knead dough on floured surface for 5 minutes or until smooth and elastic. Let rise, covered, in a warm place (85 to 90 degrees) for 1 hour or until doubled in bulk. Divide into 3 portions. Roll each portion into a 10-inch circle 1/4 inch thick. Brush with melted margarine. Cut each circle into 10 wedges. Roll as for jelly roll, starting at wide end. Place on a greased baking sheet point side down, curving in ends slightly. Let rise, covered, in warm place for 30 to 45 minutes or until doubled in bulk. Brush tops with milk or egg beaten with a small amount of water. Sprinkle with poppy seeds. Bake at 350 degrees for 20 minutes or until golden brown.

Yield: 30 servings.

Approx Per Serving: Cal 164; T Fat 8 g; 45% Calories from Fat; Prot 4 g; Carbo 19 g; Fiber 1 g; Chol 23 mg; Sod 156 mg

Michelle Lemke, Osmond

HERBED TOMATO ROLLS

2 tablespoons brown sugar
2 teaspoons salt
2 envelopes dry yeast
$5\frac{1}{2}$ cups flour
1 cup milk
5 tablespoons margarine
1 cup puréed fresh tomatoes
2 eggs
$\frac{1}{2}$ teaspoon thyme
$\frac{3}{4}$ teaspoon basil
1 clove of garlic, minced, or $\frac{1}{8}$ teaspoon garlic powder

Combine the brown sugar, salt, yeast and 1 cup of the flour in a large bowl. Combine the milk and 3 tablespoons of the margarine in a saucepan. Heat over medium heat until very warm (120 to 130 degrees), stirring frequently. Add the milk gradually to the dry ingredients, beating at low speed. Beat at medium speed for 2 minutes, scraping the side of the bowl occasionally. Beat in the puréed tomatoes, eggs, thyme, basil, garlic and $1\frac{1}{2}$ cups of the remaining flour. Stir in enough of the remaining 3 cups flour to make a soft dough. Knead on a floured surface for 10 minutes or until smooth and elastic, adding the remaining flour as needed. Shape the dough into a ball; place in a greased bowl, turning to grease all sides. Let rise, covered, in a warm place (80 to 85 degrees) for $1\frac{1}{2}$ hours or until doubled in bulk. Punch the dough down. Place on a lightly floured surface. Let rest for 15 minutes. Cut the dough into 32 equal portions; roll each portion into a ball. Place in a greased 12x18-inch baking pan. Bake at 400 degrees for 20 minutes. Brush the hot bread with the remaining margarine.

This recipe won "best of show" at our county fair in 1993.

Yield: 32 servings.

Approx Per Serving: Cal 108; T Fat 3 g; 22% Calories from Fat; Prot 3 g; Carbo 18 g; Fiber 1 g; Chol 14 mg; Sod 163 mg

Katie Kastanek, Crete

RAPID MIX ROLLS

- 4 cups flour
- 3 tablespoons sugar
- 1 teaspoon salt
- 2 envelopes rapid-rise yeast
- 1 cup milk
- 1/2 cup water
- 1/4 cup margarine

Combine 1 1/2 cups of the flour, sugar, salt and yeast in a large mixer bowl; mix well. Combine the milk, water and margarine in a saucepan. Heat over medium heat until warm (120 to 130 degrees). Add the milk mixture gradually to the dry ingredients; beat at medium speed for 2 minutes. Scrape the bowl. Add 1/2 cup of the flour; beat at high speed for 2 minutes. Stir in enough of the remaining 2 cups flour to make a soft dough. Knead the dough for 5 minutes on a floured surface. Place the dough in a greased bowl, turning to grease all sides. Let rise, covered, in a pan of warm (100 degrees) water for 15 minutes. Punch the dough down and place on a floured surface. Shape into a smooth ball. Let the dough rest for 5 minutes. Shape into 12 round rolls; place in a greased baking pan. Let rise, covered, for 15 to 20 minutes or until doubled in bulk. Bake at 425 degrees for 10 to 12 minutes or until light brown.

Yield: 12 servings.

Approx Per Serving: Cal 214; T Fat 5 g; 21% Calories from Fat; Prot 5 g; Carbo 36 g; Fiber 2 g; Chol 3 mg; Sod 234 mg

Jessica Wolff, West Point

HOMEMADE BREADSTICKS

- 2 envelopes dry yeast
- 1 1/2 cups warm (110 to 115 degrees) water
- 2 tablespoons sugar
- 1 teaspoon salt
- 4 cups all-purpose or whole wheat flour
- 1 egg, slightly beaten
- 1/4 cup sesame seeds

Dissolve the yeast and warm water in a large bowl. Add the sugar, salt and flour; mix well. Knead the dough on a floured surface until smooth. Cut the dough into 12 equal portions. Roll each portion into a stick shape; place on a greased baking sheet. Brush with egg; sprinkle with sesame seeds. Breadsticks may be baked without letting them rise. Bake at 425 degrees for 12 to 15 minutes or until brown.

The Razzamazztazz 4-H Club has enjoyed making these breadsticks for many years. They are quick and great tasting.

Yield: 12 servings.

Approx Per Serving: Cal 188; T Fat 3 g; 13% Calories from Fat; Prot 6 g; Carbo 35 g; Fiber 2 g; Chol 18 mg; Sod 186 mg

M. Jane Tonjes, Bertrand

PRETZELS

1 envelope dry yeast
$1^1/_2$ cups warm (105 to 115 degrees) water
1 teaspoon salt
1 tablespoon sugar
4 cups flour
1 egg, beaten
$^1/_4$ cup coarse salt

Soften the yeast in the warm water in a large bowl. Add 1 teaspoon salt, sugar and flour; mix well. Knead the dough on a floured surface. Divide the dough into 1-inch pieces; roll each piece into a 15-inch rope. Twist into pretzel shapes, tucking the ends under; place on a greased baking sheet. Brush with the egg; sprinkle with the coarse salt. Bake at 425 degrees for 12 to 15 minutes or until golden brown.

Yield: 20 servings.

Approx Per Serving: Cal 98; T Fat 1 g; 5% Calories from Fat; Prot 3 g; Carbo 20 g; Fiber 1 g; Chol 11 mg; Sod 1389 mg

Christine Moser, Imperial

CINNAMON ROLLS

2 envelopes rapid-rise yeast
$2^1/_2$ cups lukewarm (110 to 115 degrees) water
1 (2-layer) package yellow cake mix
$6^1/_2$ cups flour
3 eggs
$^1/_3$ cup vegetable oil
1 teaspoon salt
$^1/_2$ cup margarine, softened
2 cups packed brown sugar
1 tablespoon cinnamon
$^1/_2$ cup melted margarine
2 tablespoons milk
2 cups confectioners' sugar

Dissolve the yeast in the lukewarm water in a large mixer bowl for at least 3 minutes. Add the cake mix, 1 cup of the flour, eggs, oil and salt; beat well. Stir in enough of the remaining $5^1/_2$ cups flour to make a soft dough. Knead for 5 minutes on a floured surface. Let rise, covered, until doubled in bulk. Punch the dough down. Roll to $^1/_2$-inch thickness. Spread $^1/_2$ cup margarine over the dough; sprinkle with the brown sugar and cinnamon. Roll as for a jelly roll, sealing the edge and ends. Cut into $^1/_2$-inch slices; place in greased baking pans. Let rise, covered, until doubled in bulk. Bake at 350 degrees for 20 to 30 minutes or until brown. Combine melted margarine, milk and confectioners' sugar in a bowl; mix well. Spread over the hot rolls.

Yield: 36 servings.

Approx Per Serving: Cal 279; T Fat 9 g; 30% Calories from Fat; Prot 4 g; Carbo 45 g; Fiber 1 g; Chol 18 mg; Sod 222 mg

Karla Honke, Naper

LONG JOHNS

1/2 cup shortening
1 cup boiling water
1 cup evaporated milk or 3/4 cup milk
3 envelopes dry yeast
2 eggs, beaten
1/2 teaspoon nutmeg
1/2 cup sugar
2 teaspoons salt
1 cup whole wheat flour
7 1/2 to 8 cups all-purpose flour
Vegetable oil for deep-frying
1/4 cup margarine
1/2 cup packed brown sugar
3 tablespoons cream or milk
3 cups confectioners' sugar

Stir the shortening into the boiling water in a large mixer bowl until melted. Stir in the evaporated milk. Let stand until lukewarm (110 to 115 degrees). Dissolve the yeast in warm water using package directions. Add to the lukewarm milk mixture. Add the eggs, nutmeg, sugar, salt and whole wheat flour; beat well. Stir in enough of the all-purpose flour to make a thick dough. Let the dough rise, covered, until doubled in bulk. Punch the dough down. Roll the dough 1/2 inch thick on a floured surface. Cut into 1x6-inch strips. Let rise for 10 minutes. Fry in hot deep oil (365 to 370 degrees) in a deep fryer until brown; drain. Combine the margarine, brown sugar and cream in a saucepan. Heat over medium heat until the margarine is melted, stirring constantly. Add enough of the confectioners' sugar to make of spreading consistency. Spread over the Long Johns.

My third-grade teacher helped us make these in class. Each student received the recipe, and they have been my favorites since then. My sister won a blue ribbon with this recipe at the state fair.

Yield: 48 servings.

Approx Per Serving: Cal 171; T Fat 4 g; 23% Calories from Fat; Prot 3 g; Carbo 30 g; Fiber 1 g; Chol 12 mg; Sod 110 mg
Nutritional information does not include oil for deep-frying.

Marjean Hiebert, Imperial

KIWIFRUIT DANISH

- 1 (8-count) can crescent dinner rolls
- 3 ounces cream cheese, softened
- 1 egg yolk
- 2 tablespoons sugar
- 1 teaspoon grated orange peel
- 2 to 3 kiwifruit, peeled, sliced
- 1/3 cup apricot jam

Unroll the crescent dinner rolls; separate into 8 triangles. Combine the cream cheese, egg yolk, sugar and orange peel in a bowl; mix well. Place 1 tablespoon mixture in center of each triangle; top with 1 slice kiwifruit. Pull the points of each triangle to the center, pressing to seal; place on a greased baking sheet. Bake at 375 degrees for 12 to 15 minutes or until golden brown. Remove to a wire rack. Heat the jam in a small saucepan. Place a slice of kiwifruit on each roll. Brush the rolls with the hot apricot jam.

This recipe was used for a demonstration talk in 1990 by Heidi Lauby entitled "Fuzzy Fruit of the Future" and has become a family favorite.

Yield: 8 servings.

Approx Per Serving: Cal 191; T Fat 8 g; 34% Calories from Fat; Prot 3 g; Carbo 29 g; Fiber 1 g; Chol 41 mg; Sod 289 mg

Jessica Lauby, Lexington

SOUR CREAM TWISTS

- 1 envelope dry yeast
- 1/4 cup warm (110 to 115 degrees) water
- 4 cups flour
- 1 cup melted butter
- 1 cup sour cream
- 2 eggs, slightly beaten
- 1 teaspoon salt
- 1 teaspoon vanilla extract
- 1 cup sugar
- 1 teaspoon cinnamon

Dissolve the yeast in the warm water. Combine the flour, butter, sour cream, eggs, salt and vanilla in a large bowl; mix well. Add the yeast; beat until smooth. Cover with a damp cloth. Refrigerate for at least 2 hours or for up to 2 days. Combine the sugar and cinnamon. Sprinkle a portion of the sugar-cinnamon mixture onto a flat surface. Roll the dough into a rectangle, turning to coat both sides. Fold the dough 3 times as you would a letter. Roll into a 1/4-inch rectangle, using the remaining sugar-cinnamon to coat the surface. Cut into 1x4-inch strips. Twist each strip and place on a greased baking sheet. Bake at 375 degrees for 15 minutes.

These are very easy to make and sell well at bake sales.

Yield: 24 servings.

Approx Per Serving: Cal 203; T Fat 10 g; 45% Calories from Fat; Prot 3 g; Carbo 25 g; Fiber 1 g; Chol 43 mg; Sod 178 mg

Lynnel Fiscus, Coleridge

DESSERTS

SWEET ENDINGS
Dessert Buffet Menu

FRESH APPLE CAKE WITH CARAMEL SAUCE
page 127

ALMOND BISCOTTI
page 136

CHERRY COCONUT BALLS
page 136

RED HOT CHERRY PIE
page 140

CREAM PUFFS
page 150

SWEDISH PASTRY
page 150

CAPPUCCINO
page 36

PHOTOGRAPH BY KYLE ELLISON
Sarpy County

FRESH APPLE CAKE WITH CARAMEL SAUCE

- 3 eggs
- 1 cup vegetable oil
- 2 cups sugar
- 2 cups flour
- 2 teaspoons cinnamon
- 1 teaspoon baking soda
- 1/2 teaspoon salt
- 4 cups chopped peeled apples
- 1 cup chopped pecans
- 1 teaspoon vanilla extract
- 1/2 cup packed brown sugar
- 1/2 cup sugar
- 1 tablespoon flour
- 1/2 cup cream
- 1/2 cup butter
- 1 teaspoon vanilla extract

Beat the eggs and oil in a mixer bowl until smooth. Add 2 cups sugar gradually, beating until blended. Fold in a mixture of 2 cups flour, cinnamon, baking soda and salt. Stir in the apples, pecans and vanilla. Spoon into a 9x13-inch cake pan. Bake at 350 degrees for 50 minutes. Cool cake in the pan on a wire rack. Combine the brown sugar, 1/2 cup sugar and 1 tablespoon flour in a saucepan and mix well. Add the cream, butter and vanilla. Bring to a boil, stirring constantly. Boil for 1 to 2 minutes or until of the desired consistency, stirring frequently. Cut the cake into squares. Serve with the caramel sauce. May also top with ice cream. May omit the pecans. May substitute milk for the cream.

Yield: 15 servings.

Approx Per Serving: Cal 512; T Fat 30 g; 52% Calories from Fat; Prot 4 g; Carbo 59 g; Fiber 2 g; Chol 70 mg; Sod 207 mg

Debbie Swanson, Hickman

AMAZING CORN CAKE

- 1 (17-ounce) can cream-style corn
- 3/4 cup sugar
- 1/2 cup packed brown sugar
- 1 cup vegetable oil
- 3 eggs
- 2 1/4 cups flour
- 1 tablespoon baking powder
- 1 teaspoon baking soda
- 1 teaspoon cinnamon
- 1 teaspoon salt
- 1/2 cup raisins
- 1/2 cup chopped pecans
- 1/4 cup butter
- 1/2 cup packed brown sugar
- 1/4 cup milk
- 2 to 3 cups sifted confectioners' sugar

Combine the corn, sugar and 1/2 cup brown sugar in a mixer bowl and mix well. Add the oil and eggs, beating until well mixed. Add the flour, baking powder, baking soda, cinnamon and salt. Beat for 3 minutes or until well mixed. Stir in the raisins and pecans. Spoon into a 9x13-inch cake pan sprayed with nonstick cooking spray. Bake at 350 degrees for 30 to 35 minutes or until the cake tests done. Cool in the pan on a wire rack. Bring the butter and 1/2 cup brown sugar to a boil in a saucepan. Remove from heat. Add the milk and confectioners' sugar, stirring until of frosting consistency. Spread over the top of the cake.

Yield: 15 servings.

Approx Per Serving: Cal 470; T Fat 22 g; 41% Calories from Fat; Prot 4 g; Carbo 67 g; Fiber 1 g; Chol 51 mg; Sod 406 mg

Dorothy Bremer, Lexington

INDIAN CAKE

2 cups sugar
1/2 cup margarine, softened
2 eggs
2 cups flour
1/2 cup baking cocoa
1/2 cup cold coffee
1 teaspoon baking soda
1 teaspoon baking powder
1 teaspoon vanilla extract
1/2 teaspoon salt
1 cup boiling water
1 cup sugar
2 tablespoons baking cocoa
1 egg, beaten
3 tablespoons milk
2 tablespoons butter
1 teaspoon vanilla extract

Cream 2 cups sugar and margarine in a mixer bowl until light and fluffy. Beat in 2 eggs. Add the flour, 1/2 cup baking cocoa, coffee, baking soda, baking powder, 1 teaspoon vanilla and salt and mix well. Stir in the boiling water. Spoon into a greased and floured 9x13-inch cake pan. Bake at 350 degrees for 30 minutes or until cake tests done. Cool in the pan on a wire rack. Combine 1 cup sugar and 2 tablespoons baking cocoa in a saucepan and mix well. Stir in 1 egg, milk, butter and 1 teaspoon vanilla. Bring to a boil. Boil for 1 minute, stirring constantly. Beat the mixture in a mixer bowl until of frosting consistency. Spread over the top of the cake.

Yield: 15 servings.

Approx Per Serving: Cal 309; T Fat 9 g; 26% Calories from Fat; Prot 4 g; Carbo 55 g; Fiber 2 g; Chol 47 mg; Sod 251 mg

Brandi Hofeling, Beatrice

MISSISSIPPI MUD

1 cup margarine, softened
4 eggs
2 cups sugar
1 1/2 cups flour
1/2 cup baking cocoa
1 teaspoon vanilla extract
1/8 teaspoon salt
1 cup chopped walnuts
1 (10-ounce) package marshmallows
1/3 cup melted margarine
1/2 cup baking cocoa
1/3 cup milk
2 1/2 cups confectioners' sugar

Beat 1 cup margarine and eggs in a mixer bowl until blended. Add the sugar, flour, 1/2 cup baking cocoa, vanilla and salt; beat until smooth. Stir in the walnuts. Spoon into a 9x13-inch cake pan. Bake at 350 degrees for 20 to 25 minutes or until the cake tests done. Top with the marshmallows. Bake until the marshmallows puff. Cool in the pan on a wire rack. Beat 1/3 cup margarine, 1/2 cup baking cocoa and milk in a mixer bowl until blended. Add the confectioners' sugar gradually, beating until of frosting consistency. Spread over the top of the cake.

This is one of my favorite recipes. It brings back memories of my grandmother's kitchen. She used to take it to a lot of 4-H events.

Yield: 15 servings.

Approx Per Serving: Cal 519; T Fat 24 g; 39% Calories from Fat; Prot 6 g; Carbo 76 g; Fiber 2 g; Chol 57 mg; Sod 239 mg

Laura Hawthorne, Chadron

TURTLE NUT CAKE

1 (2-layer) package German chocolate cake mix
1 (14-ounce) package caramels
1/2 cup evaporated milk
6 tablespoons butter
1 cup chopped pecans
1 cup chocolate chips

Prepare the cake mix using package directions. Spoon 1/2 of the batter into a greased and floured 9x13-inch cake pan; store the remaining batter in the refrigerator until needed. Bake at 350 degrees for 18 minutes. Combine the caramels, evaporated milk and butter in a saucepan. Cook over low heat until smooth. Stir in the pecans. Spoon over the baked layer; sprinkle with chocolate chips. Top with the remaining batter. Bake for 20 minutes longer or until the cake tests done.

This recipe is a favorite at our house for special occasions. It's great with ice cream.

Yield: 15 servings.

Approx Per Serving: Cal 468; T Fat 26 g; 48% Calories from Fat; Prot 5 g; Carbo 58 g; Fiber 2 g; Chol 61 mg; Sod 458 mg

Anita Keys, Elsmere

POPPY SEED TEA CAKE

2 1/4 cups sugar
1 1/2 cups milk
1 1/2 cups vegetable oil
3 eggs
1 1/2 teaspoons vanilla extract
1 1/2 teaspoons butter flavoring
1 1/2 teaspoons almond extract
3 cups flour
1 1/2 teaspoons baking powder
1/2 teaspoon salt
1 1/2 teaspoons poppy seeds
3/4 cup sugar
1/4 cup orange juice
1/2 teaspoon vanilla extract
1/2 teaspoon butter flavoring
1/2 teaspoon almond extract

Combine 2 1/4 cups sugar, milk, oil, eggs, 1 1/2 teaspoons vanilla, 1 1/2 teaspoons butter flavoring and 1 1/2 teaspoons almond flavoring in a mixer bowl and mix well. Add the flour, baking powder, salt and 1 1/2 teaspoons poppy seeds, beating until mixed. Spoon into a greased bundt pan. Bake at 350 degrees for 1 hour. Cool in the pan on a wire rack for 5 minutes. Invert onto a cake plate. Combine 3/4 cup sugar, orange juice, 1/2 teaspoon vanilla, 1/2 teaspoon butter flavoring and 1/2 teaspoon almond flavoring in a saucepan. Cook until the sugar dissolves, stirring constantly. Drizzle over the hot cake.

This is a popular family recipe that is easy to prepare. My mother-in-law often makes this delicious and unique cake.

Yield: 12 servings.

Approx Per Serving: Cal 597; T Fat 30 g; 45% Calories from Fat; Prot 6 g; Carbo 77 g; Fiber 1 g; Chol 57 mg; Sod 162 mg

Janet Latta, Stratton

Candy Mud Balls

- **1½ (1-pound) packages confectioners' sugar**
- **1 (14-ounce) can sweetened condensed milk**
- **½ cup melted butter**
- **1 cup flaked coconut**
- **1 cup chopped pecans**
- **¼ cup melted food grade wax**
- **2 cups chocolate chips**

Combine 1 package of the confectioners' sugar, condensed milk and butter in a bowl and mix well. Stir in the coconut. Add the remaining confectioners' sugar and mix well; mixture will be stiff. Stir in the pecans. Shape into 1-inch balls. Combine the food grade wax and chocolate chips in a double boiler. Cook over hot water until smooth, stirring frequently. Dip the balls into the chocolate mixture; place on waxed paper. Let stand until set.

This recipe was given to me by a very dear friend. I have had this candy at Christmas for over 35 years.

Yield: 32 servings.

Approx Per Serving: Cal 234; T Fat 10 g; 38% Calories from Fat; Prot 2 g; Carbo 36 g; Fiber 1 g; Chol 12 mg; Sod 47 mg

Dora Lee Bates, Whitney

Cocoa Applesauce Bars

- **1½ cups sugar**
- **½ cup margarine, softened**
- **2 eggs**
- **2 cups flour**
- **2 cups applesauce**
- **2 tablespoons baking cocoa**
- **1 teaspoon baking soda**
- **½ teaspoon salt**
- **½ teaspoon cinnamon**
- **1 cup chocolate chips**
- **½ cup chopped pecans**
- **2 tablespoons sugar**

Beat 1½ cups sugar, margarine and eggs in a mixer bowl until creamy, scraping the bowl occasionally. Add the flour, applesauce, baking cocoa, baking soda, salt and cinnamon and mix well. Spoon into a 10x15-inch baking pan. Sprinkle with the chocolate chips, pecans and 2 tablespoons sugar. Bake at 350 degrees for 30 minutes. Let stand until cool. Cut into bars.

Yield: 48 servings.

Approx Per Serving: Cal 99; T Fat 4 g; 36% Calories from Fat; Prot 1 g; Carbo 16 g; Fiber 1 g; Chol 9 mg; Sod 65 mg

Sandra K. Stockall, Hershey

ZUCCHINI BROWNIES

- $1^1/_2$ cups sugar
- $^1/_2$ cup margarine, softened
- 2 eggs
- 2 cups flour
- 2 tablespoons baking cocoa
- 1 teaspoon baking soda
- $^1/_2$ teaspoon cinnamon
- 2 cups grated zucchini
- 1 cup chocolate chips
- 2 teaspoons sugar

Beat $1^1/_2$ cups sugar, margarine and eggs in a mixer bowl until creamy, scraping the bowl occasionally. Add the flour, baking cocoa, baking soda and cinnamon and mix well. Stir in the zucchini. Add the chocolate chips, stirring until mixed. Spoon into a greased and floured 9x13-inch baking pan. Sprinkle with 2 teaspoons sugar. Bake at 350 degrees for 45 minutes. Let stand until cool. Cut into bars.

Yield: 36 servings.

Approx Per Serving: Cal 110; T Fat 4 g; 34% Calories from Fat; Prot 2 g; Carbo 18 g; Fiber 1 g; Chol 12 mg; Sod 57 mg

Dorothy Bremer, Lexington

CHOCOLATE CHEESE LAYER BARS

- $^1/_2$ cup butter, softened
- 1 ounce unsweetened chocolate, melted
- 1 cup sugar
- 2 eggs
- 1 teaspoon vanilla extract
- 1 cup flour
- 1 teaspoon baking powder
- $^1/_2$ cup chopped walnuts
- 8 ounces cream cheese, softened
- $^1/_4$ cup butter, softened
- $^1/_2$ cup sugar
- 1 egg
- 2 tablespoons flour
- $^1/_2$ teaspoon vanilla extract
- $^1/_4$ cup chopped walnuts
- 1 cup chocolate chips
- 3 cups miniature marshmallows
- $^1/_4$ cup butter
- 1 ounce unsweetened chocolate
- 2 tablespoons milk
- 3 cups confectioners' sugar
- 1 teaspoon vanilla extract

Beat $^1/_2$ cup butter, 1 ounce unsweetened chocolate, 1 cup sugar, 2 eggs, 1 teaspoon vanilla, 1 cup flour and baking powder in the order listed in a mixer bowl until blended. Stir in $^1/_2$ cup walnuts. Spoon into a greased 9x13-inch baking pan. Reserve 2 ounces of the cream cheese. Beat the remaining cream cheese, $^1/_4$ cup butter, $^1/_2$ cup sugar, 1 egg, 2 tablespoons flour and $^1/_2$ teaspoon vanilla in a mixer bowl until smooth. Stir in $^1/_4$ cup walnuts. Spread over the prepared layer; sprinkle with the chocolate chips. Bake at 350 degrees for 20 to 25 minutes or until the edges pull from the sides of the pan. Sprinkle with the marshmallows. Bake for 2 minutes longer. Remove from the oven; swirl marshmallows with a knife. Let stand until cool. Combine the reserved cream cheese, $^1/_4$ cup butter, 1 ounce unsweetened chocolate and milk in a saucepan. Cook over low heat until blended, stirring constantly. Remove from heat. Add the confectioners' sugar and 1 teaspoon vanilla, beating until of spreading consistency. Swirl the frosting over the baked layer. Cut into $1^1/_2$-inch bars. Refrigerate until serving time.

Yield: 54 servings.

Approx Per Serving: Cal 146; T Fat 8 g; 46% Calories from Fat; Prot 2 g; Carbo 19 g; Fiber 1 g; Chol 26 mg; Sod 59 mg

Edee Lindstrom, Holdrege

DOUBLE CHOCOLATE CRUMBLE BARS

- 3/4 cup sugar
- 1/2 cup butter, softened
- 2 eggs
- 1 teaspoon vanilla extract
- 3/4 cup flour
- 1/2 cup chopped pecans
- 2 tablespoons baking cocoa
- 1/4 teaspoon baking powder
- 1/4 teaspoon salt
- 2 cups miniature marshmallows
- 1 cup semisweet chocolate chips
- 1 cup creamy peanut butter
- 1 1/2 cups crisp rice cereal

Beat the sugar and butter in a mixer bowl until creamy. Add the eggs and vanilla, beating until blended. Stir in a mixture of the flour, pecans, baking cocoa, baking powder and salt. Spread in a greased 9x13-inch baking pan. Bake at 350 degrees for 15 to 20 minutes or until the edges pull from the sides of the pan. Sprinkle the baked layer with the marshmallows. Bake for 3 minutes longer. Let stand until cool. Combine the chocolate chips and peanut butter in a saucepan. Cook over low heat until blended, stirring constantly. Stir in the cereal. Spread over the baked layer. Chill until set. Cut into bars. Refrigerate until serving time.

Yield: 36 servings.

Approx Per Serving: Cal 141; T Fat 9 g; 54% Calories from Fat; Prot 3 g; Carbo 14 g; Fiber 1 g; Chol 19 mg; Sod 96 mg

Alicia Janzen, Beatrice

CHOCOLATE FILLING BARS

- 2 cups semisweet chocolate chips
- 1 (14-ounce) can sweetened condensed milk
- 2 tablespoons margarine
- 1/2 teaspoon salt
- 2 teaspoons vanilla extract
- 2 cups packed brown sugar
- 1 cup margarine, softened
- 2 eggs
- 2 teaspoons vanilla extract
- 2 1/2 cups flour
- 1 teaspoon baking soda
- 1 teaspoon salt
- 3 cups rolled oats
- 1 cup chopped pecans

Combine the chocolate chips, condensed milk, 2 tablespoons margarine and 1/2 teaspoon salt in a double boiler. Cook over hot water until smooth, stirring frequently. Remove from heat. Stir in 2 teaspoons vanilla. Cream the brown sugar, 1 cup margarine, eggs and 2 teaspoons vanilla in a mixer bowl until light and fluffy. Add a sifted mixture of the flour, baking soda and 1 teaspoon salt. Stir in the oats. Add the pecans and mix well. Spread 2/3 of the dough in a greased 10x15-inch baking pan; spread with the chocolate mixture. Dot with the remaining dough. Bake at 350 degrees for 20 to 25 minutes or until light brown. Cut into bars. Let stand until cool.

Yield: 72 servings.

Approx Per Serving: Cal 127; T Fat 6 g; 43% Calories from Fat; Prot 2 g; Carbo 17 g; Fiber 1 g; Chol 8 mg; Sod 101 mg

Kelsey Watkins, Benkelman

"M & M'S" BARS

2 cups quick-cooking oats
$1^1/_2$ cups flour
1 cup packed brown sugar
1 teaspoon baking soda
$^3/_4$ teaspoon salt
1 cup melted margarine
1 (14-ounce) can sweetened condensed milk
$^1/_3$ cup peanut butter
1 cup "M & M's" Chocolate Candies

Combine the oats, flour, brown sugar, baking soda and salt in a bowl and mix well. Add the margarine, stirring until crumbly. Reserve $1^1/_2$ cups of the crumb mixture. Press the remaining crumb mixture over the bottom of a 10x15-inch baking pan. Bake at 350 degrees for 10 to 12 minutes or until light brown. Spread a mixture of the condensed milk and peanut butter over the baked layer. Top with a mixture of the reserved oat mixture and the "M & M's" Chocolate Candies. Bake for 15 to 20 minutes longer or until brown. Let stand until cool. Cut into bars.

Yield: 48 servings.

Approx Per Serving: Cal 131; T Fat 7 g; 44% Calories from Fat; Prot 2 g; Carbo 17 g; Fiber 1 g; Chol 3 mg; Sod 120 mg

Sherry Steele, Hickman

ORANGE BARS

1 (6-ounce) can frozen orange juice concentrate
3 cups slivered pecans
1 (1-pound) package confectioners' sugar
$^1/_2$ cup margarine, softened
1 (1-pound) package vanilla wafers, crushed
$1^1/_2$ cups chopped orange-flavor prunes

Thaw the orange juice concentrate in the refrigerator overnight. Sprinkle $^1/_2$ of the pecans in the bottom of a 9x13-inch baking pan. Combine the orange juice concentrate, confectioners' sugar and margarine in a mixer bowl. Beat until blended. Stir in the vanilla wafer crumbs and prunes. Spread over the pecans. Sprinkle with the remaining pecans; press into the mixture. Refrigerate for several hours. Cut into bars. Serve cold. May shape mixture into 1-inch balls and roll in chopped pecans.

Yield: 36 servings.

Approx Per Serving: Cal 216; T Fat 11 g; 45% Calories from Fat; Prot 2 g; Carbo 29 g; Fiber 1 g; Chol 7 mg; Sod 71 mg

Rebecca Meyer, Beatrice

SALTED PEANUT CHEWS

$1\frac{1}{2}$ cups flour
$\frac{2}{3}$ cup packed brown sugar
$\frac{1}{2}$ teaspoon salt
$\frac{1}{4}$ teaspoon baking soda
$\frac{1}{2}$ cup margarine, softened
2 egg yolks, beaten
1 teaspoon vanilla extract
2 cups peanut butter chips
$\frac{2}{3}$ cup corn syrup
$\frac{1}{4}$ cup margarine
2 teaspoons vanilla extract
2 cups crisp rice cereal
2 cups salted peanuts
3 cups miniature marshmallows

Combine the flour, brown sugar, salt and baking soda in a bowl and mix well. Stir in the $\frac{1}{2}$ cup margarine, egg yolks and 1 teaspoon vanilla. Press over the bottom of a lightly greased 9x13-inch baking pan. Bake at 350 degrees for 12 to 15 minutes or until light brown. Combine the peanut butter chips, corn syrup and $\frac{1}{4}$ cup margarine in a saucepan while the crust is baking. Cook until blended, stirring frequently. Stir in 2 teaspoons vanilla. Add the cereal and peanuts and mix well. Sprinkle the baked layer with the marshmallows. Bake for 2 to 3 minutes longer or until the marshmallows soften. Spread the peanut mixture over the hot baked layers. Let stand until cool. Cut into bars.

I make these to take to rodeos and fair events.

Yield: 36 servings.

Approx Per Serving: Cal 199; T Fat 11 g; 48% Calories from Fat; Prot 5 g; Carbo 22 g; Fiber 1 g; Chol 12 mg; Sod 168 mg

Mrs. Tim Wills, Hemingford

HARVEST PUMPKIN BARS

2 cups flour
2 cups sugar
1 tablespoon pumpkin pie spice
2 teaspoons cinnamon
2 teaspoons baking powder
1 teaspoon baking soda
$\frac{1}{2}$ teaspoon salt
1 (16-ounce) can pumpkin
$\frac{3}{4}$ cup vegetable oil
4 eggs, beaten
3 ounces cream cheese, softened
6 tablespoons margarine, softened
1 teaspoon milk
1 teaspoon vanilla extract
2 cups confectioners' sugar

Combine the flour, sugar, pumpkin pie spice, cinnamon, baking powder, baking soda and salt in a bowl and mix well. Stir in the pumpkin, oil and eggs. Spread in a greased 10x15-inch baking pan. Bake at 350 degrees for 20 to 25 minutes or until the edges pull from sides of pan. Let stand until cool. Beat the cream cheese, margarine, milk and vanilla in a mixer bowl until smooth. Add the confectioners' sugar, beating until of spreading consistency. Spread over the baked layer. Refrigerate until serving time. Cut into bars. May freeze for future use.

Yield: 48 servings.

Approx Per Serving: Cal 130; T Fat 6 g; 41% Calories from Fat; Prot 1 g; Carbo 18 g; Fiber <1 g; Chol 20 mg; Sod 81 mg

Jane Qualm, Ericson

RAISIN CREAM BARS

$1^3/_4$ cups rolled oats
$1^3/_4$ cups flour
1 cup packed brown sugar
1 teaspoon baking soda
1 cup margarine, softened
1 cup raisins
$^1/_2$ cup water
$^1/_4$ teaspoon salt
2 cups sour cream
$1^1/_2$ cups sugar
4 egg yolks, beaten
3 tablespoons cornstarch

Combine the oats, flour, brown sugar and baking soda in a bowl and mix well. Add the margarine, stirring until crumbly. Reserve $^1/_3$ of the crumb mixture. Press the remaining crumb mixture over the bottom of a 9x13-inch baking pan. Bake at 350 degrees for 15 minutes. Combine the raisins, water and salt in a saucepan. Cook over low heat for 5 minutes. Stir in a mixture of the sour cream, sugar, egg yolks and cornstarch. Cook until thickened, stirring constantly. Spread over the baked layer; sprinkle with the reserved crumb mixture. Bake until brown. Refrigerate until serving time. Cut into bars.

Yield: 36 servings.

Approx Per Serving: Cal 184; T Fat 9 g; 41% Calories from Fat; Prot 2 g; Carbo 25 g; Fiber 1 g; Chol 29 mg; Sod 108 mg

Sue Finke, Cozad

S'MORES COOKIE BARS

$^3/_4$ cup sugar
$^1/_2$ cup margarine, softened
1 egg
$^1/_2$ teaspoon vanilla extract
$1^1/_3$ cups flour
$^3/_4$ cup graham cracker crumbs
1 teaspoon baking powder
$^1/_4$ teaspoon salt
1 cup milk chocolate chips
1 cup marshmallow creme

Beat the sugar and margarine in a mixer bowl until light and fluffy. Add the egg and vanilla, beating until smooth. Stir in a mixture of the flour, graham cracker crumbs, baking powder and salt. Spread $^1/_2$ of the dough in a greased 8x8-inch baking pan. Sprinkle with the chocolate chips; spread with the marshmallow creme. Drop bits of the remaining dough over the top; spread carefully. Bake at 350 degrees for 30 minutes. Let stand until cool. Cut into bars.

This recipe won a purple ribbon and a Best of Junior Foods trophy at the Sioux County Fair in 1995.

Yield: 25 servings.

Approx Per Serving: Cal 172; T Fat 6 g; 33% Calories from Fat; Prot 2 g; Carbo 28 g; Fiber <1 g; Chol 10 mg; Sod 116 mg

Brian Rapier, Harrison

ALMOND BISCOTTI

1 tablespoon butter
1 cup sugar
1/2 cup butter or margarine, softened
3 eggs
1 teaspoon vanilla extract or anise flavoring
2 cups flour
2 teaspoons baking powder
1/8 teaspoon salt
1/2 cup chopped almonds
1/4 cup sugar

Line the bottom of a 9x13-inch baking pan with foil; spread 1 tablespoon butter over the foil. Beat 1 cup sugar and 1/2 cup butter in a mixer bowl until creamy. Beat in the eggs 1 at a time. Stir in the vanilla. Stir in a mixture of the flour, baking powder and salt. Add the almonds and mix well. Pat the dough into two 3x12-inch rectangles on the foil; sprinkle with 1/4 cup sugar. Bake at 375 degrees for 15 to 20 minutes or until brown and firm. Remove from the oven; reduce the oven temperature to 300 degrees. Cool on a wire rack for 15 minutes. Cut each rectangle diagonally into 1/2-inch slices. Place cut side down on an ungreased baking sheet. Bake for 10 minutes on each side. Turn off the oven. Let stand with the oven door ajar until cool. Store in airtight containers.

Yield: 42 servings.

Approx Per Serving: Cal 81; T Fat 4 g; 40% Calories from Fat; Prot 1 g; Carbo 11 g; Fiber <1 g; Chol 22 mg; Sod 52 mg

Ashley Bergt, Norfolk

CHERRY COCONUT BALLS

1 cup sugar
3/4 cup margarine, softened
1 egg
1 teaspoon vanilla extract
2 cups sifted flour
1/2 teaspoon baking powder
1/2 teaspoon salt
1/2 cup chopped maraschino cherries
1/2 cup grated coconut
1/2 cup chopped pecans
1 1/2 cups sifted confectioners' sugar
2 tablespoons maraschino cherry juice
1/4 teaspoon salt

Beat the sugar and margarine in a mixer bowl until creamy. Add the egg and vanilla, beating until smooth. Add a sifted mixture of the flour, baking powder and 1/2 teaspoon salt and mix well. Stir in the maraschino cherries, coconut and pecans. Drop by teaspoonfuls onto a lightly greased cookie sheet. Bake at 375 degrees for 10 minutes or until brown. Remove to a wire rack to cool. Spread each cookie with a mixture of the confectioners' sugar, maraschino cherry juice and 1/4 teaspoon salt. May omit the pecans.

Yield: 48 servings.

Approx Per Serving: Cal 88; T Fat 4 g; 42% Calories from Fat; Prot 1 g; Carbo 12 g; Fiber <1 g; Chol 4 mg; Sod 72 mg

JoLynn Funk, Grand Island

WHITE CHOCOLATE BROWNIE DROPS

- 1/2 cup butter-flavor shortening
- 1/2 cup sugar
- 2 eggs
- 1 teaspoon vanilla extract
- 1 cup semisweet chocolate chips, melted
- 1 cup rolled oats
- 3/4 cup flour
- 1 teaspoon baking powder
- 1/2 cup chopped white chocolate

Beat the shortening, sugar, eggs and vanilla in a mixer bowl until smooth. Add the chocolate and mix well. Stir in a mixture of the oats, flour and baking powder. Add the white chocolate and mix well. Drop by rounded teaspoonfuls onto an ungreased cookie sheet. Bake at 350 degrees for 7 to 9 minutes or until the cookies are almost set; centers should be moist. Cool on cookie sheet for 2 minutes. Remove to a wire rack to cool completely. May substitute vanilla milk chips for the white chocolate.

Yield: 36 servings.

Approx Per Serving: Cal 93; T Fat 5 g; 50% Calories from Fat; Prot 1 g; Carbo 11 g; Fiber 1 g; Chol 12 mg; Sod 15 mg

Jerryl Rowse, Burwell

CHOCOLATE THUMBPRINT COOKIES

- 2/3 cup sugar
- 1/2 cup butter or margarine, softened
- 1 egg yolk
- 2 tablespoons milk
- 1 teaspoon vanilla extract
- 1 cup flour
- 1/3 cup baking cocoa
- 1/4 teaspoon salt
- 1 egg white, beaten
- 1 cup chopped pecans
- 1/2 cup confectioners' sugar
- 1 tablespoon butter or margarine, softened
- 2 teaspoons milk
- 1/4 teaspoon vanilla extract
- 24 chocolate candy kisses

Beat the sugar, 1/2 cup butter, egg yolk, 2 tablespoons milk and 1 teaspoon vanilla in a mixer bowl until creamy. Stir in a mixture of the flour, baking cocoa and salt. Chill for 1 hour or until the dough is firm and can be easily handled. Shape into 1-inch balls. Dip in the egg white; roll in the pecans. Place the balls on a lightly greased cookie sheet. Make an indention in the center of each ball with the thumb. Bake at 350 degrees for 10 to 12 minutes or until brown. Beat the confectioners' sugar, 1 tablespoon butter, 2 teaspoons milk and 1/4 teaspoon vanilla in a mixer bowl until smooth. Spoon 1/4 teaspoon into each thumbprint indention. Press a candy kiss gently into the center of each cookie. Remove to a wire rack to cool. May substitute pecan halves or candied cherry halves for the chocolate kisses.

I used this recipe in a 4-H demo-talk entitled "Affectionate Kisses."

Yield: 24 servings.

Approx Per Serving: Cal 153; T Fat 10 g; 54% Calories from Fat; Prot 2 g; Carbo 16 g; Fiber 1 g; Chol 22 mg; Sod 74 mg

Jessica Lauby, Lexington

SOUR CREAM SUGAR COOKIES

2 cups sugar
1 cup sour cream
1 cup butter, softened
2 eggs
2 teaspoons vanilla extract
1 teaspoon baking soda
4 cups flour
1 teaspoon baking powder
1/8 teaspoon salt

Combine the sugar, sour cream, butter, eggs, vanilla and baking soda in a bowl and mix well. Stir in the flour, baking powder and salt. Refrigerate, covered, overnight. Roll dough 1/4 inch thick on a floured surface; cut with cookie cutter. Place on ungreased cookie sheet. Bake at 400 degrees for 5 to 7 minutes or until light brown. Remove to a wire rack to cool. May spread cookies with your favorite frosting.

These cookies melt in your mouth.

Yield: 36 servings.

Approx Per Serving: Cal 157; T Fat 7 g; 39% Calories from Fat; Prot 2 g; Carbo 22 g; Fiber <1 g; Chol 28 mg; Sod 99 mg

Brett Esau, Beatrice

WHOLE WHEAT HOLIDAY COOKIES

1 cup sugar
1/2 cup margarine, softened
3 tablespoons milk
1 egg
1 tablespoon grated lemon or orange peel
1 teaspoon vanilla extract
1 teaspoon baking powder
1/2 teaspoon baking soda
1/2 teaspoon salt
1/2 teaspoon nutmeg
2 cups whole wheat flour
2 tablespoons sugar
1/2 teaspoon cinnamon

Combine 1 cup sugar, margarine, milk, egg, lemon peel, vanilla, baking powder, baking soda, salt and nutmeg in a mixer bowl and mix well. Add the whole wheat flour gradually, beating until blended. Chill, covered, for 1 hour. Roll the dough 1/8 inch thick on a lightly floured surface; cut with a floured cookie cutter. Place 2 inches apart on an ungreased cookie sheet. Sprinkle with a mixture of 2 tablespoons sugar and cinnamon. Bake at 375 degrees for 8 to 10 minutes or until light brown. Cool on a cookie sheet for 1 minute. Remove to a wire rack to cool completely. Store in an airtight container.

The whole wheat flour improves the cookies nutritionally and the citrus peel give them a special flavor.

Yield: 36 servings.

Approx Per Serving: Cal 72; T Fat 3 g; 34% Calories from Fat; Prot 1 g; Carbo 11 g; Fiber 1 g; Chol 6 mg; Sod 83 mg

Linda Buethe, Tecumseh

APPLE PIE

- 1/2 teaspoon salt
- 1 1/2 cups flour
- 1/2 cup shortening
- 1/4 cup (or less) ice water
- 2 tablespoons orange juice
- 1/3 cup packed brown sugar
- 1/3 cup sugar
- 1 teaspoon cinnamon
- 3 tablespoons flour
- 1/4 teaspoon salt
- 6 cups sliced peeled Granny Smith or Jonathan apples
- 2 tablespoons butter
- 1 tablespoon milk
- 1 teaspoon sugar

Mix 1/2 teaspoon salt and 1 1/2 cups flour in a bowl. Cut in the shortening until crumbly. Add enough ice water 1 tablespoon at a time to form a soft dough. Roll dough into 2 thin circles on a floured surface. Line a 9-inch pie plate with 1 circle, trimming to fit. Mix the orange juice, brown sugar, 1/3 cup sugar, cinnamon, 3 tablespoons flour and 1/4 teaspoon salt in a large bowl. Add apples, tossing to coat. Spoon into pastry-lined pie plate; dot with the butter. Top with remaining pastry, fluting edge and cutting vents. Brush with milk; sprinkle with 1 teaspoon sugar. Bake, covered with foil, at 400 degrees for 40 minutes. Bake, uncovered, for 10 to 20 minutes longer or until golden brown. Store in refrigerator.

This recipe came from a cookbook my aunt gave me called "For Boys Only." My grandma taught me how to make a thin flaky crust.

Yield: 8 servings.

Approx Per Serving: Cal 347; T Fat 16 g; 41% Calories from Fat; Prot 3 g; Carbo 49 g; Fiber 2 g; Chol 8 mg; Sod 234 mg

Patrick Anderson, Omaha

CHERRY RASPBERRY PIE

- 1 (16-ounce) can pitted red cherries
- 1 (10-ounce) package frozen raspberries
- 3/4 cup sugar
- 3 tablespoons cornstarch
- 3 tablespoons butter or margarine
- 1/4 teaspoon almond extract
- 1/4 teaspoon red food coloring
- 1 recipe (2-crust) pie pastry

Drain cherries and raspberries, reserving 1 1/4 cups juice. Combine the sugar and cornstarch in a saucepan. Stir in the reserved juice, mixing well. Bring to a boil over medium heat, stirring constantly. Remove from heat. Stir in the butter, almond extract and food coloring. Fold in the cherries and raspberries. Line a 9-inch pie plate with 1 pie pastry. Add filling. Top with remaining pastry, sealing edge and cutting vents. Bake at 375 degrees for 45 minutes. Refrigerate.

My grandmother found this recipe in a magazine. It was from a lady who had won $100,000 with it in a recipe contest. Now it is our family favorite.

Yield: 8 servings.

Approx Per Serving: Cal 416; T Fat 18 g; 39% Calories from Fat; Prot 3 g; Carbo 62 g; Fiber 3 g; Chol 12 mg; Sod 263 mg

Anthony Kulhanek, Broken Bow

RED HOT CHERRY PIE

$1^1/_2$ cups flour
$^1/_2$ teaspoon salt
$^1/_2$ cup shortening
1 egg
1 teaspoon vinegar
$2^1/_2$ tablespoons water
1 (16-ounce) can cherry pie filling
$^1/_2$ cup red hot cinnamon candies
$^1/_3$ cup coconut
1 teaspoon sugar

Combine the flour and salt in a bowl. Cut in the shortening until crumbly. Mix the egg, vinegar and water in a small bowl. Pour into the flour mixture; mix well. Divide into 2 portions. Shape each portion into a ball. Roll out very thin between sheets of waxed paper. Line a 9-inch pie plate with 1 portion of the pastry. Layer pie filling, candies and coconut in prepared pie plate. Top with remaining pastry, sealing edge and cutting vents. Sprinkle with sugar. Bake at 400 degrees for 15 minutes. Reduce oven temperature to 350 degrees. Bake for 30 minutes longer or until golden brown. May use a purchased 2-crust pie pastry.

This recipe was developed by my mom, a Home Economist. This recipe won a purple ribbon for me in the pie competition at the Dawes County Fair.

Yield: 8 servings.

Approx Per Serving: Cal 353; T Fat 15 g; 38% Calories from Fat; Prot 4 g; Carbo 51 g; Fiber 1 g; Chol 27 mg; Sod 174 mg

Angie Hawthorne, Chadron

MUD PIE

1 cup sugar
$^1/_2$ cup melted margarine
1 teaspoon vanilla extract
$^1/_4$ teaspoon salt
2 eggs
$^1/_3$ cup flour
$^1/_3$ cup baking cocoa
1 cup chopped pecans
$^1/_4$ cup fudge sauce
2 tablespoons confectioners' sugar
4 ounces whipped topping

Combine the sugar, margarine, vanilla, salt and eggs in a mixer bowl; beat well. Add the flour and cocoa; mix well. Stir in the pecans. Spoon into a greased 8-inch pie plate. Bake at 325 degrees for 25 minutes or until the pie tests done. Pierce holes in the top of pie with a wooden pick. Spread fudge sauce over top. Cool in refrigerator. Fold the confectioners' sugar into the whipped topping in a bowl. Spread over cool pie. May drizzle top with additional fudge sauce if desired. Store pie in the refrigerator.

This prize winning dessert is a chocolate lover's favorite.

Yield: 8 servings.

Approx Per Serving: Cal 433; T Fat 28 g; 56% Calories from Fat; Prot 5 g; Carbo 45 g; Fiber 2 g; Chol 54 mg; Sod 235 mg

Joe Valasek, Comstock

FUDGE BROWNIE PIE

2 eggs
1 cup sugar
1/2 cup melted butter or margarine
1/2 cup flour
1/3 cup baking cocoa
1/4 teaspoon salt
1 teaspoon vanilla extract
1/2 cup chopped pecans
1 quart vanilla ice cream
Hot Fudge Sauce

Beat the eggs in a mixer bowl. Add the sugar and melted butter; beat well. Mix the flour, cocoa and salt together. Add to the egg mixture; mix well. Stir in the vanilla and pecans. Spoon into a lightly greased 8-inch pie plate. Bake at 350 degrees for 25 to 30 minutes or until almost set. Pie will not test done in the center. Cool slightly and refrigerate until serving time. Cut into wedges. Spoon ice cream on top and drizzle with the Hot Fudge Sauce.

HOT FUDGE SAUCE

3/4 cup sugar
1/2 cup baking cocoa
1 (5-ounce) can evaporated milk
1/3 cup light corn syrup
1/3 cup butter or margarine
1 teaspoon vanilla extract

Combine the sugar and cocoa in a small saucepan. Stir in the evaporated milk and corn syrup. Bring to a boil over medium heat, stirring constantly. Boil for 1 minute, stirring constantly. Remove from heat. Stir in the butter and vanilla. Serve warm.

A very rich dessert for any chocolate lover.

Yield: 6 servings.

Approx Per Serving: Cal 868; T Fat 47 g; 46% Calories from Fat; Prot 11 g; Carbo 112 g; Fiber 5 g; Chol 185 mg; Sod 491 mg

Jessica Lauby, Lexington

OATMEAL PIE

3 eggs
2/3 cup sugar
1 cup packed brown sugar
2 tablespoons melted butter
2/3 cup rolled oats
2/3 cup coconut
1/2 cup chopped walnuts
1 teaspoon vanilla extract
1 unbaked (9-inch) pie shell

Beat the eggs in a mixer bowl. Add the sugar, brown sugar and melted butter; beat well. Stir in the oats, coconut, walnuts and vanilla. Spoon into the unbaked pie shell. Bake at 350 degrees for 30 minutes. May top with whipped topping or vanilla ice cream.

This recipe was submitted in memory of Mary Kienke.

Yield: 6 servings.

Approx Per Serving: Cal 566; T Fat 26 g; 41% Calories from Fat; Prot 8 g; Carbo 77 g; Fiber 3 g; Chol 116 mg; Sod 248 mg

Pam Munk, Springview

FRESH PEACH PIE

- $1^1/_2$ cups flour
- $1^1/_2$ teaspoons sugar
- 1 teaspoon salt
- $^1/_2$ cup vegetable oil
- 2 tablespoons milk
- $^3/_4$ cup sugar
- 2 tablespoons cornstarch
- 1 cup water
- 2 tablespoons orange or peach gelatin
- 3 cups sliced fresh peaches

Combine the flour, $1^1/_2$ teaspoons sugar and salt in a bowl; mix well. Add the oil; mix well. Add the milk; mix well. Press pastry into a 9-inch pie plate; flute the edge. Bake at 400 degrees for 25 minutes or until brown. Cool to room temperature. Combine $^3/_4$ cup sugar, cornstarch and water in a saucepan; mix well. Cook over medium heat until clear, stirring constantly. Stir in the gelatin. Cool slightly. Spoon the peaches into the cooled crust. Pour the cooled gelatin filling over peaches. Chill in the refrigerator.

Yield: 6 servings.

Approx Per Serving: Cal 433; T Fat 19 g; 38% Calories from Fat; Prot 6 g; Carbo 62 g; Fiber 2 g; Chol <1 mg; Sod 363 mg

Eileen Krumbach, Shelby

PECAN PIE

- $1^1/_4$ cups flour
- $^1/_4$ teaspoon salt
- $^1/_3$ cup shortening
- 3 to 4 tablespoons cold water
- 3 eggs
- 1 cup corn syrup
- $^2/_3$ cup sugar
- $^1/_3$ cup melted margarine or butter
- 1 teaspoon vanilla extract
- $1^1/_4$ cups pecan halves

Combine the flour and salt in a bowl. Cut in the shortening until the mixture is crumbly. Add cold water 1 tablespoon at a time, tossing gently to moisten flour. Shape the dough into a ball. Roll into a 12-inch circle on a lightly floured surface. Fit into a 9-inch pie plate. Trim to $^1/_2$ inch beyond edge of pie plate. Fold under extra pastry; flute edge. Beat the eggs in a mixer bowl. Add corn syrup, sugar, margarine and vanilla; mix well. Stir in pecan halves. Spoon into prepared pie plate. Cover edge of pastry with foil. Bake at 350 degrees for 25 minutes. Remove the foil. Bake for 20 to 25 minutes longer or until a knife inserted comes out clean. Cool on a wire rack. Store, covered, in refrigerator.

Yield: 8 servings.

Approx Per Serving: Cal 535; T Fat 30 g; 48% Calories from Fat; Prot 6 g; Carbo 66 g; Fiber 2 g; Chol 80 mg; Sod 230 mg

Evelyn Fox, Elwood
Christie Mall, Franklin

CHARLIE'S SOUR CREAM PINEAPPLE PIE

1 cup sour cream
1 cup undrained crushed pineapple
3 egg yolks
1/4 cup flour
1 cup sugar
1 teaspoon vanilla extract
1 baked (9-inch) pie shell
3 egg whites
1/4 teaspoon cream of tartar
1/4 cup sugar

Combine the sour cream, pineapple and egg yolks in a saucepan; mix well. Bring to a boil over medium heat, stirring frequently. Add a mixture of flour and 1 cup sugar; mix well. Cook until thickened, stirring constantly. Stir in vanilla. Spoon into the baked pie shell. Beat eggs whites and cream of tartar in a mixer bowl until soft peaks form. Add 1/4 cup sugar gradually, beating until stiff peaks form. Spoon over pie, sealing to edge. Bake at 325 degrees for 10 minutes or until brown.

This recipe was given to me by a fellow named Charlie (of course) and he asked me to make it for him. He said it was as good as his mother's was. One piece and you can't leave it alone.

Yield: 8 servings.

Approx Per Serving: Cal 369; T Fat 16 g; 38% Calories from Fat; Prot 5 g; Carbo 53 g; Fiber 1 g; Chol 92 mg; Sod 161 mg

Barbara Nilson, Springview

SOUR CREAM RAISIN PIE

1 cup sugar
1 cup sour cream
2 eggs, beaten
1 teaspoon vanilla extract
1/8 teaspoon salt
1 cup raisins
1/2 cup walnuts, chopped or crushed
1 unbaked (9-inch) pie shell

Combine the sugar, sour cream, eggs, vanilla and salt in a mixer bowl; beat well. Stir in the raisins and walnuts. Spoon into the unbaked pie shell. Bake at 300 degrees for 1 hour. Store in refrigerator.

Yield: 8 servings.

Approx Per Serving: Cal 406; T Fat 20 g; 43% Calories from Fat; Prot 6 g; Carbo 55 g; Fiber 2 g; Chol 66 mg; Sod 190 mg

Linda Stoner, McCook

SWEET POTATO PIE

3 eggs
2 cups mashed cooked sweet potatoes
3/4 cup sugar
1/2 teaspoon salt
1 teaspoon cinnamon
1/2 teaspoon nutmeg
1 (8-ounce) can evaporated milk
1/4 cup melted butter
1 unbaked (9-inch) pie shell

Beat the eggs lightly in a bowl. Add the sweet potatoes and sugar; mix well. Add the salt, cinnamon and nutmeg; mix well. Stir in the evaporated milk and melted butter. Spoon into the unbaked pie shell. Bake at 350 degrees for 35 minutes or until a knife inserted in center comes out clean. Refrigerate. Serve with whipped cream.

Yield: 6 servings.

Approx Per Serving: Cal 479; T Fat 24 g; 44% Calories from Fat; Prot 9 g; Carbo 59 g; Fiber 3 g; Chol 138 mg; Sod 497 mg

Jessica Bickford, Omaha

BAVARIAN APPLE CHEESECAKE

1/3 cup sugar
1/3 cup margarine or butter
1 tablespoon shortening
1/4 teaspoon vanilla extract
1 cup flour
1/8 teaspoon salt
4 cups sliced peeled Granny Smith apples
16 ounces cream cheese, softened
1/2 cup sugar
1/2 teaspoon vanilla extract
2 eggs
1/3 cup sugar
1 teaspoon ground cinnamon

Combine 1/3 cup sugar, margarine, shortening and 1/4 teaspoon vanilla in a mixer bowl. Beat at medium speed until mixed. Add the flour and salt, mixing until crumbly. Pat into a 9-inch springform pan and set aside. Arrange the apples in a single layer in a shallow baking pan. Bake, covered with foil, at 400 degrees for 15 minutes. Beat the cream cheese, 1/2 cup sugar and 1/2 teaspoon vanilla in a mixer bowl until light and fluffy. Add the eggs, beating at low speed just until mixed. Pour into the prepared springform pan. Arrange the warm apples over the cream cheese mixture. Sprinkle with a mixture of 1/3 cup sugar and cinnamon. Bake at 400 degrees for 40 minutes. Cool in the pan. Remove the sides of the pan and place the cheesecake on a serving plate. Chill, covered, for 4 to 24 hours. May sprinkle with 1/4 cup sliced almonds before baking.

I used this as a snack at some of our 4-H meetings. It's a family favorite.

Yield: 12 servings.

Approx Per Serving: Cal 333; T Fat 20 g; 54% Calories from Fat; Prot 5 g; Carbo 34 g; Fiber 1 g; Chol 77 mg; Sod 204 mg

Jessica Lauby, Lexington

MINI CHOCOLATE CHIP CHEESECAKES

1 1/3 cups graham cracker crumbs
1/3 cup sugar
1/4 cup baking cocoa
1/3 cup melted butter
24 ounces cream cheese
1 (14-ounce) can sweetened condensed milk
1 cup melted miniature semisweet chocolate chips
3 eggs
2 teaspoons vanilla extract
1 cup miniature semisweet chocolate chips

Mix the crumbs, sugar, cocoa and butter in a bowl. Use the bottom of a small glass to press equal portions of the crumb mixture into 30 paper-lined muffin cups. Beat the softened cream cheese in a mixer bowl until fluffy. Beat in the condensed milk and melted chocolate gradually. Add the eggs and vanilla and mix well. Spoon into the muffin cups. Top with 1 cup chocolate chips. Bake at 300 degrees for 20 minutes. Let stand until cool. Refrigerate until serving time; refrigerate any leftovers. May spray the muffin cups with nonstick cooking spray; but freeze the cooled cheesecakes for 15 minutes before removing from the muffin cups with a narrow spatula.

These are very rich but very good!

Yield: 30 servings.

Approx Per Serving: Cal 265; T Fat 17 g; 55% Calories from Fat; Prot 5 g; Carbo 25 g; Fiber 1 g; Chol 56 mg; Sod 143 mg

Barbara Ehlers, Leigh

LEAN AND LUSCIOUS CHEESECAKE

1 1/2 cups reduced-fat vanilla wafer crumbs
1 egg white
40 ounces fat-free cream cheese, softened
1 cup sugar
3 tablespoons flour
2 teaspoons grated lemon peel
2 teaspoons vanilla extract
5 eggs
1 egg yolk
1/4 cup evaporated skim milk

Press a mixture of the crumbs and egg white into a lightly greased 9-inch springform pan. Chill thoroughly. Combine the next 5 ingredients in a large mixer bowl. Beat at high speed until fluffy. Beat in the eggs and egg yolk 1 at a time. Beat in the evaporated milk. Pour into the prepared pan. Bake at 500 degrees for 10 minutes. Reduce the oven temperature to 250 degrees. Bake for 50 to 60 minutes or until cheesecake tests done. Cool on a wire rack. Chill for 8 hours to overnight or until firm. Remove the side of the pan. Cut the cheesecake into wedges. Refrigerate any leftovers.

This was the second place winner in the junior division at the 1995 State Fair 4-H Egg Preparation Demonstration Contest.

Yield: 12 servings.

Approx Per Serving: Cal 241; T Fat 4 g; 15% Calories from Fat; Prot 18 g; Carbo 31 g; Fiber <1 g; Chol 123 mg; Sod 652 mg

Erica Nisley, Smithfield

STRAWBERRY CHEESECAKE

1 (2-layer) package pudding-recipe yellow cake mix
1/3 cup margarine
3 eggs
3/4 cup sugar
2 teaspoons vanilla extract
16 ounces cream cheese, softened
2 cups sour cream
1/4 cup sugar
1 tablespoon vanilla extract
1 to 2 cups strawberries
1 tablespoon cornstarch
2 to 3 tablespoons water

Beat the cake mix, margarine and 1 egg at low speed in a mixer bowl until crumbly. Press lightly into an ungreased 9x13-inch baking pan. Beat 2 eggs, 3/4 cup sugar, 2 teaspoons vanilla and cream cheese in a mixer bowl until light and fluffy. Spread over the crumb mixture. Bake at 350 degrees for 20 to 25 minutes or until a knife inserted near the center comes out clean. Mix the sour cream, 1/4 cup sugar and 1 tablespoon vanilla in a bowl. Spread over the baked layer. Let stand until cool. Break the strawberries up with a pastry cutter. Combine a mixture of cornstarch and water with most of the strawberries in a microwave-safe bowl. Microwave on Medium for 1 to 2 minutes or until thickened. Stir in the remaining strawberries and spread over the top of the cheesecake. Chill thoroughly. May substitute cherry or blueberry pie filling for the strawberries.

Yield: 15 servings.

Approx Per Serving: Cal 430; T Fat 26 g; 53% Calories from Fat; Prot 6 g; Carbo 45 g; Fiber 1 g; Chol 89 mg; Sod 400 mg

Janice Mehl, North Platte

PEANUT BUTTER-APPLE DESSERT

1 1/2 cups graham cracker crumbs
1/2 cup packed brown sugar
1/2 cup peanut butter
1/4 cup melted margarine
1/3 cup peanut butter
3/4 cup confectioners' sugar
8 ounces cream cheese, softened
3/4 cup sugar
18 ounces whipped topping
2 (21-ounce) cans apple pie filling
1 teaspoon cinnamon

Mix the crumbs, brown sugar, 1/2 cup peanut butter and margarine in a bowl. Press into a 9x13-inch baking pan. Refrigerate until needed. Mix 1/3 cup peanut butter and confectioners' sugar in a bowl until crumbly. Beat the cream cheese in a mixer bowl until light and fluffy. Blend in the sugar and whipped topping. Layer half the cream cheese mixture and all the pie filling in prepared pan. Sprinkle with the cinnamon. Layer half the peanut butter mixture, remaining cream cheese mixture and remaining peanut butter mixture over the pie filling. Refrigerate until serving time.

Be ready to give out copies of this recipe!

Yield: 15 servings.

Approx Per Serving: Cal 475; T Fat 24 g; 45% Calories from Fat; Prot 6 g; Carbo 62 g; Fiber 2 g; Chol 17 mg; Sod 266 mg

Sherry Steele, Lincoln

BLINTZES WITH RASPBERRY SAUCE

- 1 (16-ounce) package frozen raspberries, thawed in refrigerator
- 2 tablespoons sugar
- 1 cup flour
- 1 cup skim milk
- 1/2 cup egg substitute
- 1 tablespoon melted margarine
- 16 ounces low-fat cottage cheese
- 3 tablespoons egg substitute
- 1/2 teaspoon sugar

Purée the raspberries in a securely covered blender; strain into a bowl. Stir in 2 tablespoons sugar and set aside. Blend the flour, skim milk, 1/2 cup egg substitute and margarine in a medium bowl. Let stand for 30 minutes. Heat a lightly greased 8-inch nonstick skillet or crepe pan over medium-high heat. Pour in a scant 1/4 cup batter, tilting the pan to allow the batter to cover the bottom. Cook for 1 to 2 minutes or until the edges begin to lightly brown. Turn crepe. Cook for 30 to 60 seconds longer or until light brown. Place on waxed paper. Stir the batter and repeat the process until 10 crepes are made. Mix the cottage cheese, 3 tablespoons egg substitute and 1/2 teaspoon sugar in a small bowl. Spread 2 tablespoons of the mixture down the center of each crepe. Fold the crepes into thirds by folding the top and bottom of each crepe to meet in the center, forming blintzes. Place the blintzes seam side down in a lightly greased nonstick skillet. Cook over medium heat for 4 minutes per side or until golden brown. Top with the raspberry sauce. Store leftovers in the refrigerator.

This recipe was my 1995 Favorite Foods entry for our Cuming County Contest.

Yield: 10 servings.

Approx Per Serving: Cal 176; T Fat 3 g; 14% Calories from Fat; Prot 11 g; Carbo 27 g; Fiber 2 g; Chol 4 mg; Sod 242 mg

Rachel Broekemeier, West Point

BERRY PARFAIT

- 2 pints strawberries, rinsed, hulled
- 1 1/2 pints raspberries
- 1 pint blueberries
- 1/4 cup frozen unsweetened apple juice concentrate, thawed in refrigerator
- 1/8 teaspoon ground cinnamon, or to taste
- 3 1/2 cups nonfat plain yogurt, drained slightly

Cut half the strawberries into 1/2-inch slices; coarsely chop the remaining strawberries. Combine the sliced strawberries, raspberries and blueberries in a large bowl and set aside. Combine the chopped strawberries, apple juice concentrate and cinnamon in a heavy saucepan. Cook over low heat for 10 minutes. Cool to room temperature. Pureé the sauce in a securely covered blender until very smooth. Toss 1 cup of the sauce with the sliced strawberry mixture. Store the remaining sauce in the refrigerator for another use. Layer 1/4 cup berry mixture, 1/4 cup yogurt, 1/4 cup berry mixture, 1/4 cup yogurt and 1/2 cup berry mixture in each of six 12-ounce parfait glasses or tall tumblers. Top each with 1 tablespoon yogurt. Garnish each with a berry. Store in refrigerator until serving time.

Yield: 6 servings.

Approx Per Serving: Cal 185; T Fat 1 g; 5% Calories from Fat; Prot 10 g; Carbo 36 g; Fiber 7 g; Chol 3 mg; Sod 116 mg
Nutritional information includes the entire amount of sauce.

Barbara Schlickbernd, West Point

CHERRIES IN THE SNOW

- 1/2 cup melted butter
- 1 to 1 1/2 cups finely crushed graham crackers
- 3 ounces cream cheese, softened
- 1/2 cup sugar
- 1 teaspoon vanilla extract
- 1 cup whipped cream
- 1 cup miniature marshmallows
- 1 (21-ounce) can cherry pie filling

Mix the butter and graham crackers in a bowl. Press into a 9-inch pie plate. Blend the cream cheese, sugar and vanilla in a bowl. Fold in the whipped cream and marshmallows. Spoon into the prepared pie plate. Chill for several hours to overnight. Spread the pie filling over the top. Store in refrigerator.

Yield: 6 servings.

Approx Per Serving: Cal 587; T Fat 32 g; 47% Calories from Fat; Prot 4 g; Carbo 75 g; Fiber 1 g; Chol 84 mg; Sod 442 mg

Lucinda Els, Benkelman

BUSTER BAR DESSERT

2 cups confectioners' sugar
$^{2}/_{3}$ cup chocolate chips
1 (12-ounce) can evaporated milk
$^{1}/_{2}$ cup margarine
1 teaspoon vanilla extract
1 (1-pound) package Oreo cookies, crushed
$^{1}/_{2}$ cup melted margarine
$1^{1}/_{2}$ cups salted peanuts
$^{1}/_{2}$ gallon vanilla ice cream, softened

Combine the confectioners' sugar, chocolate chips, evaporated milk and $^{1}/_{2}$ cup margarine in a saucepan. Boil for 8 minutes, stirring constantly. Beat in the vanilla. Cool in the refrigerator. Mix the cookie crumbs and $^{1}/_{2}$ cup margarine in a bowl. Spread in a 9x13-inch pan. Sprinkle with the peanuts and refrigerate until set. Spread with the ice cream. Cover with the cooled sauce. Freeze until firm.

Yield: 15 servings.

Approx Per Serving: Cal 606; T Fat 37 g; 53% Calories from Fat; Prot 10 g; Carbo 64 g; Fiber 3 g; Chol 38 mg; Sod 470 mg

Sherry Steele, Lincoln

DOUBLE CHOCOLATE MINT DESSERT

1 cup flour
1 cup sugar
$^{1}/_{2}$ cup butter, softened
4 eggs
1 (16-ounce) can chocolate syrup
2 cups confectioners' sugar
$^{1}/_{2}$ cup butter, softened
1 tablespoon water
$^{1}/_{2}$ teaspoon mint extract
3 drops of green food coloring
6 tablespoons butter
1 cup mint or semisweet chocolate chips

Combine the flour, sugar, $^{1}/_{2}$ cup butter, eggs and chocolate syrup in a mixer bowl; beat until smooth. Pour into a greased 9x13-inch baking pan. Bake at 350 degrees for 25 to 30 minutes or until the top springs back when lightly touched. Cool in the pan. Beat the confectioners' sugar, $^{1}/_{2}$ cup butter, water, mint flavoring and food coloring in a mixer bowl until smooth. Spread over the baked layer. Chill slightly. Combine 6 tablespoons butter and mint chocolate chips in a small microwave-safe bowl. Microwave on High for 1 to $1^{1}/_{2}$ minutes or until the mixture is smooth when stirred. Pour over the dessert. Chill, covered, until serving time. May omit the food coloring.

This recipe is a great holiday dessert. I have also made a multi-layer cake by doubling the mint and chocolate layer ingredients. If you like mint and chocolate, you'll love this dessert!

Yield: 20 servings.

Approx Per Serving: Cal 325; T Fat 17 g; 43% Calories from Fat; Prot 3 g; Carbo 46 g; Fiber 1 g; Chol 77 mg; Sod 165 mg

Tracy J. Behnken, Omaha

CREAM PUFFS

- **1 (4-ounce) package vanilla instant pudding mix**
- **2 cups milk**
- **1 cup boiling water**
- **$\frac{1}{2}$ cup butter or margarine**
- **$\frac{1}{4}$ teaspoon salt**
- **1 cup sifted flour**
- **4 eggs**
- **8 ounces whipped topping**

Prepare the pudding mix with milk using the package directions. Chill. Combine the water, butter and salt in a saucepan. Bring to a rolling boil. Add the flour all at once; mix until the mixture forms a smooth ball. Remove from the heat. Beat in the eggs 1 at a time. Shape into mounds on a greased baking sheet, leaving 2 inches between each cream puff. Bake at 450 degrees for 15 minutes. Reduce the oven temperature to 350 degrees. Bake for 20 to 25 minutes longer or until light brown. Cool on a wire rack. Fold the whipped topping into the chilled pudding. Fill the cream puffs. Refrigerate until serving time.

Yield: 16 servings.

Approx Per Serving: Cal 201; T Fat 12 g; 54% Calories from Fat; Prot 4 g; Carbo 19 g; Fiber <1 g; Chol 74 mg; Sod 264 mg

Kristi Hanna, Burwell
Jessica Mager, Wilber

SWEDISH PASTRY

- **1 egg, beaten**
- **3 tablespoons sugar**
- **$\frac{1}{4}$ teaspoon salt**
- **$\frac{1}{2}$ teaspoon almond extract**
- **1 envelope dry yeast**
- **1 cup warm (110 to 155 degrees) milk**
- **$2\frac{1}{2}$ cups flour**
- **$\frac{1}{2}$ cup margarine, softened**
- **1 egg, beaten**
- **1 cup confectioners' sugar**
- **$\frac{1}{4}$ teaspoon almond extract**
- **2 tablespoons water**

Combine the first 4 ingredients in a bowl; beat well. Dissolve the yeast in the warm milk in a large bowl. Stir in the egg mixture. Add the flour, beating until a shiny dough forms. Knead slightly. Roll into a rectangle $\frac{1}{4}$ inch thick on a floured surface. Spread with $\frac{1}{3}$ of the margarine. Fold over $\frac{1}{3}$ of each long side; fold over $\frac{1}{3}$ of each short side. Refrigerate for 15 minutes or until the dough rises slightly. Repeat the rolling, spreading with margarine and folding process twice. Roll $\frac{1}{2}$ inch thick on a floured surface. Cut into triangles. Roll the triangles from the long side, tucking point ends under. Place on a baking sheet. Let rise until doubled in bulk. Brush with beaten egg. Bake at 375 degrees for 10 minutes or until lightly browned. Frost with a mixture of the remaining ingredients. May add 1 tablespoon favorite pie filling on the dough before rolling.

Yield: 15 servings.

Approx Per Serving: Cal 192; T Fat 8 g; 35% Calories from Fat; Prot 4 g; Carbo 27 g; Fiber 1 g; Chol 31 mg; Sod 124 mg

Melanie Kouma, Dwight

Fast, Easy and Fun

Just Kiddin' Around
After the Game Party Menu

Tacos Gringo-Style
page 30

Go Anywhere Snack
page 154

Smothered Burritos
page 70
or
Sloppy Joe Pizza
page 75
or
Old-Fashioned Ham and Bean Soup
page 39

Earthquake Cake
page 157

Prom Punch
page 36

PHOTOGRAPH BY JASON HIRSCHFELD
York County

OUT-OF-THIS-WORLD FRUIT DIP

- **2 cups mixed pineapple, apple and banana chunks**
- **1 orange, cut into halves horizontally**
- **8 ounces cream cheese, softened**
- **1/2 cup whipped topping**
- **1/2 cup marshmallow creme**
- **2 to 3 drops of red food coloring**

Dip the fruit in lemon or orange juice to prevent discoloration. Place the orange halves cut side down on a serving plate. Thread the fruit pieces alternately onto wooden skewers. Insert the skewers randomly into the orange halves. Cover and chill until serving time. Mix the cream cheese, whipped topping and marshmallow creme in a bowl. Stir in the food coloring. Spoon into a small serving dish. Serve with the fruit. Do not allow to stand at room temperature for more than 2 hours; refrigerate any leftovers. May use any favorite fruit.

Yield: 4 servings.

Approx Per Serving: Cal 407; T Fat 23 g; 48% Calories from Fat; Prot 5 g; Carbo 50 g; Fiber 2 g; Chol 62 mg; Sod 197 mg

Linda Raddatz, Sidney

EDIBLE LEGOS

- **2 (3-ounce) packages strawberry gelatin**
- **1 cup boiling water**
- **2 (3-ounce) packages lime gelatin**
- **1 cup boiling water**
- **3 ounces cream cheese, softened**
- **1 teaspoon milk**

Combine the strawberry gelatin and 1 cup water in a bowl, stirring until the gelatin dissolves. Pour into an 8x8-inch dish. Combine the lime gelatin and 1 cup water in a bowl, stirring until the gelatin dissolves. Pour into an 8x8-inch dish. Chill the mixtures for 3 hours or until set. Cut into blocks. Mix the cream cheese with the milk in a small bowl. Build your design, spreading cream cheese between the gelatin blocks to hold the design together. Store in refrigerator.

This was my 1993 Cuming County Favorite Foods Contest entry.

Yield: 6 servings.

Approx Per Serving: Cal 266; T Fat 5 g; 16% Calories from Fat; Prot 6 g; Carbo 52 g; Fiber 0 g; Chol 16 mg; Sod 186 mg

David Heftie, Wisner

GO ANYWHERE SNACK

16 cups mixed cereal
2 cups raisins
2 cups chopped mixed nuts
1/2 cup wheat germ
1/2 cup margarine
1/4 cup light corn syrup
1/4 cup honey
1 cup packed brown sugar
1/2 teaspoon salt

Mix the cereal, raisins, mixed nuts and wheat germ in a large bowl; set aside. Place the margarine in a microwave-safe bowl. Microwave on Medium until melted; stir. Add the corn syrup, honey, brown sugar and salt. Microwave until the brown sugar is dissolved. Pour over the cereal mixture, mixing well. Pour onto a baking sheet. Bake at 275 degrees for 2 hours, stirring every 30 minutes.

This was my own idea. My mom helped me decide on the quantity of each item. My family really enjoys it.

Yield: 40 servings.

Approx Per Serving: Cal 220; T Fat 11 g; 41% Calories from Fat; Prot 4 g; Carbo 30 g; Fiber 3 g; Chol 0 mg; Sod 185 mg

Kassandra K. Voboril, Primrose

GORP BARS

2 cups corn Chex
2 1/2 cups pretzel sticks, broken into halves
1 1/2 cups "M & M's" Chocolate Candies
3/4 cup raisins
5 cups miniature marshmallows
1/2 cup margarine
1/2 cup peanut butter

Mix the cereal, pretzels, candies and raisins in a large bowl; set aside. Combine the marshmallows and margarine in a large microwave-safe bowl. Microwave for 3 to 4 minutes or until the marshmallows are melted. Stir in the peanut butter. Add the marshmallow mixture to the cereal mixture, stirring well. Press into a lightly buttered 9x13-inch pan. Let stand until set. Cut into bars.

Yield: 12 servings.

Approx Per Serving: Cal 388; T Fat 19 g; 42% Calories from Fat; Prot 6 g; Carbo 53 g; Fiber 2 g; Chol 0 mg; Sod 365 mg

Carmen Schlickbernd, West Point

GO-BIG-RED POPCORN

- 1 (12-ounce) package red hot cinnamon candies
- 1/2 cup (about) sugar
- 1 cup margarine
- 1/2 cup light corn syrup
- 1 teaspoon salt
- 1/2 teaspoon baking soda
- 1 teaspoon butter flavoring
- 1 teaspoon oil of cinnamon, or to taste
- 6 to 7 quarts popped popcorn

Combine the candies with enough of the sugar to measure 2 cups. Combine the candy mixture, margarine, corn syrup and salt in a large saucepan. Bring to a full rolling boil. Boil for 5 minutes; remove from the heat. Add the baking soda, flavoring and cinnamon oil; mix well. Pour over the popcorn in a large roaster, stirring carefully. Bake at 250 degrees for 1 hour, stirring every 15 minutes. Spread on waxed paper or a baking sheet to cool. Store in an airtight container or plastic bag.

We make this recipe at least once during the holiday season. It makes great gifts and is also a great munchie while watching the Big Red football games.

Yield: 20 servings.

Approx Per Serving: Cal 234; T Fat 10 g; 36% Calories from Fat; Prot 1 g; Carbo 37 g; Fiber 2 g; Chol 0 mg; Sod 248 mg

Jeff Buethe, Tecumseh
Kim Harris, Pawnee City

HARVEST POPCORN

- 2 quarts unsalted freshly popped popcorn
- 2 (1-ounce) cans potato sticks
- 1 cup salted mixed nuts
- 1 teaspoon lemon pepper
- 1 teaspoon Worcestershire sauce
- 1/2 teaspoon onion powder
- 1/2 cup melted butter
- 1 teaspoon dried whole dillweed
- 1/2 teaspoon garlic powder

Combine the popcorn, potato sticks and mixed nuts in a 10x15-inch jelly roll pan. Mix the lemon pepper, Worcestershire sauce, onion powder, butter, dillweed and garlic powder in a bowl. Pour over the popcorn mixture, stirring until evenly coated. Bake at 350 degrees for 6 to 8 minutes or until heated through, stirring once.

Yield: 6 servings.

Approx Per Serving: Cal 373; T Fat 32 g; 75% Calories from Fat; Prot 6 g; Carbo 19 g; Fiber 4 g; Chol 41 mg; Sod 479 mg

Kimberly Lake, Fairbury

MEXI-CORN

2 tablespoons margarine
1 teaspoon salt
1/2 teaspoon onion salt
1/4 teaspoon chili powder
1 teaspoon grated Parmesan cheese
2 quarts popped popcorn

Place the margarine in a 6-ounce microwave-safe bowl. Microwave until melted. Stir in the salt, onion salt, chili powder and cheese. Pour over the popcorn in a large bowl, tossing to coat evenly.

Yield: 6 servings.

Approx Per Serving: Cal 77; T Fat 4 g; 50% Calories from Fat; Prot 1 g; Carbo 8 g; Fiber 2 g; Chol <1 mg; Sod 539 mg

Shirley Rippe, Hebron

GRAND-SLAM PIZZA STICKS

2 breadsticks
1/4 cup pizza sauce
10 slices pepperoni
4 ounces string cheese, torn into halves

Cut each breadstick into halves lengthwise without cutting completely through. Spread 1 tablespoon of the pizza sauce on each cut side. Layer the pepperoni and cheese over the sauce. Place on a microwave-safe plate. Microwave, loosely covered, on High for 30 to 60 seconds or until the cheese is melted.

We used this recipe in an intergenerational dairy foods demonstration called "A Royal Treat." In our menu, we emphasized a snack to be eaten before a baseball game. We received a purple ribbon. This was Amber's first demonstration; she was eight years old.

Yield: 2 servings.

Approx Per Serving: Cal 335; T Fat 22 g; 60% Calories from Fat; Prot 21 g; Carbo 12 g; Fiber <1 g; Chol 55 mg; Sod 1027 mg

Amber and Debbie Goossen, Beatrice

FRUITY ANGEL CAKE

1 (21-ounce) can cherry pie filling
1 angel food cake mix

Combine the pie filling and cake mix in a bowl; mix well. Pour into an angel food cake pan or a 10x13-inch cake pan. Bake using the package directions; may take up to an additional 10 minutes to bake.

Anyone can make this cake. It tastes very good and is low in fat.

Yield: 16 servings.

Approx Per Serving: Cal 150; T Fat <1 g; 2% Calories from Fat; Prot 3 g; Carbo 35 g; Fiber <1 g; Chol 0 mg; Sod 228 mg

La Shon DeHart, Wauneta

CHOCOLATE CRAZY CAKE

3 cups flour
2 cups sugar
1/4 cup baking cocoa
2 teaspoons baking soda
2 cups water
2 teaspoons vanilla extract
2/3 cup vegetable oil
1 teaspoon salt
2 tablespoons vinegar

Combine the flour, sugar, cocoa, baking soda, water, vanilla, oil, salt and vinegar in a bowl; mix well. Pour into a greased 9x12-inch cake pan. Bake at 350 degrees for 35 to 40 minutes or until cake tests done.

This recipe is good for those on an egg-free diet. It is the first recipe I made as a child.

Yield: 15 servings.

Approx Per Serving: Cal 283; T Fat 10 g; 32% Calories from Fat; Prot 3 g; Carbo 47 g; Fiber 1 g; Chol 0 mg; Sod 253 mg

Diana Kehrli, Schuyler

EARTHQUAKE CAKE

1 cup coconut
1 cup chopped pecans
1 (2-layer) package German chocolate cake mix
1/2 cup margarine, softened
1 (1-pound) package confectioners' sugar
8 ounces cream cheese, softened

Cover the bottom of a greased 3 inch deep 9x13-inch cake pan with coconut; sprinkle with the pecans. Prepare the cake mix using the package directions. Pour over the pecans. Blend the margarine, confectioners' sugar and cream cheese in a bowl. Spoon over the cake mix; do not stir. Bake at 350 degrees for 1 hour or until the cake tests done.

Yield: 15 servings.

Approx Per Serving: Cal 509; T Fat 28 g; 49% Calories from Fat; Prot 4 g; Carbo 62 g; Fiber 1 g; Chol 61 mg; Sod 453 mg

Sherry Steele, Hickman

LEMON YUMMY CAKE

1 (2-layer) package lemon cake mix
1 (4-ounce) package lemon instant pudding mix
3/4 cup vegetable oil
1 cup water
4 eggs
Juice of 2 lemons
Grated peel of 1 lemon
2 cups confectioners' sugar

Combine the cake mix, pudding mix, oil, water and eggs in a bowl. Beat until smooth. Pour into a nonstick 9x13-inch cake pan. Bake at 350 degrees for 20 to 30 minutes or until the cake tests done. Prick the warm cake several times with a fork. Combine the lemon juice, lemon peel and confectioners' sugar in a bowl, stirring until of a glaze consistency. Pour over the warm cake.

Yield: 16 servings.

Approx Per Serving: Cal 327; T Fat 15 g; 39% Calories from Fat; Prot 3 g; Carbo 49 g; Fiber <1 g; Chol 53 mg; Sod 301 mg

Marilyn Burkhalter, Elwood

BUCKEYES

1/2 cup margarine
2 cups confectioners' sugar
3 cups crisp rice cereal
1 1/2 cups chunky peanut butter
2 cups chocolate chips
1/2 bar food-grade wax

Melt the margarine in a saucepan. Add the confectioners' sugar, cereal and peanut butter; mix well. Shape into golf ball-size balls. Freeze until firm. Melt the chocolate chips and wax in a double boiler, stirring until smooth. Dip the frozen balls into the chocolate mixture. Let cool.

This is a favorite on both sides of the family.

Yield: 36 servings.

Approx Per Serving: Cal 166; T Fat 11 g; 54% Calories from Fat; Prot 3 g; Carbo 17 g; Fiber 1 g; Chol 0 mg; Sod 111 mg

Stephanie Alm, Omaha

MARSHMALLOW PUFFS

36 large marshmallows
1 1/2 cups semisweet chocolate chips
1/2 cup chunky peanut butter
2 tablespoons butter or margarine

Line a 9x9-inch pan with foil or waxed paper. Arrange the marshmallows in the pan. Combine the chocolate chips, peanut butter and butter in a microwave-safe bowl. Microwave until melted. Pour evenly over the marshmallows. Chill completely. Cut into servings between the marshmallows.

These tasty treats are so simple even the kids or grandkids can make them! The only thing they like better is eating them.

Yield: 36 servings.

Approx Per Serving: Cal 83; T Fat 5 g; 45% Calories from Fat; Prot 1 g; Carbo 11 g; Fiber 1 g; Chol 2 mg; Sod 28 mg

Fran Obermire, Atkinson

PEANUT CLUSTERS

1 pound almond bark
2 cups semisweet chocolate chips
1 pound dry roasted salted peanuts

Melt the almond bark and chocolate chips in a double boiler. Stir in the peanuts. Drop by tablespoonfuls onto a baking sheet lined with waxed paper. Chill until set.

This easy candy is made all during the year for family and friends.

Yield: 60 servings.

Approx Per Serving: Cal 112; T Fat 8 g; 59% Calories from Fat; Prot 2 g; Carbo 10 g; Fiber <1 g; Chol 0 mg; Sod 69 mg

Blair Uden, Lexington

DAD'S FAVORITE PEANUT BRITTLE

1 cup raw peanuts
1/2 cup light corn syrup
1 cup sugar
1/8 teaspoon salt
1 teaspoon butter or margarine
1 teaspoon vanilla extract
1 teaspoon baking soda

Combine the first 4 ingredients in a microwave-safe bowl. Microwave on High for 4 minutes, stirring occasionally. Microwave for 3 minutes longer. Add the butter and vanilla. Microwave for 1 to 2 minutes longer or until heated through. Stir in the baking soda. Pour onto a buttered baking sheet. Let cool. Break into pieces. Store in an airtight container.

Yield: 10 servings.

Approx Per Serving: Cal 210; T Fat 8 g; 31% Calories from Fat; Prot 4 g; Carbo 35 g; Fiber 1 g; Chol 1 mg; Sod 136 mg

Susan Stevenson, Petersburg
Mary and Leah Wendorff, Callaway

RICE KRISPIE DOTS

1/4 cup butter
4 1/2 cups miniature marshmallows
5 1/2 cups Rice Krispies
1/2 cup chocolate chips

Place the butter in a microwave-safe 3-quart glass dish. Microwave until melted. Stir in the marshmallows. Microwave on High for 1 minute; stir. Microwave for 30 seconds or until most of the marshmallows are melted. Add the cereal, stirring until well coated. Stir in the chocolate chips. Spread in a buttered 9x13-inch pan. Pat down with a buttered spoon. Chill thoroughly. Cut into squares.

Yield: 24 servings.

Approx Per Serving: Cal 86; T Fat 3 g; 30% Calories from Fat; Prot 1 g; Carbo 15 g; Fiber <1 g; Chol 5 mg; Sod 101 mg

Kelsey Eitel, Crawford

ROCKY ROAD CANDY

2 cups semisweet chocolate chips
2 cups butterscotch chips
1 cup peanut butter
1 (10-ounce) package miniature marshmallows
1 cup dry roasted salted peanuts

Combine the chocolate chips, butterscotch chips and peanut butter in a large glass bowl. Microwave on High for 1 1/2 minutes; stir. Microwave for 1 1/2 minutes longer; stir. Fold in the marshmallows and peanuts. Spread in a buttered 9x13-inch pan. Refrigerate for 2 hours or until set.

Yield: 36 servings.

Approx Per Serving: Cal 184; T Fat 11 g; 51% Calories from Fat; Prot 3 g; Carbo 21 g; Fiber 1 g; Chol <1 mg; Sod 80 mg

Sarah Effken Purcell, Broken Bow

WATERMELON COOKIES

3/4 cup butter, softened
1/2 cup sugar
1 (3-ounce) package watermelon gelatin
2 eggs
1 teaspoon vanilla extract
2 1/2 cups flour
1 teaspoon baking powder
1 teaspoon salt
1/2 cup sugar

Combine the butter, 1/2 cup sugar and gelatin in a mixer bowl. Beat until light and fluffy. Add the eggs and vanilla, beating until mixed. Add the flour, baking powder and salt; mix well. Chill thoroughly. Shape into 3/4-inch balls. Dip in the remaining 1/2 cup sugar. Place on a nonstick cookie sheet and press down slightly. Bake at 375 degrees for 8 to 10 minutes or until lightly browned.

Yield: 48 servings.

Approx Per Serving: Cal 75; T Fat 3 g; 37% Calories from Fat; Prot 1 g; Carbo 11 g; Fiber <1 g; Chol 17 mg; Sod 88 mg

Amanda and Melissa Hansen, Ceresco

CHOCOLATE CRINKLE COOKIES

2 cups flour
2 teaspoons baking powder
1/2 teaspoon salt
1/2 cup vegetable oil
4 ounces unsweetened chocolate, melted
2 cups sugar
4 eggs
2 teaspoons vanilla extract
1 cup confectioners' sugar

Mix the flour, baking powder and salt together. Mix the oil, chocolate and sugar in a bowl. Beat in the eggs 1 at a time. Add the vanilla. Add the flour mixture and mix well. Chill for 4 hours or longer. Drop by teaspoonfuls into the confectioners' sugar; roll and shape into balls. Place on a greased cookie sheet. Bake at 350 degrees for 10 to 12 minutes or until lightly browned.

Yield: 72 servings.

Approx Per Serving: Cal 67; T Fat 3 g; 35% Calories from Fat; Prot 1 g; Carbo 10 g; Fiber <1 g; Chol 12 mg; Sod 28 mg

Fran Allacher, McCook

LEMON WHIPPERSNAPPERS

1 (2-layer) package lemon cake mix
2 cups whipped topping
1 egg
1/2 cup confectioners' sugar

Combine the cake mix, whipped topping and egg in a bowl; mix well. Drop by teaspoonfuls into the confectioners' sugar. Roll in the sugar and shape into balls. Place 1 1/2 inches apart on a nonstick cookie sheet. Bake at 350 degrees for 10 to 15 minutes or until lightly browned.

Yield: 48 servings.

Approx Per Serving: Cal 61; T Fat 2 g; 27% Calories from Fat; Prot 1 g; Carbo 11 g; Fiber 0 g; Chol 4 mg; Sod 70 mg

Jo Ann Sharpe, Pawnee City

NO-BAKE COOKIES

2 cups sugar
1/2 cup margarine
1/2 cup milk
1/2 cup peanut butter
1/4 cup baking cocoa
1 teaspoon vanilla extract
3 cups rolled oats

Bring the sugar, margarine and milk to a boil in a saucepan. Boil for 3 minutes; remove from the heat. Add the peanut butter, cocoa and vanilla; mix well. Stir in the oats. Drop by tablespoonfuls onto waxed paper. Let cool.

I found this when I took my first cooking project.

Yield: 30 servings.

Approx Per Serving: Cal 139; T Fat 6 g; 37% Calories from Fat; Prot 3 g; Carbo 20 g; Fiber 1 g; Chol <1 mg; Sod 59 mg

Jennifer Maddux, Wauneta
Angie Petersen, Hemingford

PIZZA COOKIE

1/2 cup butter, softened
1/2 cup packed brown sugar
1 egg
1 1/4 cups flour
1 teaspoon baking soda
1/2 teaspoon salt
1 cup miniature chocolate chips
1 (16-ounce) can ready-to-spread frosting
1 (16-ounce) can chocolate syrup

Combine the butter, brown sugar and egg in a large mixer bowl. Beat at medium speed for 2 minutes or until light and fluffy. Add the flour, baking soda and salt, beating until combined. Stir in 1/2 cup chocolate chips. Spread on a lightly greased 12-inch pizza pan. Bake at 350 degrees for 15 minutes. Cool on a wire rack. Spread with the frosting. Swirl the chocolate syrup over the frosting. Sprinkle with the remaining 1/2 cup chocolate chips.

Yield: 8 servings.

Approx Per Serving: Cal 745; T Fat 30 g; 35% Calories from Fat; Prot 6 g; Carbo 119 g; Fiber 4 g; Chol 58 mg; Sod 471 mg

Erin Bales, Grand Island

BUTTERY CINNAMON SKILLET APPLES

1/3 cup butter
1/2 to 3/4 cup sugar
2 tablespoons cornstarch
1 1/2 cups water
1/4 to 1/2 teaspoon cinnamon
4 medium cooking apples, cored, cut into slices

Melt the butter in a nonstick skillet over medium heat. Stir in the sugar and cornstarch. Add the water, cinnamon and apples and mix well. Cook, covered, over medium heat until the apples are tender, spooning sauce over the apples occasionally. Serve the sauce over the apples.

Yield: 4 servings.

Approx Per Serving: Cal 369; T Fat 16 g; 37% Calories from Fat; Prot <1 g; Carbo 60 g; Fiber 2 g; Chol 41 mg; Sod 157 mg

Kinsey DeBoer, Smithfield

BANANA BUTTERFINGER DESSERT

- 3 large Butterfinger candy bars, frozen, finely crushed
- 3 bananas, sliced
- 1 cup chopped pecans
- 16 ounces whipped topping

Combine the candy, bananas, pecans and whipped topping in a large bowl; mix well. Chill thoroughly in the refrigerator.

Yield: 6 servings.

Approx Per Serving: Cal 660; T Fat 43 g; 55% Calories from Fat; Prot 7 g; Carbo 70 g; Fiber 4 g; Chol <1 mg; Sod 93mg

Mary Manion, Crawford

PRONTO CHERRY CRUNCH ❀ *from The 4-H Friends' Cookbook*

- 2 (21-ounce) cans cherry pie filling
- 1 (2-layer) package white cake mix
- 1 cup melted butter or margarine
- 1 cup quick-cooking oats
- 1 cup chopped pecans

Spread the cherry pie filling in a 9x13-inch baking pan. Sprinkle with the cake mix; drizzle with the butter. Sprinkle with a mixture of the oats and pecans. Bake at 350 degrees for 45 to 50 minutes. Serve topped with whipped cream or vanilla ice cream.

Yield: 15 servings.

Approx Per Serving: Cal 421; T Fat 22 g; 47% Calories from Fat; Prot 4 g; Carbo 54 g; Fiber 2 g; Chol 33 mg; Sod 392 mg

Lonna Axthelm; Mrs. Donald Hayes
Mrs. William Karre; Diane Propst
Jacquie Schliep; Joanie Starck

PEANUT BUTTER PIE

- 3 ounces cream cheese
- 1/4 cup confectioners' sugar
- 1/2 cup chunky peanut butter
- 1/2 cup milk
- 8 ounces whipped topping
- 1 (9-inch) graham cracker pie shell
- 1/4 cup chopped peanuts

Whip the cream cheese in a mixer bowl until soft. Beat in the confectioners' sugar and peanut butter. Add the milk gradually, beating well after each addition. Fold in the whipped topping. Pour into the pie shell. Sprinkle with the peanuts. Freeze until firm.

Yield: 8 servings.

Approx Per Serving: Cal 465; T Fat 31 g; 58% Calories from Fat; Prot 8 g; Carbo 42 g; Fiber 2 g; Chol 14 mg; Sod 356 mg

Conni Bales, Grand Island

APPENDIX

EQUIVALENT CHART

page 164

SUBSTITUTION CHART

page 166

FOOD SAFETY

page 167

FOOD GUIDE PYRAMID

page 168

WHAT COUNTS AS A SERVING?

page 169

APPLYING THE PYRAMID

page 170

EQUIVALENT CHART

	When the recipe calls for	Use
Baking	1/2 cup butter	4 ounces
	2 cups butter	1 pound
	4 cups all-purpose flour	1 pound
	4 1/2 to 5 cups sifted cake flour	1 pound
	1 square chocolate	1 ounce
	1 cup semisweet chocolate chips	6 ounces
	4 cups marshmallows	1 pound
	2 1/4 cups packed brown sugar	1 pound
	4 cups confectioners' sugar	1 pound
	2 cups granulated sugar	1 pound
Cereal – Bread	1 cup fine dry bread crumbs	4 to 5 slices
	1 cup soft bread crumbs	2 slices
	1 cup small bread cubes	2 slices
	1 cup fine cracker crumbs	28 saltines
	1 cup fine graham cracker crumbs	15 crackers
	1 cup vanilla wafer crumbs	22 wafers
	1 cup crushed cornflakes	3 cups uncrushed
	4 cups cooked macaroni	8 ounces uncooked
	3 1/2 cups cooked rice	1 cup uncooked
Dairy	1 cup shredded cheese	4 ounces
	1 cup cottage cheese	8 ounces
	1 cup sour cream	8 ounces
	1 cup whipped cream	1/2 cup heavy cream
	2/3 cup evaporated milk	1 small can
	1 2/3 cups evaporated milk	1 13-ounce can
Fruit	4 cups sliced or chopped apples	4 medium
	1 cup mashed bananas	3 medium
	2 cups pitted cherries	4 cups unpitted
	2 1/2 cups shredded coconut	8 ounces
	4 cups cranberries	1 pound
	1 cup pitted dates	1 8-ounce package
	1 cup candied fruit	1 8-ounce package
	3 to 4 tablespoons lemon juice plus 1 tablespoon grated lemon rind	1 lemon
	1/3 cup orange juice plus 2 teaspoons grated orange peel	1 orange
	4 cups sliced peaches	8 medium
	2 cups pitted prunes	1 12-ounce package
	3 cups raisins	1 15-ounce package

	When the recipe calls for	Use
Meats	4 cups chopped cooked chicken	1 5-pound chicken
	3 cups chopped cooked meat	1 pound, cooked
	2 cups cooked ground meat	1 pound, cooked
Nuts	1 cup chopped nuts	4 ounces shelled 1 pound unshelled
Vegetables	2 cups cooked green beans	1/2 pound fresh or 1 16-ounce can
	2 1/2 cups lima beans or red beans	1 cup dried, cooked
	4 cups shredded cabbage	1 pound
	1 cup grated carrot	1 large
	8 ounces fresh mushrooms	1 4-ounce can
	1 cup chopped onion	1 large
	4 cups sliced or chopped potatoes	4 medium
	2 cups canned tomatoes	1 16-ounce can

Measurement Equivalents

1 tablespoon = 3 teaspoons
2 tablespoons = 1 ounce
4 tablespoons = 1/4 cup
5 1/3 tablespoons = 1/3 cup
8 tablespoons = 1/2 cup
12 tablespoons = 3/4 cup
16 tablespoons = 1 cup
1 cup = 8 ounces or 1/2 pint
4 cups = 1 quart
4 quarts = 1 gallon

1 6 1/2 to 8-ounce can = 1 cup
1 10 1/2 to 12-ounce can = 1 1/4 cups
1 14 to 16-ounce can = 1 3/4 cups
1 16 to 17-ounce can = 2 cups
1 18 to 20-ounce can = 2 1/2 cups
1 29-ounce can = 3 1/2 cups
1 46 to 51-ounce can = 5 3/4 cups
1 6 1/2 to 7 1/2-pound can or Number 10 = 12 to 13 cups

Metric Equivalents

Liquid

1 teaspoon = 5 milliliters
1 tablespoon = 15 milliliters
1 fluid ounce = 30 milliliters
1 cup = 250 milliliters
1 pint = 500 milliliters

Dry

1 quart = 1 liter
1 ounce = 30 grams
1 pound = 450 grams
2.2 pounds = 1 kilogram

NOTE: *The metric measures are approximate benchmarks for purposes of home food preparation.*

SUBSTITUTION CHART

	Instead of	Use
Baking	1 teaspoon baking powder	1/4 teaspoon baking soda plus 1/2 teaspoon cream of tartar
	1 tablespoon cornstarch (for thickening)	2 tablespoons flour or 1 tablespoon tapioca
	1 cup sifted all-purpose flour	1 cup plus 2 tablespoons sifted cake flour
	1 cup sifted cake flour	1 cup minus 2 tablespoons sifted all-purpose flour
	1 cup dry bread crumbs	3/4 cup cracker crumbs
Dairy	1 cup buttermilk	1 cup sour milk or 1 cup yogurt
	1 cup heavy cream	3/4 cup skim milk plus 1/3 cup butter
	1 cup light cream	7/8 cup skim milk plus 3 tablespoons butter
	1 cup sour cream	7/8 cup sour milk plus 3 tablespoons butter
	1 cup sour milk	1 cup milk plus 1 tablespoon vinegar or lemon juice or 1 cup buttermilk
Seasoning	1 teaspoon allspice	1/2 teaspoon cinnamon plus 1/8 teaspoon cloves
	1 cup catsup	1 cup tomato sauce plus 1/2 cup sugar plus 2 tablespoons vinegar
	1 clove of garlic	1/8 teaspoon garlic powder or 1/8 teaspoon instant minced garlic or 3/4 teaspoon garlic salt or 5 drops of liquid garlic
	1 teaspoon Italian spice	1/4 teaspoon each oregano, basil, thyme, rosemary plus dash of cayenne
	1 teaspoon lemon juice	1/2 teaspoon vinegar
	1 tablespoon mustard	1 teaspoon dry mustard
	1 medium onion	1 tablespoon dried minced onion or 1 teaspoon onion powder
Sweet	1 1-ounce square chocolate	1/4 cup baking cocoa plus 1 teaspoon shortening
	1 2/3 ounces semisweet chocolate	1 ounce unsweetened chocolate plus 4 teaspoons granulated sugar
	1 cup honey	1 to 1 1/4 cups sugar plus 1/4 cup liquid or 1 cup corn syrup or molasses
	1 cup granulated sugar	1 cup packed brown sugar or 1 cup corn syrup, molasses or honey minus 1/4 cup liquid

FOOD SAFETY

What we think is the flu can sometimes be caused by harmful bacteria that may be in food. Bacteria on foods can grow and make you sick. You can't always see, smell, or taste if food is contaminated with bacteria—so it's important to buy safe food and keep it safe when you get home.

These are some foods that bacteria like best: milk and other dairy products, eggs, meat, poultry, and seafood. When buying, storing, and preparing foods, it's important to use safe food handling practices. Here are some tips to follow:

At the Store:

- Buy cans and jars that look perfect. Don't buy dented, rusted cans or cans with bulging ends. Check the carton of eggs to see if any are broken or cracked.
- Keep dripping meat juices away from other foods. Put raw meat, poultry, and seafood into plastic bags before they go into your cart.
- Pick up milk and other cold foods last. This gives food less time to warm up before you get home. Pick up hot chicken and other hot foods just before you go to the checkout lane. This will give hot food less time to cool off before you get home.

Storing Food:

- Return home as soon as you can after shopping for food. Put food into the refrigerator or freezer right away. Eggs always go in the refrigerator.

Preparing Food:

- Wash your hands with warm water and soap before and after you handle food. Wash anything that comes in contact with food, such as utensils, counters, equipment, etc. Use paper towels to wipe up cupboard spills, especially meat juices.
- If you use a dishcloth, use one that has been freshly laundered and dried in your dryer. Rinse with hot soapy water after each use and hang to dry. Change dishcloths frequently. A dirty dishcloth can add more bacteria than it removes.
- Rinse fresh fruits and vegetables under running water to wash away dirt. Do not use dish detergent or hand soap to wash fruits and vegetables.
- Keep raw meat, poultry, and seafood and their juices away from other foods. These foods can spread bacteria in your kitchen.
- Keep meat, poultry, and seafood cold while they thaw. Thaw them:
  - **In the refrigerator**, 1 to 2 days before you will cook the food.
  - **In the microwave**, using the "defrost" setting. Then cook the food right away.
- Cook raw meat, poultry, seafood, and eggs until they are done. Use an oven temperature of at least 325 degrees F. to destroy bacteria.
- Cook red meat, especially ground meat, until it looks brown inside and the juices look clear, not pink.
- Poke cooked chicken with a fork. The juices should look clear, not pink.
- Stick a fork into cooked fish. The fish should flake.
- Cook eggs until whites and yolks are firm, not runny.

Handling Leftovers:

- Store leftovers in the refrigerator or freezer as soon as you finish eating. If food is left out for 2 or more hours, bacteria can grow. Put leftovers in shallow dishes so they cool faster. Eat leftovers in the next 2 days.
- IF IN DOUBT, THROW IT OUT!

Source: Alice Henneman, M.S., R.D., Lancaster County Extension Educator, and Julie Albrecht, Ph.D., R.D., Associate Professor, Extension Food Specialist, University of Nebraska. Adapted from: *Keep Your Food Safe*, FDA, 1991.

FOOD GUIDE PYRAMID

A Guide to Daily Food Choices

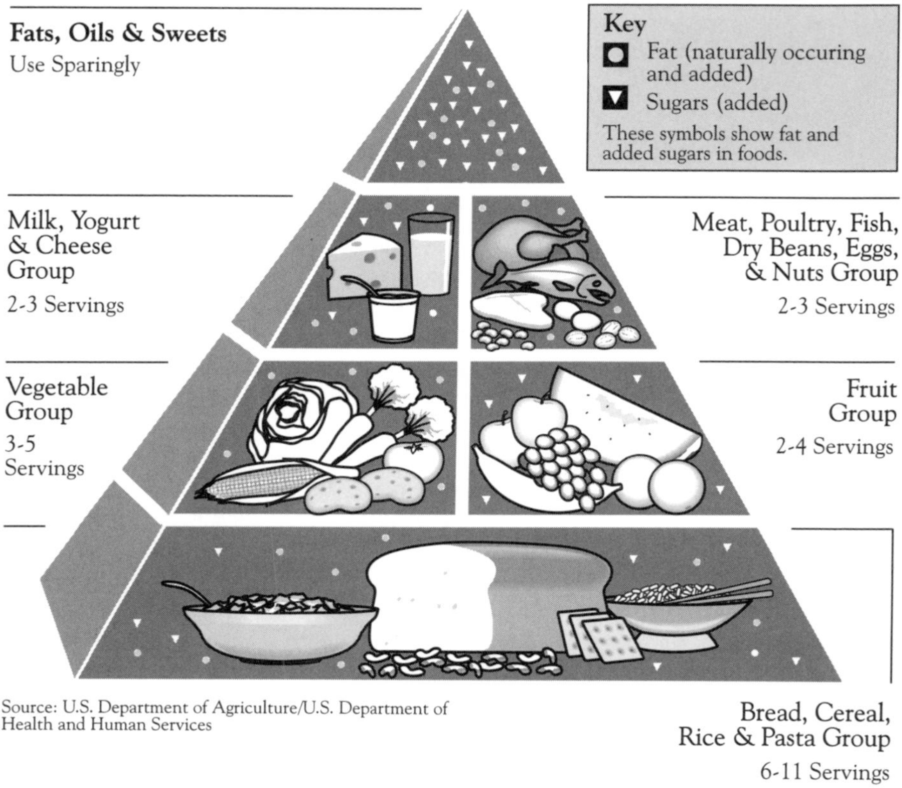

Fats, Oils & Sweets
Use Sparingly

Key
Fat (naturally occuring and added)
Sugars (added)
These symbols show fat and added sugars in foods.

Milk, Yogurt & Cheese Group
2-3 Servings

Meat, Poultry, Fish, Dry Beans, Eggs, & Nuts Group
2-3 Servings

Vegetable Group
3-5 Servings

Fruit Group
2-4 Servings

Bread, Cereal, Rice & Pasta Group
6-11 Servings

Source: U.S. Department of Agriculture/U.S. Department of Health and Human Services

Use the Food Guide Pyramid to help you eat better every day . . . the Dietary Guidelines way. Start with plenty of Breads, Cereals, Rice, and Pasta; Vegetables; and Fruits. Add two to three servings from the Milk group and two to three servings from the Meat group.

Each of these food groups provides some, but not all, of the nutrients you need. No one food group is more important than another—for good health you need them all. Go easy on fats, oils, and sweets—the foods in the small tip of the Pyramid.

What Counts as a Serving?

Bread group servings:
1 slice of bread
1 ounce of ready-to-eat cereal
1/2 cup cooked cereal, rice, or pasta
1/2 English muffin or hamburger bun

Vegetable group servings:
1 cup of raw, leafy green vegetables
1/2 cup cooked vegetables
1/2 cup chopped raw vegetables
3/4 cup vegetable juice

Fruit group servings:
3/4 cup fruit juice
1 medium apple or orange
1 small banana
1/2 large grapefruit
1 1/2 cups raw, cooked, or canned fruit

Milk group servings:
1 cup whole, 2%, or skim milk
1/2 cup evaporated milk
1 cup plain or flavored yogurt
1 1/2 ounces natural cheese
2 ounces process cheese

Meat group servings:
2 to 3 ounces of cooked lean meat, fish, or poultry
one egg, 1/2 cup cooked beans, or 2 tablespoons peanut butter may be substituted for 1 ounce of meat.

Individuals differ in their nutrient and calorie needs as shown by the range in numbers of servings. A teenage boy should eat more servings from the bread group than the 65-year-old woman. And, with the exception of the milk group, young children should eat the lower number of servings and smaller serving sizes. If you eat a larger portion, count it as more than one serving. For example, a dinner-size portion of spaghetti (1 to 1 1/2 cups) counts as two to three servings from the bread group.

Fats and sweets have a group of their own at the tip of the pyramid. Many of our favorite foods—desserts, snacks and spreads, and beverages—are high in sugars and fats or oils but low in nutrients. The fat ◘ and added sugar ▼ symbols are found throughout the other food groups. By choosing foods from each food group that are low in fat and sugar and by limiting added fats and sweets, you can have a diet that supplies needed vitamins and minerals without too many calories.

APPLYING THE PYRAMID

The pyramid is based on the principles of variety, relative proportions, and moderation.

Variety

The best nutrition protection comes from eating a variety of foods. In the grain group, substitute some whole grain for part of the white flour. Try the new white whole wheat flour and experiment with quick-cooking brown rice, barley, or bulgur as starch in soups and casseroles.

Proportions

The pyramid indicates the relative amount to eat. Make most of your food choices from the two lower levels—the grains and the fruits and vegetables. These plant foods provide needed vitamins, minerals, and dietary fiber, as well as energy (measured in calories) mainly from carbohydrates and protein. Most are naturally low in fat and calories. Starchy foods are not fattening. It's the added fat and sugar that boosts the calorie count.

You need 2 to 3 servings from the animal food groups of milk and meat. Animal foods are especially good sources of protein, zinc, and vitamin B12, with milk providing calcium and meat providing iron. Choose low-fat versions to reduce calories, fat, saturated fat, and dietary cholesterol.

Moderation

There are no "good" or "bad" foods. All make some contribution to a healthy diet; however, those limited in nutrients or containing too much fat or sugar should be eaten less frequently.

Making good-tasting, healthful food

- Check out the spices and herbs on your shelves. They're a great, low-fat way to enhance flavor. More generous use of cinnamon and nutmeg can substitute for part of the sugar. Lower-sodium seasoning blends are now available.
- Pay attention to eye appeal. We eat with our eyes as well as our taste buds. Garnish food with color and texture contrasts.
- Make changes gradually but permanently. Eating is for a lifetime.

Material excerpted from:
Essence of KANSAS . . . Taste Two! 4-H Cookbook
as prepared by
Mary P.Clarke, Ph.D., R.D. L.D., C.H.E.
Paula Peters, Ph.D.
Kansas Extension nutrition specialists

INDEX

APPETIZERS. *See also* Dips; Snacks; Spreads
- Buffalo Wings Original New York-Style, 32
- Confetti Bars, 33
- Mozzarella Sticks, 32
- Rumaki, 33
- Tortilla Roll-Ups, 34

BARBECUE
- Barbecue Bison Meatballs, 82
- Barbecued Beef Brisket, 57
- Barbecued Meatballs, 63
- Barbecued Meat Loaf, 66
- Barbecued Minute Steak, 58
- Barbecued Ribs, 87
- Barbecued Trout, 102
- Honey Barbecue-Style Baked Beans, 16

BEANS
- Bacon Bean Ground Beef Casserole, 68
- Campfire Baked Beans, 50
- Homemade Pork and Beans, 14
- Honey Barbecue-Style Baked Beans, 16
- Old-Fashioned Ham and Bean Soup, 39

BEEF. *See also* Ground Beef
- Barbecued Beef Brisket, 57
- "Bohemian" Teriyaki Beef, 11
- Chicken and Chipped Beef, 93
- Chili, 12
- Dried Beef Log, 31
- Pumpkin Stew, 62
- Reuben Casserole, 62

BEEF, KABOBS
- Beef Kabobs in Lemon Marinade, 61
- Beef Shish Kabobs, 60

BEEF, ROASTS
- Italian Roast Beef, 57
- Pepsi Pot Roast, 58

BEEF, STEAKS
- Barbecued Minute Steak, 58
- Company Round Steak, 59
- Green Pepper Steak, 60
- Perfect Marinated Steaks, 61
- Round Steak Meal-in-One, 59

BEVERAGES
- Almond Tea, 36
- Banana Milk Shake, 35
- Cappuccino Mix, 36
- Prom Punch, 36
- Purple Cow Shakes, 35
- Slush Punch, 35

BISON
- Barbecue Bison Meatballs, 82
- Bison Stew, 82

BREADS, QUICK. *See also* Corn Bread; Muffins
- Carrot Bread, 109
- Monkey Bread, 110
- Pumpkin Biscuits with Maple Butter, 109

BREADS, YEAST
- Award-Winning Honey Whole Wheat Loaves, 117
- Bulgur Bread, 112
- Colonial Yeast Bread, 112
- Cornish Saffron Christmas Bread, 20
- Herbed Sour Cream Batter Bread, 116
- Homemade Breadsticks, 121
- Houska-Czech Braided Bread, 21
- Multigrain Bread, 113
- Onion Bread, 113
- Onion Dill Bread, 114
- Peaches and Cream Coffee Cake, 115
- Pretzels, 122
- Purple Ribbon Three-Wheat Batter Bread, 117
- Runzas, 77
- Sour Cream Poppy Seed Bread, 116
- Stuffed Vienna Bread, 118
- Swedish Rye Bread, 114

CAKES. *See also* Coffee Cakes
- Amazing Corn Cake, 127
- Chocolate Crazy Cake, 157
- Coconut Pecan Cake, 24
- Earthquake Cake, 157
- Fresh Apple Cake with Caramel Sauce, 127
- Fruity Angel Cake, 156
- Lemon Yummy Cake, 157
- Melba's Oatmeal Cake, 25
- Poppy Seed Tea Cake, 129

CAKES, CHOCOLATE
- Indian Cake, 128
- Mississippi Mud, 128
- Turtle Nut Cake, 129

CANDY
- Buckeyes, 158
- Candy Mud Balls, 130
- Dad's Favorite Peanut Brittle, 159
- Marshmallow Puffs, 158
- Peanut Clusters, 158
- Rice Krispie Dots, 159
- Rocky Road Candy, 159

CHEESECAKES
- Bavarian Apple Cheesecake, 144
- Lean and Luscious Cheesecake, 145
- Mini Chocolate Chip Cheesecakes, 145
- Strawberry Cheesecake, 146

CHICKEN. *See also* Salads, Chicken
- Alta's Chicken Casserole, 95
- Baked Chicken Breasts Supreme, 92
- Buffalo Wings Original New York-Style, 32
- Cashew Chicken, 92

Chicken and Broccoli Soup, 40
Chicken and Chipped Beef, 93
Chicken and Rice Balls, 97
Chicken Casserole, 96
Chicken Pockets, 98
Chicken Roll-Ups with Noodles, 94
Chicken Spaghetti, 99
Hawaiian Chicken, 93
Hot and Spicy Casserole, 96
Oven-Baked Chicken, 91
Polynesian Honey Pineapple Chicken, 91
Scalloped Chicken, 98
Southern Corn Bread Chicken Sandwiches, 95
Stir-Fried Chicken and Zucchini, 94

COFFEE CAKES
Monkey Bread, 110
Peaches and Cream Coffee Cake, 115

COOKIES
Almond Biscotti, 136
Cherry Coconut Balls, 136
Chocolate Crinkle Cookies, 160
Chocolate Thumbprint Cookies, 137
Date Nut Balls, 26
Favorite Oatmeal Cookies, 26
Lemon Whippersnappers, 160
No-Bake Cookies, 161
Pizza Cookie, 161
Sour Cream Sugar Cookies, 138
Watermelon Cookies, 160
White Chocolate Brownie Drops, 137
Whole Wheat Holiday Cookies, 138

COOKIES, BAR
Chocolate Cheese Layer Bars, 131
Chocolate Filling Bars, 132
Cocoa Applesauce Bars, 130
Double Chocolate Crumble Bars, 132
Harvest Pumpkin Bars, 134
Low-Fat Brownies, 25
"M & M's" Bars, 133
Orange Bars, 133
Raisin Cream Bars, 135
Salted Peanut Chews, 134
S'Mores Cookie Bars, 135
Zucchini Brownies, 131

CORN BREAD
Southern Corn Bread Chicken Sandwiches, 95
Taco Turkey Corn Bread, 16

DESSERTS. *See also* Cakes; Candy; Cheesecakes; Cookies; Pies
Banana Butterfinger Dessert, 162
Berry Parfait, 148
Blintzes with Raspberry Sauce, 147
Buster Bar Dessert, 149
Buttery Cinnamon Skillet Apples, 161
Cherries in the Snow, 148
Cream Puffs, 150
Double Chocolate Mint Dessert, 149
Hot Fudge Sauce, 141
Peanut Butter-Apple Dessert, 146
Pronto Cherry Crunch, 162
Swedish Pastry, 150

DIPS
Berry Good Dip, 29
Fruit Dip, 29
Melissa's Tacos Gringo-Style, 30
Out-of-this-World Fruit Dip, 153
Salsa Sauce, 29
Tex-Mex Dip, 30

EGG DISHES
Breakfast Casserole, 104
Breakfast Strata, 104
Chiles Rellenos Casserole, 106
Chili and Cheese Bake, 103
Sausage and Potato Breakfast Casserole, 104

FISH. *See also* Tuna
Barbecued Trout, 102

4-H FRIENDS RECIPES
Lasagna, 63
Pork Chops and Potatoes, 83
Pronto Cherry Crunch, 162
Swedish Rye Bread, 114
Turkey Tetrazzini, 101

FROSTINGS
Coconut Frosting, 24

GROUND BEEF. *See also* Meatballs; Meat Loaves
Bacon Bean Ground Beef Casserole, 68
Baked Spaghetti, 80
Beefy Enchilada Casserole, 70
Enchiladas, 71
Hamburger Spud Casserole, 76
Hearty Beef and Potato Casserole, 76
Hungry Man Casserole, 78
Lasagna, 63
Mary's Miracle, 78
Melissa's Tacos Gringo-Style, 30
Miniature Cheese Patties, 67
Quick-and-Easy Chinese Casserole, 68
Quick Cheeseburger Pie, 69
Ranch Burgers, 79
Runzas, 77
Sloppy Joe Pizza, 75
Sloppy Joes, 79
Smothered Burritos, 70
Spaghetti Pie, 80
Super Nachos, 71
Taco Bake, 72
Taco Beef Quiche, 72
Tostado Casserole, 73
Upside-Down Pizza, 75
Western Casserole, 81
Zucchini Casserole, 81

GROUND BEEF, NOODLES
Beef Noodle Casserole, 74
Crusty Ground Beef Noodle Casserole, 73

French Beef, 69
Yum-a-Setta, 74

HAM
Barrett's Hearty Ham and Vegetable Casserole, 13
Breakfast Casserole, 104
Breakfast Strata, 104
Cheesy Potato and Ham Chowder, 40
Fruited Ham and Rice Pilaf, 53
Glazed Ham Balls, 85
Ham and Mandarin Salad, 48
Ham Balls, 85
Noodle and Ham Casserole, 86
Old-Fashioned Ham and Bean Soup, 39

LAMB
Festive Holiday Lamb, 15

MEATBALLS
Barbecue Bison Meatballs, 82
Barbecued Meatballs, 63
Cheesy Porcupine Meatballs, 64
Company Meatballs, 12
Glazed Ham Balls, 85
Ham Balls, 85
Meatballs in Gingersnap Sauce, 13
Polynesian Meatballs, 65
Porcupine Meatballs, 65
Spicy Meatballs, 64
Swedish Meatballs, 66

MEATLESS MAIN DISHES
Angel Hair Pasta with Tomatoes and Basil, 105
Cheese Enchiladas with Chili Powder Sauce, 106
Chiles Rellenos Casserole, 106
Three-Cheese Enchiladas, 105

MEAT LOAVES
Barbecued Meat Loaf, 66
Cheese-Filled Meat Loaf, 67
Party Pride Ham Loaf, 86

MEXICAN
Beefy Enchilada Casserole, 70
Cheese Enchiladas with Chili Powder Sauce, 106
Chiles Rellenos Casserole, 106
Enchiladas, 71
Hot and Spicy Casserole, 96
Melissa's Tacos Gringo-Style, 30
Salsa Sauce, 29
Smothered Burritos, 70
Super Nachos, 71
Taco Bake, 72
Taco Beef Quiche, 72
Tex-Mex Dip, 30
Tex-Mex Turkey Enchiladas, 100
Three-Cheese Enchiladas, 105
Tortilla Roll-Ups, 34
Tostado Casserole, 73

MUFFINS
Lemon Poppy Seed Muffins, 110
Orangey Cranberry Muffins, 111
Strawberry Muffins, 111

NOODLES
Alta's Chicken Casserole, 95
Chicken Roll-Ups with Noodles, 94
Noodle and Ham Casserole, 86

PASTA. *See also* Salads, Pasta; Spaghetti
Angel Hair Pasta with Tomatoes and Basil, 105
Arlene's Macaroni and Cheese, 19
Lasagna, 63

PHEASANT
Pheasant Potpie, 99

PIES
Apple Pie, 139
Charlie's Sour Cream Pineapple Pie, 143
Cherry Raspberry Pie, 139
Fresh Peach Pie, 142
Fudge Brownie Pie, 141
Mud Pie, 140
Oatmeal Pie, 141
Peanut Butter Pie, 162
Pecan Pie, 142
Red Hot Cherry Pie, 140
Sour Cream Raisin Pie, 143
Sweet Potato Pie, 144

PIZZA
Sloppy Joe Pizza, 75
Upside-Down Pizza, 75

PORK. *See also* Ham; Sausage
Barbecued Ribs, 87
Fruited Pork, 84
Fruited Pork Roast, 14
Homemade Pork and Beans, 14
Sweet-and-Sour Pork, 84

PORK, CHOPS
Breakfast Casserole, 104
"Chicken Lickin' Good" Pork Chops, 83
Marinated Pork Chops, 83
Pork Chops and Potatoes, 83

POTATOES
Cheesy Potato and Ham Chowder, 40
Roger's Mashed Potatoes, 18
Stuffed Potatoes, 51
Texas Potatoes, 19
Three-Cheese Scalloped Potatoes, 18

RICE
Cheesy Rice and Zucchini Casserole, 54
Fruited Ham and Rice Pilaf, 53
Harvest Celebration Sausage and Rice Stuffing, 54

ROLLS
"Best of Show" Dinner Rolls, 119
Broccoli Rolls, 118
Butterhorn Rolls, 119
Crescent Rolls, 23

Herbed Tomato Rolls, 120
Rapid Mix Rolls, 121

ROLLS, SWEET
Caramel Cinnamon Rolls, 22
Cinnamon Rolls, 122
Kiwifruit Danish, 124
Long Johns, 123
Sour Cream Twists, 124

SALADS, CHICKEN
Chicken Salad with Pecans, 47
Luncheon Chicken Salad, 45
Pasta Chicken Salad, 46
Summer Chicken Salad, 46

SALADS, FRUIT
Applesauce Gelatin Salad, 41
Club Raspberry Salad, 43
Cranberry Salad, 41
Fresh Fruit Salad, 44
Frog-Eye Salad, 44
Garden Glow Salad, 42
Leprechaun Salad, 45
Orange Pudding Salad, 42
Peaches and Cream Salad, 43

SALADS, MAIN DISH
Ham and Mandarin Salad, 48
Tuna Macaroni Salad, 48

SALADS, PASTA
Frog-Eye Salad, 44
Pasta Chicken Salad, 46
Tuna Macaroni Salad, 48

SALADS, SPINACH
Strawberry Spinach Salad, 49
Sweet-and-Sour Spinach Salad, 50

SALADS, VEGETABLE
Broccoli Raisin Salad, 11
Lentil Vegetable Salad, 49

SANDWICHES
Ranch Burgers, 79
Sloppy Joes, 79
Southern Corn Bread Chicken Sandwiches, 95
Tuna Burgers, 102

SAUSAGE
Chili and Cheese Bake, 103
German Sauerkraut Casserole, 88
Harvest Celebration Sausage and Rice Stuffing, 54
Italian Rice Bake, 87
Sausage and Potato Breakfast Casserole, 104
Sausage-Stuffed Acorn Squash, 88

SIDE DISHES
Arlene's Macaroni and Cheese, 19
Fruit and Herb Turkey Dressing, 53

SNACKS. *See also* Sandwiches
Edible Legos, 153
Go Anywhere Snack, 154
Go-Big-Red Popcorn, 155
Gorp Bars, 154
Grand-Slam Pizza Sticks, 156
Harvest Popcorn, 155
Hot and Sweet Snack Mix, 34
Mexi-Corn, 156

SOUPS
Cheesy Potato and Ham Chowder, 40
Chicken and Broccoli Soup, 40
Chili, 12
Old-Fashioned Ham and Bean Soup, 39
Vegetable Cheese Soup, 39

SPAGHETTI
Baked Spaghetti, 80
Chicken Spaghetti, 99
Spaghetti Pie, 80
Turkey Tetrazzini, 101

SPREADS
Cheese Logs, 31
Cheese Spread, 31
Dried Beef Log, 31
Maple Butter, 109

SQUASH
Sausage-Stuffed Acorn Squash, 88
South-of-the-Border Squash, 52

STEWS
Bison Stew, 82
Pumpkin Stew, 62

TUNA
Cheese and Tuna Crescents, 103
Tuna Burgers, 102
Tuna Macaroni Salad, 48

TURKEY
Polynesian Turkey, 100
Taco Turkey Corn Bread, 16
Tex-Mex Turkey Enchiladas, 100
Turkey Tetrazzini, 101

VEGETABLES. *See also* Names of Vegetables; Salads, Spinach; Salads, Vegetable
Celery and Water Chestnut Casserole, 17
Oriental Mushrooms, 51
Scalloped Corn, 17
Stir-Fry Vegetables, 52

ZUCCHINI
Cheesy Rice and Zucchini Casserole, 54
Stir-Fried Chicken and Zucchini, 94
Zucchini Brownies, 131
Zucchini Casserole, 81

SHARING OUR BEST RECIPES FROM NEBRASKA 4-H

c/o Nebraska 4-H Development Foundation
114 Agricultural Hall, University of Nebraska
Lincoln, Nebraska 68583-0700

Make checks payable to: Nebraska 4-H Development Foundation

Name: ______________________________

Address: ______________________________

City/State/Zip: ______________________________

Please send _____ copies @ $11.95 each ________

Postage and handling @ $ 2.00 each ________

Total $ ________

Cookbooks may be purchased directly at
County Extension Offices or the State 4-H Office.

SHARING OUR BEST RECIPES FROM NEBRASKA 4-H

c/o Nebraska 4-H Development Foundation
114 Agricultural Hall, University of Nebraska
Lincoln, Nebraska 68583-0700

Make checks payable to: Nebraska 4-H Development Foundation

Name: ______________________________

Address: ______________________________

City/State/Zip: ______________________________

Please send _____ copies @ $11.95 each ________

Postage and handling @ $ 2.00 each ________

Total $ ________

Cookbooks may be purchased directly at
County Extension Offices or the State 4-H Office.